# Understanding drugs, alcohol and crime

## Trevor Bennett and Katy Holloway

Open University Press

Open University Press
McGraw-Hill Education
McGraw-Hill House
Shoppenhangers Road
Maidenhead
Berkshire
England
SL6 2QL

email: enquiries@openup.co.uk
world wide web: www.openup.co.uk

and Two Penn Plaza, New York, NY 10121-2289, USA

First published 2005

A catalogue record of this book is available from the British Library

ISBN-13 978 0335 21257 6 (pb)      978 0335 21258 3 (hb)
ISBN-10 0 335 21257 3 (pb)      0 335 21258 1 (hb)

Library of Congress Cataloging-in-Publication Data
CIP data has been applied for

Typeset by RefineCatch Ltd, Bungay, Suffolk
Printed in Poland EU by OZGraf. S.A.
www.polskabook.pl

# Understanding drugs, alcohol and crime

WITHDRAWN

# CRIME AND JUSTICE
## Series editor: Mike Maguire
Cardiff University

*Crime and Justice* is a series of short introductory texts on central topics in criminology. The books in this series are written for students by internationally renowned authors. Each book tackles a key area within criminology, providing a concise and up-to-date overview of the principal concepts, theories, methods and findings relating to the area. Taken as a whole, the *Crime and Justice* series will cover all the core components of an undergraduate criminology course.

*Published titles*

Understanding criminology,
2nd edition
Sandra Walklate

Understanding justice, 2nd edition
Barbara A. Hudson

Understanding victims and
restorative justice
James Dignan

Understanding risk in criminal
justice
Hazel Kemshall

Understanding youth and crime
Sheila Brown

Understanding crime data
Clive Coleman and
Jenny Moynihan

Understanding white collar crime
Hazel Croall

Understanding crime prevention
Gordon Hughes

Understanding violent crime
Stephen Jones

Understanding community
penalties
Peter Raynor and Maurice
Vanstone

Understanding social control
Martin Innes

Understanding psychology and
crime
James McGuire

Understanding drugs, alcohol
and crime
Trevor Bennett and Katy Holloway

# Contents

# Preface

It is widely believed that drug use causes crime. One of the main aims of the current UK drug strategy is to reduce crime by reducing the availability and use of illicit substances (Home Office 2002). However, it is not at all certain whether there is such a connection between drug use and crime. It is possible that the two are not connected at all or even that the two are connected in a direction opposite to that hypothesized and that drug use causes *less* crime. This might occur when drugs impair the functioning or de-motivate the individual. While it might appear intuitively obvious that drug use causes *more* crime, it might not be the case in practice. It is important to take a critical view and to find out what the research actually says on this subject. The aim of this book is to do just that and to look at the research literature as a whole to determine whether the view that drug use causes crime is correct.

The book has been inspired in part by two large research projects that the authors have recently completed for the Home Office on the connection between drug use and crime. The first project was the NEW-ADAM (New English and Welsh Arrestee Drug Abuse Monitoring) programme, which aimed to look at drug use and crime among samples of arrestees (see, among others, Holloway and Bennett 2004). This study was based on interviews with and urine samples collected from arrestees held in police custody suites. The research was conducted in 16 locations in England and Wales and sought to determine the extent to which arrestees (most of whom were current offenders) were involved in drug use. The second project was a systematic review of the literature in two areas of research relevant to the 'drugs–crime' connection. One of the reviews aimed to investigate the strength and nature of the link between drug use and crime. The other review aimed to investigate the effectiveness of interventions that might (among other things) reduce criminal behaviour among drug users. The book draws heavily on our knowledge generated as part of conducting these reviews. However, we have not presented the findings of these projects in this book, as these can be found elsewhere in Home Office reports and other publications. Instead, the book includes a large amount of original analysis and reworking of the material collected as part of these projects. It has also been informed by our broader knowledge of work in this area.

There have been other reviews of the literature on drug use and crime. Existing reviews have tended to produce mixed conclusions. One of the best and one of the earliest reviews was conducted by Gandossy *et al.* (1980). The review concluded that heroin addicts engage in substantial amounts of income-generating crimes. However, the authors were reticent to say much more than this. They concluded that the relationship was clearer for heroin users than for users of other drugs. However, they were particularly concerned about the variation across studies in methods and results that made generalization difficult. Hough (1996) conducted a more recent review and was also somewhat circumspect in his conclusions. He thought that current research was patchy and that all that could be said with certainty was that drug misuse was responsible for at least some crime. Chaiken and Chaiken (1990) were sceptical of the existence of a general association between drug use and crime. In their review of the literature on the relationship between drug use and predatory crime, they concluded that they found no evidence of a simple or unified association between drug use and participation in crime.

However, there has been a considerable amount written on the drugs–crime connection that has suggested a relationship between the two. The edited volume on drug use and crime by Tonry and Wilson (1990) is well worth reading and documents a number of examples of the drugs–crime connection. One of the earliest and most influential edited volumes on the topic by Inciardi (1981) also provides evidence for various connections between drug use and crime.

The aims of this book are to provide an up-to-date overview of the literature on drug use and crime and to try to arrive at a conclusion about the nature of the relationship. This book is different from other books on the subject in a number of ways. It focuses strongly on research conducted in the UK, but pays due attention to work conducted in other countries, especially in areas where UK research is more limited. It also aims to pay particular attention to base comments on the evidence of published research and to include all cited research within the references at the end of the book. This has resulted in quite a long list of references for a book of this size. However, it is hoped that, as a result, the book might be a useful reference source for anyone working in the area. The book is also slightly different in that it includes information on alcohol use and crime. The alcohol and crime connection and the drugs and crime connection are usually discussed in separate volumes and read by separate audiences. This is perhaps unfortunate in that there are clear similarities between the two topics. To provide a context for the discussion, the book also considers related areas of interest, including the historical development of policy and law relating to drug misuse, the extent of drug misuse in the UK and its associated problems, and explanations and theories of drug misuse and the drugs–crime connection.

Acknowledgements to others who have assisted in preparing this publication are made after this Preface. However, it is worth noting by way of a conclusion that most scientific work is the result of taking small steps and that most of the preceding steps have been climbed by others. We are indebted to these others for the pre-existing work on this topic and for current debates and discussions that have informed our thinking. We hope that we in turn will contribute to this knowledge base by consolidating existing work into an accessible volume.

*Trevor Bennett and Katy Holloway*
*October 2004*

# Series editor's foreword

This book by Trevor Bennett and Katy Holloway is the latest in the successful *Crime and Justice* series published by Open University Press/ McGraw-Hill. The series is well established as a key resource in universities teaching criminology or criminal justice, especially in the UK but increasingly also overseas. The aim from the outset has been to give undergraduates and graduates both a solid grounding in the relevant area and a taste to explore it further. Although aimed primarily at students new to the field, and written as far as possible in plain language, the books are not over-simplified. On the contrary, the authors set out to 'stretch' readers and to encourage them to approach criminological knowledge and theory in a critical and questioning frame of mind.

Bennett and Holloway's book focuses on the major debates surrounding the relationship between drugs (including alcohol) and crime. The book is notable for its careful use of research evidence; indeed, one of the authors' great skills is to bring order, sense and clarity to the results of the large amount of research material on this subject that has accumulated around the world. The text demonstrates that there are no straightforward answers to questions such as whether drug taking 'causes' crime or vice versa. One has first to define what one means by 'drugs', 'causes' and 'crime'. The taking of *some* types of substance (legal or illegal) appears to be statistically related to the commission of *some* types of offence, but the relationship may be mediated by all kinds of other personal, social, environmental and cultural factors. As they rightly emphasize, establishing statistical correlations is only part of the story: empirical evidence should be used to develop and test theoretical explanation. Bennett and Holloway lead the reader sure-footedly across this fascinating if sometimes tricky landscape, in what should become a key 'state-of-the-art' text for this field of study.

In addition to their analysis of the drugs–crime relationship, the authors provide valuable succinct overviews of current knowledge about levels and patterns of drug and alcohol use across the world; the nature and extent of 'addiction'; international and local drug markets; the various governmental strategies adopted to control, reduce or manage substance abuse; and the 'effectiveness' of various kinds of intervention. The latter section looks closely, for example, at evidence on how successful various criminal justice and treatment programmes have been in reducing both addiction and drug-related offending.

Other books previously published in the *Crime and Justice* series – all of whose titles begin with the word 'Understanding' – have covered criminological theory (Sandra Walklate), penal theory (Barbara Hudson), crime data and statistics (Clive Coleman and Jenny Moynihan), youth and crime (Sheila Brown), crime prevention (Gordon Hughes), violent crime (Stephen Jones), community penalties (Peter Raynor and Maurice Vanstone), white collar crime (Hazel Croall), risk and crime (Hazel Kemshall), social control (Martin Innes), psychology and crime (James McGuire), and victims and restorative justice (James Dignan). Two are already in second editions and other second editions are planned. Other new books in the pipeline include texts on prisons, policing, social attitudes to crime, criminological research methods, race and crime, 'cybercrime' and political violence. All are topics which are either already widely taught or are growing in prominence in university degree courses on crime and criminal justice, and each book should make an ideal foundation text for a relevant module. As an aid to understanding, clear summaries are provided at regular intervals. In addition, to help students expand their knowledge, recommendations for further reading are given at the end of each chapter.

*Mike Maguire*
*December 2004*

# Acknowledgements

We noted in the Preface that we are indebted to the hundreds and perhaps even thousands of authors who have worked in the area of drug misuse and crime. However, our contribution to this debate has also been influenced by people closer to us who have affected our thinking in various ways. These include the various staff at the Home Office with whom we have worked in the area of drugs and crime for nearly a decade. We are also grateful, of course, to the Home Office for funding research that has helped us to review and conduct research in this area. We are particularly indebted to the various researchers who have worked with us over the years. They are too numerous to mention by name (the NEW-ADAM programme employed over 30 researchers at various times). However, we would like to note our thanks to the research staff who worked with us most recently on the systematic reviews of the literature, including Catherine Appleton, Stephen Brown and Tracy Pitman. We are also grateful to the series editor, Mike Maguire, for his very helpful comments on earlier drafts of the book. It goes almost without saying that he is in no way responsible for our errors. We would also like to thank the many other people who have given us ideas, influenced our thinking, or suggested references.

# The nature of the problem

## Introduction

This book is about the relationship between drug misuse and crime. It is prompted by the idea that drug use might actually *cause* crime. If drug use did cause crime, then one way of tackling crime might be to tackle drug use. However, until we know the facts of the relationship, we cannot know whether there is any meaningful link between the two. It might be the case that crime causes drug use or something else causes both of them.

The book is primarily a review of the research literature on drug misuse and crime. In particular, it focuses on research on the statistical association and causal connection between drug misuse and criminal behaviour. However, it also looks at the main theories that have attempted to explain the relationship. To provide a context for the discussion, the book investigates a number of related issues, including the extent of drug misuse, the way in which drug misuse has changed over time, the effects of drugs on perceptions and behaviour, and the ways in which drugs are misused by drug users.

The focus of the book is on the relation between *drugs* and crime rather than *alcohol* and crime, but in most discussions some information on alcohol misuse also will be included. The book focuses on what is happening in the UK rather than elsewhere, although developments in other countries are considered when appropriate.

This aim of this introductory chapter is to consider those issues that need to be covered before one can make sense of the chapters that follow. The first section looks at a few definitions that are often confused or misunderstood. The second section looks at the nature of the problem of drug misuse and discusses why the topic is worth our attention. The third section considers the nature of the drugs–crime connection and opens the debate on the central theme of the book. The final section gives the broad direction that the argument will follow and summarizes the main chapters.

## Definitional issues

It might be useful to begin by looking at some definitional issues that are sometimes problematic, but are central to understanding this body of literature.

### What are drugs?

This first question might seem simplistic and easy to answer. However, the word 'drugs' can be applied to almost any substance that can modify one or more of the functions of a living organism. In this case, it might be necessary to confine the concept of 'living organisms' to refer to higher forms of life to exclude chemicals that might affect only insects or simpler organisms (e.g. pesticides or fungicides). In practice, the term is generally used to refer to substances that are normally taken for therapeutic purposes. However, it is widely accepted that these same substances might be used for non-therapeutic purposes. One glossary of terms describes 'drugs' as: 'Any chemical compound that is used in the prevention, diagnosis, treatment, or cure of disease, for the relief of pain, or to control or improve any physiological or pathological disorder in humans or animals' (Cabinet Office 2001). The word is also used to refer to other chemicals that might be taken solely for recreational purposes and might not be used in medical treatment. For example, cannabis has been used recreationally in the UK since the 1950s. However, it has only recently been incorporated into medical treatment.

Drugs can be categorized in various ways. Hence, it is important to know which categories of drugs are being referred to in the context of discussion about drugs and crime. One such system is the pharmacological method of classification, which is based on the nature of the effects of the drug on the user. One common version of this classification is the division of drugs into stimulants, depressants, analgesics and hallucinogens. *Stimulant* drugs activate the central nervous system and increase wakefulness and physical activity. They include cocaine, crack and amphetamines, all of which may induce a feeling of euphoria and excitement. *Depressants* depress the activity of the central nervous system and are used to relieve stress, induce sleep and allay anxiety. Depressants include benzodiazepines and barbiturates. *Analgesics* are used mainly to relieve pain. The strongest analgesics are opium, morphine and heroin.

*Hallucinogens* affect perceptions, sensations, thinking and emotions. They include drugs such as LSD, magic mushrooms and ecstasy. Another method of grouping drugs is the legal system of classification based on the severity of the penalties attached to breaches of drug laws. Under current legislation in the UK, drugs are categorized into three groups: Class A, Class B and Class C. Class A drugs cover the most serious drugs, including heroin and cocaine. Class C drugs cover the least serious drugs, including diazepam and (after a downgrading from Class B) cannabis (these will be discussed in more detail later).

Alcohol is not necessarily any easier to define. In part, this is because it can be defined in a number of ways depending on whether the definition is chemical, biological, medical or social. In a chemical sense, alcohol refers to any organic chemical containing one or more hydroxyl group molecules. The most common forms of alcohol are ethanol (made from grain) and methanol (made from wood). The distinction is important when defining the term or consuming the product. Ethanol is the basis of beers, wines and spirits and is used in many countries around the world for its physical and social effects. Methanol is the basis of antifreeze and some solvents and can cause blindness and other nervous system damage if ingested. Hence, it is important to know which form of alcohol is being considered.

Another definitional issue that needs to be addressed is whether alcohol is a drug. Again, this is not quite so straightforward as it might seem. This is because some classifications of drugs omit alcohol. Alcohol and drugs are often discussed separately as if they were different in some way. The difference might be understood in terms of the classificatory systems used. In terms of biological systems of classification, alcohol would be regarded as a drug as it has a clear depressant effect on the central nervous system. In this sense, it is commonly defined as a sedative-hypnotic. In terms of medical systems of classification, alcohol might not be viewed like other drugs, as it is not often used for therapeutic purposes (although some Victorian general practitioners recommended that their patients used alcohol or cigarettes as methods of relieving stress). If there were such a thing as a criminological system of classification, it is likely that alcohol would be kept separate from other drugs. The research literature on alcohol and crime and drugs and crime are quite separate and in many respects do not overlap. The research is typically conducted by different groups of academics. There is also some evidence (discussed later) that the relationship between alcohol and crime and that between drugs and crime is different. Hence, in the current book, drugs and alcohol are discussed separately.

### What are 'illegal drugs'?

The simplest answer to this question is that 'illegal drugs' are those prohibited under current drugs legislation. There are two main statutes that define the current legal status of drugs in the UK: the Medicines Act 1968 and the Misuse of Drugs Act 1971 (although there are many more recent

Acts that amend and extend the principles of these Acts). The Medicines Act 1968 is less relevant to the current debate in that it mainly concerns the manufacture and supply of medicinal products. Under this Act, medicines are divided into three categories. The first is 'prescription-only' drugs, which are the most restricted and can only be sold or supplied by a pharmacist if ordered by a doctor or dentist. The second is 'pharmacy medicines', which can be sold or supplied without a prescription, but only by a pharmacist. The third is drugs on the 'general sales list', which are the least restricted drugs and can be sold or supplied without a prescription by any shop. The Misuse of Drugs Act 1971 is much more important to the current discussions in that its main aim is to prevent the misuse of 'controlled drugs'. This legislation classifies controlled drugs as falling into Class A, B or C drug groups (as mentioned earlier). Class A drugs include heroin, ecstasy, LSD and cocaine, Class B drugs include amphetamines and less potent opioid painkillers (e.g. codeine), and Class C drugs include temazepam, diazepam and, more recently, cannabis.

In terms of legal classification, 'illegal drugs' can be defined as those drugs listed in these and more recent updates of these Acts. However, the definition can become a little more complex when the method of use is taken into account. It is not uncommon for drug users to be prescribed legally a drug such as methadone and to use it illegally. This might be done by injecting the prescribed drug rather than consuming it orally. It might also be done by taking larger quantities than prescribed. This can be achieved by saving up dosages and consuming the saved dosages all at once. It is also common for some heroin users to purchase legally certain cough medicines containing traces of opium or codeine 'over-the-counter' and consume the whole bottle in one go.

### What are drug offences?

This is a similar question to the one above. However, it serves to identify the precise nature of the offences involving drugs that are proscribed by law. It is also useful to distinguish drug offences from drug-related crime (to be discussed in the next section). In practice, most official data on the drugs–crime connection come from government statistics on drug offences. Much less is known about drug-related crime other than drug offences.

Drug offences are usually regarded as those offences defined by the Misuse of Drugs Act 1971. The Act defines a number of offences concerning 'controlled drugs', which comprise those drugs listed as Class A, B or C in the schedules of the Act. The offences that can be committed are: importation, exportation, production or concerned in the production, supply or offer to supply, possession and cultivation. The Act also prohibits an occupier or manager of premises to permit or suffer any of these offences being committed on the premises. One of the notable aspects of the Act is that, generally speaking, it does not prohibit *use* of controlled substances. However, there is a sub-section of the Act that specifically prohibits opium smoking (which is interesting considering that pure opium is rarely smoked in the UK). It might also be assumed that use at some point must involve possession. Nevertheless, it is not illegal to have consumed drugs (with the exception of driving a vehicle under the influence of drugs). This provision in the law means that drug users often swallow drugs in their possession if they believe they are about to be arrested.

Alcohol offences are somewhat different to drug offences, which reinforces the idea that alcohol and drugs are often seen as distinct. Interestingly, alcohol is not controlled by the Medicines Act 1968 or the Misuse of Drugs Act 1971. In fact, alcohol offences are defined through a different set of laws. The Licensing Act 1964 governs the manufacture, sale, distribution and purchase of alcohol. The 1964 Act mainly defines where and when alcohol can be sold and consumed. 'On licences' permit the sale and consumption of alcohol on the premises. 'Off licences' permit shops to sell alcohol, but do not permit the consumption of alcohol on the premises. Licences have to be approved by magistrates, although the police can object if they think the applicant is not fit to sell alcohol. There are also laws restricting the age at which alcohol can be consumed. In the UK, it is an offence to give alcohol to a child under 5 years of age. Children aged over 14 can go into pubs unaccompanied by adults, but they cannot be served alcohol until they are 18. Young people aged 16 and over can buy and drink beer or cider (but not spirits) in a pub, but only if they are having a meal. There are also laws relating to alcohol and motor vehicles. Under the Road Traffic Act 1988, it is an offence to drive a motor vehicle on a road or other public place when under the influence of alcohol. The legal limit for drinking and driving in the UK is 80 milligrams of alcohol per 100 millilitres of blood, 35 micrograms of alcohol per 100 millilitres of breath, and 107 milligrams of alcohol per 100 millilitres of urine. There are also restrictions relating to alcohol and street disorder and other public drunkenness offences.

In some countries, the alcohol laws are more restrictive than in the UK. In some Middle Eastern countries, both the sale and consumption of alcohol are banned. In some European countries, the sale and consumption of alcohol are tightly controlled. In Sweden, for example, there is a state monopoly on the sale of alcohol and it can only be supplied from approved outlets. The minimum age for the purchase of all alcoholic drinks with the exception of beer is 20 (International Center for Alcohol Policy 2002). The maximum blood-alcohol level at which someone can legally drive is so low that it is only just above that produced naturally in the body. It might also be overlooked that the United States has a tradition for strict alcohol policies. The current minimum drinking age set by the Federal Minimum Legal Drinking Age Laws is 21 years.

### What is drug-related crime?

One of the central aims of the government's updated drugs strategy is to reduce 'drug-related crime' (Home Office 2002: 6). However, the term is not precisely defined. This is a common problem and there is some indication that the term may be used differently across different publications.

One possible definition of 'drug-related' crime is that it is those offences covered by the Misuse of Drugs Act 1971. In other words, 'drug offences' and 'drug-related crime' could mean the same thing. In practice, the terms are used slightly differently. 'Drug offences' refer specifically to the offences defined in the Act. 'Drug-related crime' refers to a wide range of offences that are in some way caused by drug use. For example, it is widely believed that some burglaries, robberies and shopliftings are caused by drug users seeking illegal means of financing their drug use. The concept is also sometimes used to describe offences committed as part of the operation of drug markets and the supply of illegal drugs. One of the most wide-ranging definitions of 'drug-related' crime has been devised by the European Monitoring Centre for Drugs and Drug Addiction (EMCDDA 2003). The definition has the advantage that it integrates most of the different ways in which the term is currently used. The definition is as follows:

> Drug-related crime can be considered to include criminal offences in breach of drug legislation, crimes committed under the influence of illicit drugs, crimes committed by users to support their drug habit (mainly acquisitive crime and drug dealing) and systemic crimes committed as part of the functioning of illicit markets (fight for territories, bribing of officials, etc.).
>
> (EMCDDA 2003: 33)

A similar kind of discussion has taken place in relation to the concept of 'alcohol-related crime'. At one level it could include just those alcohol offences specifically defined in law. This would have the same disadvantages as discussed above in relation to drugs. In practice, the concept is used more widely to consider other offences committed under the influence of alcohol or in some other way influenced by alcohol (e.g. moderate use of alcohol to provide the courage to offend). The UK government has identified action against 'alcohol-related crime' in its strategy document 'Alcohol Harm Reduction Strategy for England' (Cabinet Office 2004). The document does not define the concept as such. However, it describes the broad areas covered by the term. These include crime and disorder in which alcohol use is implicated. It is specified that alcohol misuse might not be the direct cause of these offences. However, the concept refers to those cases in which alcohol might be a contributory factor. These include various kinds of street disorder and violence of the street associated with drinking.

## The nature of the problems of drug misuse

This book is mainly about the possible connection between drug misuse and crime. However, drug misuse is a problem in its own right in that it can adversely affect both the individual and society. In the following sub-sections, we shall look at some of the problems of drug misuse and some of the problems of clearly defining them.

### What is drug misuse?

There are a number of fairly similar concepts currently being used to describe different kinds of inappropriate drug use. One of the most common ways of describing this kind of drug use is to refer to the problem of 'drug misuse'.

Perhaps the most relevant starting point in answering the question is to consider what exactly is 'drug use'. According to DrugScope, 'drug use' refers to 'the taking of a drug, either by swallowing, smoking, injecting or any other way of getting the drug into the blood stream'. It may also include insufflation (inhaling the drug contained in a fine spray). They explain that 'drug use' refers to drug taking that is not necessarily wrong or dangerous. In other words, the term 'drug use' should only be used to describe taking a legal drug that has been legally prescribed or legally obtained in the manner recommended by the doctor or pharmacist. Any other use would be defined as 'drug misuse' or 'drug abuse'.

The concepts of 'drug misuse' and 'drug abuse' are sometimes used interchangeably. However, according to dictionary definitions, the terms are slightly different. Proctor (1995) defines 'misuse' and 'abuse' as follows:

Misuse:
'. . . to use something in an unsuitable way or in a way that was not intended'.

Abuse:
'. . . to use or treat someone or something wrongly or badly, especially in a way that is to your own advantage'.

The use of the term drug 'misuse' in the drugs literature tends to reflect these general definitions. 'Drug misuse' is often used to refer to inappropriate use of legal drugs and 'drug abuse' is often used to refer to excessive use of legal drugs ('bad use') or any use of illegal drugs ('wrong use'). 'Drug misuse' might arise, therefore, as a result of using legal drugs for reasons other than their intended purpose, such as taking laxatives to achieve weight loss. 'Drug abuse' might arise when legal drugs are used excessively to such an extent that they could result in harm to the user. Use of cannabis would be considered 'drug abuse' because, in most cases, it is an illegal drug and any use would be regarded as abuse. Hence, it would be expected that the term 'drug abuse' would be most common in the drugs literature. However, the current fashion is to use the term 'misuse' rather than 'abuse'. The preference is reflected in the choice of terms used in the naming of the Misuse of Drugs Act 1971, which, by the above definition, should be called the 'Abuse of Drugs Act 1971'. However, it has been argued that the term 'misuse' is preferred to 'abuse' because it is seen as less judgemental.

The terms 'misuse' and 'abuse' are also applied to alcohol consumption. In this case, 'alcohol misuse' would refer to inappropriate use of alcohol. This might include drinking to get drunk or drinking at work. 'Alcohol abuse' would refer more specifically to excessive use of alcohol (such as binge drinking or at a level that might lead to harm) and illegal use of alcohol (such as under age drinking). However, the term 'alcohol misuse' is currently preferred for its non-judgemental associations, which means that the two terms are often used interchangeably.

### What is problematic drug use?

The term 'problematic drug use' is widely used in the literature. Nevertheless, its meaning is also somewhat variable across studies. In a recent National Institute on Drug Abuse report, 'problematic drug use' is defined as: 'The use of a substance to modify or control mood or state of mind in a manner that is illegal or harmful to oneself or others' (Trachtenberg and Fleming 2004: 1). In this case, the definition is very similar to the definition of 'drug abuse', mentioned above, in that it refers to drug use that might lead to harm. In a report from Belgium, the authors note that the government defines 'problematic use' as a 'pattern of use that is beyond one's control' (Kaminski and Decorte 2004). In other words, the emphasis is on whether users find aspects of their drug use detrimental. Other publications have focused more on dependency. In these cases, 'problematic drug use' applies mainly to users of addictive drugs, such as heroin, crack and cocaine. The European Monitoring Centre for Drugs and Drug Addiction define 'problem drug use' as 'injecting drug use or long duration/regular use of opiates, cocaine and/or amphetamines' (EMCDDA 2003: 10). Perhaps the simplest meaning of 'problematic drug use' is to consider it as drug use that generates problems, either for the user or for society.

The concept is also commonly applied in relation to alcohol use. 'Problematic alcohol use' is often defined as alcohol use that adversely affects the user or others. In practice, researchers and practitioners have developed a wide range of indicators of adverse effects of alcohol that might define 'problematic alcohol use'. These include whether the person uses alcohol to function 'properly', whether they regularly become intoxicated, whether they go to work or drive a car while intoxicated, whether they have experienced any injuries as a result of being intoxicated, whether the person feels that their life is affected adversely by alcohol, whether they want to give up or cut down but cannot. Hence, a problem drinker is anyone whose drinking causes a problem to themselves or others.

**What is drug dependence?**

The concept of 'drug dependence' also has many meanings in the research literature. It is sometimes used interchangeably with the concept of 'addiction' and the two terms are often combined by using a slash to show that either term would do (e.g. 'dependence/addiction'). Other writers make a distinction between the two terms and argue that it is possible to have 'dependence' without 'addiction' and 'addiction' without 'dependence'. To differentiate between the terms it is necessary to introduce two more related concepts of 'tolerance' and 'withdrawal'.

A common medical definition of addiction is something that occurs when the following three criteria are met:

1 There is an increased tolerance for the drug.
2 There are signs of physical and/or psychological dependence.
3 There are signs of withdrawal symptoms following cessation of drug use.

'Tolerance' refers to the phenomenon of needing more of a drug to obtain the same effect. The user becomes tolerant to the existing level of consumption of the drug and the effect is reduced. To return to the same effect, the level of consumption needs to be increased. The existence of 'tolerance' explains why some drug users (typically heroin users) can consume amounts of the drug that would be lethal to non-tolerant users. In fact, some heroin users returning from periods of imprisonment may become ill or even die if they use heroin at the same levels before imprisonment. The concept of 'dependence' can be split into physical and psychological dependence. Physical dependence refers to the experience of a physical need for the drug in order to function normally. One sign of physical dependence is the presence of withdrawal symptoms (see below) following cessation of drug use. Psychological dependence refers more to a belief that the person needs a particular drug to function normally. It is possible that psychological dependence is just as compelling as physical dependence in determining continued drug use. 'Withdrawal symptoms' comprise physical manifestations that arise as a result of termination of drug use. In the case of heroin addiction, drug termination can cause a variety of symptoms, including nausea, weakness, anxiety, perspiration, headaches, cramps, vomiting, diarrhoea, hallucinations, shaking and physical shock.

The choice of terms tends to reflect current fashions. The term 'dependence' is currently preferred in the literature over the word 'addiction'. Again, it is thought to be less judgemental. The word 'addiction' is also associated with the word 'addict', which is currently thought among practitioners to be an unhelpful label that might inhibit effective treatment. Hence, the concept of 'drug dependence' is preferred and typically it is used to refer to a perceived need for a particular drug (regardless of whether the need is physical or psychological in origin). One advantage of the concept of 'dependence' over 'addiction' is that it is much easier to measure 'dependence' (which can be done through a standard interview schedule) than addiction (which might need medical tests to be measured with any accuracy).

These definitional principles can also be applied to the study of 'alcohol dependence' and 'alcohol addiction' (usually referred to as 'alcoholism'). Alcohol addicts develop a tolerance for alcohol, they are dependent on alcohol, and they develop withdrawal symptoms when alcohol use is terminated. The main difference is that 'alcohol addicts' have their own descriptive label of 'alcoholics' and their own descriptive condition of 'alcoholism'. In other words, there appears to be less sensitivity to the concept of 'addiction' in relation to alcohol use. However, the term itself is rarely used and is generally referred to as 'alcoholism'. It is also interesting that there are no comparable terms for 'alcoholics' and 'alcoholism' among drug users, in the sense that there are no 'drugics' or 'drugism'. This may be because of the different history of the two conditions. The concept of 'alcoholism' has a long history and its origins are strongly embedded in the medical model. The modern conception of 'drug addiction' is more recent and its history spans both criminal and medical models.

## Why is drug misuse a social problem?

The previous sections have discussed the problem of drug misuse from the point of view of the individual user. However, drug misuse also generates problems for society, including social and economic problems. The problem of the possible connection between drug misuse and crime is a central issue of the book and will be discussed in detail later.

One problem associated with drug misuse is the problem of health. Health problems such as dependency and the risk of infection and death have already been discussed in the context of individual user problems. However, other health issues have broader social implications. Many drug users administer their drugs by intravenous injection and at least some of them dispose of their used equipment in inappropriate ways. Used syringes can be found on the streets of some neighbourhoods and can be washed up on beaches or river banks. There is some evidence that HIV infection in the UK is in part spread through transmission by the shared syringes of drug users. Another disease spread through sharing equipment is hepatitis B, which carries the risk that the disease might be transmitted to the non-drug-using population. Another problem of drug misuse is the economic and social costs to society. These include costs to the health service, work-related costs, state benefits and the costs of community care.

Similar arguments can be brought to bear in relation to alcohol misuse. Alcohol misuse generates problems not only for the user, but also for the rest of society. According to Alcohol Concern (2004), 1.7 million working days a year are lost as a result of alcohol-related absence and sickness. It is estimated that alcohol use costs businesses almost £300 million a year. It also generates costs for the health service in terms of accident and emergency admissions. Alcohol misuse is also responsible for drink driving accidents and traffic-related deaths.

## The nature of the drugs–crime connection

The main aim of this book is to investigate the 'drugs–crime connection'. To achieve this, it is useful to know something about what the 'drugs–crime connection' means in practice.

The term 'drugs–crime connection' refers to the relationship between drug misuse and criminal behaviour. It is used by the government in its strategy documents to suggest that drug use and crime are linked in some way. Hence, the first question to ask is, 'What kind of link?' There are many ways in which drug use and criminal behaviour might be connected. The research literature investigates four main types of connection. First, drug use might cause crime. This might occur when drug users seek illegal funds to pay for their drug use. Second, crime might cause drug use. This might occur when surplus funds from crime are used to purchase drugs. Third, drug use and criminal behaviour might both be caused by a third variable. This might be a common individual or social characteristic (poor parenting) or a cluster of variables that affect both drug use and crime (e.g. various variables relating to social disadvantage). Fourth, drugs and crime might not be causally linked at all. This might occur when certain kinds of deviant behaviour co-exist among individuals or groups. The forms of behaviour may be connected, but no one can be seen as the cause of the others.

Research on the 'drugs–crime connection' has also investigated different types of drugs and different types of crimes. Hence, the second question to ask is, 'What kinds of drugs and what kinds of crime?' It is unlikely that all kinds of drugs and all kinds of crimes are connected. Drug use covers a wide range of drugs from aspirins to heroin. Criminal behaviour covers a wide range of crimes from tax evasion to homicide. In practice, drugs and crime research tends to be limited to just certain types of drugs and crime. These drugs and offences tend to be those that are linked to the main theoretical perspectives on the connection (discussed below). In practice, the most common drugs investigated in the drugs–crime connection are heroin, crack and cocaine, and the most common offences are burglary, theft and robbery.

As mentioned above, research on the drugs–crime connection tends to be influenced by the major theories that have been developed to explain the connection. Hence, the third question to ask is, 'How can the drugs–crime connection be explained?' One of the most influential theories explaining the connection is the 'economic necessity' argument. This specifies that drug users will commit crimes to finance their drug use. The relationship is thus largely a financial one. The amount of illegal income generated is proportionate to the expenditure on drugs. Another important theory is the 'hedonistic pursuits' argument. This argues that criminal behaviour provides surplus funds that can be spent on leisure activities. The hedonistic pursuits of offenders include alcohol use and drug taking. Hence, in this case, crime can be thought of as the cause of drug misuse.

The concept of the 'alcohol–crime connection' is similar in many ways to the 'drugs–crime connection'. It refers to a statistical association and causal connection between alcohol use and crime. Alcohol use can be linked to crime directly through various alcohol offences, including drinking driving offences, drunkenness offences and public order offences involving alcohol. However, it also refers to other kinds of connection in which alcohol use might be associated with other kinds of offences. We could ask similar questions as those asked in relation to the drugs–crime connection. First, 'What kinds of crime are implicated in the alcohol–crime connection?' One of the main differences between the drugs–crime connection and the alcohol–crime connection is that the former focuses mainly on property offences, while the latter focuses mainly on violent offences. There have been a number of longitudinal studies that have shown that homicide rates rise and fall in accordance with the rise and fall of alcohol consumption (e.g. Norström 1998). Studies have also shown longitudinal links with other violent offences, including assaults and family violence. There have also been studies that have investigated the links between alcohol use and football hooliganism and alcohol use and criminal damage. However, there have been some studies that have investigated the links between alcohol use and property crimes, such as vehicle crime and burglary (see Bennett and Wright 1984a).

The second question that could be asked is, 'How can the alcohol–crime connection be explained?' The major theories of the links between alcohol and crime tend to be oriented around the same causal models as research on the links between drugs and crime. In other words, alcohol use might cause crime, crime might cause alcohol use, both alcohol and crime might be caused by a third variable or set of variables, or the relationship might be spurious with no causal link between the two. However, the specific theories used to explain these connections are slightly different. There is greater emphasis placed in alcohol studies compared with drug studies on the pharmacological effects of alcohol in precipitating criminal behaviour. These include the effects of alcohol in stimulating aggression and the ability of alcohol to give the courage to offend. The alcohol research also considers in more detail than the drugs research the importance of the setting in linking alcohol use and crime. In particular, research has looked at the role of 'pubs' and clubs and their environmental characteristics in precipitating criminal behaviour.

## The nature of the book

As mentioned earlier, the main aim of the book is to investigate the links between drug misuse and crime. However, some attention will be paid to the links between alcohol use and crime. One reason for looking at the problem of drugs and crime is the current importance given to the topic in terms of both research and government policy. There is currently considerable concern that a large proportion of crime in the UK is drug-related and there is considerable interest in attempting to do something about it. Hence, one of the aims of the book is to provide a context for this debate by reviewing the nature of the problem and the nature of possible solutions.

The current chapter has outlined some of the definitional issues involved in the debate and has generally outlined the context. Chapter 2 investigates the legal and policy context of the discussion and describes the evolution of the law and policy relating to drug misuse. The chapter argues that it is only in recent years that drug use has been defined as a social problem and until that time drugs were widely consumed without constraint or control. To some extent, law and policy define the nature of the problem. However, not all countries see the problem in the same way and some have developed relatively lenient policies and some have developed relatively severe policies.

Chapter 3 investigates the extent of drug misuse in the UK and the problems generated by it. In particular, it examines the extent of the demand for drugs and the various ways in which this demand is satisfied by suppliers. It looks at different types of drug markets and distribution methods, and the success of the police and customs and excise in tackling supply. It also looks at the common problems associated with drug misuse both for the individual and society.

Chapter 4 examines different types of drug misuse and the different types of drugs misused and their effects. It also looks at patterns of drug misuse, including type, frequency and amount, and patterns of multiple drug misuse, including drug combinations and their effects. The chapter also considers motives for drug misuse and users' reasons for starting and stopping.

Chapter 5 outlines the various theories that attempt to explain the drugs–crime connection. This includes a discussion on the different causal models and the nature of the explanations offered. It then reviews the major theories relating to each of the causal models.

Chapter 6 investigates what the research literature tells us about the statistical association between drug misuse and crime. It looks at previous reviews of the literature and what is already known about the nature of the association. The chapter makes a distinction between the links between involvement in drug use and involvement in crime and frequency of drug use and frequency of crime. It then goes on to look at research which has disaggregated the findings to show the relationship between specific types of drug use and specific types of crime. It also looks at the relationship between multiple drug use and crime.

Chapter 7 investigates what the research literature can tell us about the causal connection between drug misuse and crime. This is done by looking at 'age-of-onset' studies, which determine whether drug use preceded crime or crime preceded drug misuse, and 'changes-over-time' studies, which determine whether changes in drug misuse are associated with changes in criminal behaviour. The chapter also looks at what offenders and drug users have said about the causal connection between drug misuse and crime.

Chapter 8 focuses on methods for tackling the drugs–crime connection. It identifies the main treatment programmes and criminal justice programmes and considers the findings of research that have evaluated their effectiveness. The chapter looks at research on treatment programmes and criminal justice programmes separately and compares the two. It then looks at possible variations in effectiveness in relation to different types of programme and different types of subject.

The final chapter summarizes what has been learned about the drugs and crime connection and reviews current attempts to tackle the problem. It identifies gaps in the research literature and in government policies and makes proposals about ways in which the problem might be researched and tackled in the future.

## Further reading

A good source of general information on the nature of drugs and drug misuse is the DrugScope website (http://www.drugscope.org.uk). General information about government policy on drug misuse can be found on the Home Office website (http://www.homeoffice.gov.uk). A useful introductory publication on drug misuse and criminal behaviour is the book *Drugs and Crime* (Bean 2001). This is one of the few books on drugs and crime that has a dominantly UK focus. Another useful UK source is *Drug Misuse and the Criminal Justice System: A Review of the Literature* (Hough 1996). The edited volume *Drugs and Crime: A Review of Research* (Tonry and Wilson 1990) is one of the most widely cited books in the area.

# chapter two

# Policy context: from defining to reducing harm

## Introduction

This chapter looks at the process by which drug use became defined as a problem. It begins by looking at drug use before it was thought of as deviant or harmful. It then looks at the process by which drug use became defined first as a medical problem and later as a criminal problem. It reports on more recent perceptions of drug misuse and the attempts of governments to control it. The final section compares government policies across countries and identifies differences in approaches to tackling drug misuse.

## When drug use was not a problem

It is only in recent years that drug use has been defined as a social problem. Previously, drugs had been used in many countries over many centuries for self-medication, religious experience, creative inspiration and recreation with little or no moral condemnation and few social controls. The first systematic account of the medicinal properties of cannabis appeared in China nearly 5000 years ago. Chewing coca leaves for strength and energy has been common practice in South America for several thousand years.

The opium poppy was used by ordinary people in ancient civilizations to ease pain and to sedate and can be found in the pharmacopoeias of the Egyptians, Greeks and Romans (Robson 1999). However, by the early twentieth century opium and many other drugs were morally condemned and legally proscribed. This chapter will explore the way in which drug use became defined as a social problem and the more recent attempts of governments to control it. Particular attention will be paid to drug policy in the UK, although some comparisons will be made with the drug policies of other European countries and the United States.

In the nineteenth century, opium was widely used as a medicine and was viewed largely in terms of its benefits. Doctors thought of opium as central to medicine and one of the most important and powerful drugs available for the treatment of disease (Berridge and Edwards 1981). At the time, the medical profession was fairly ineffective and offered little more than palliatives and common sense. Opiates were one of the few drugs that had any clear medicinal effects and were used widely by doctors. Their power and effectiveness in relieving pain and providing comfort resulted in some physicians describing them as 'God's own medicine' (Osler 1892). In terms of popularity and availability, it has been argued that opium products were similar to current over-the-counter drugs such as aspirin (Stimson and Oppenheimer 1982).

Opium-based medicines and tonics were used in Britain, Europe and the United States for much of the nineteenth century as analgesics, sedatives, febrifuges and remedies for cholera (South 1994). Opium products were viewed by ordinary people as everyday household items and were available in most grocer shops and pharmacists. Other drugs were also widely available, including cannabis tinctures and hashish pastes, some of which included cocaine or opium extracts. Cocaine could be bought in the form of pastilles, lozenges, wines or teas, along with psychedelics such as mescaline. Morphine and heroin could be purchased over the counter, along with hand-tooled syringes and injection kits (Jay 2000). It might now seem ironic that during the reign of Queen Victoria and the high point of the British Empire, periods considered as the height of propriety and respectability, the country was awash with mind-altering drugs (Jay 2000). Respected literary figures such as Thomas de Quincey, who wrote *Confessions of an English Opium Eater*, and Coleridge both helped to bring a level of acceptability to what was the equivalent to recreational drug use.

It is perhaps slightly misleading to describe drug use in general or opium use in particular during the nineteenth century as wholly acceptable. Opiates tended to be consumed under fairly limited conditions. It was acceptable to use opium-based products in the treatment of disease and in tackling various physical ailments. Workers sometimes used opium to alleviate the pains of physical work. Opium use among fen workers in East Anglia was widespread as a means of ameliorating the effects of working in the damp and cold marshlands (Berridge and Edwards 1981). Opium was also commonly used as baby 'soothers' or 'quieteners' to aid sleep and as an effective cough suppressant. It was also accepted that some writers and artists used psychoactive drugs for artistic and creative reasons. However, this does not mean that all forms of use would have been tolerated. According to Edwards (1981), opiate use was not the object of moral opprobrium, mainly because it was associated with medical and not 'luxurious' use (Edwards 1981). The Victorians in particular were disapproving of inebriety and signs of public lasciviousness. They were also uncomfortable with over-indulgence and public drunkenness and excesses of alcohol use were widely condemned.

The first signs of change in public attitudes towards drug use occurred towards the end of the nineteenth century. According to South (1994), there were at least three reasons for the change of moral attitudes. The first was the progression of the industrial revolution and the growing concern about public health and the conditions of the new urban working class. The second was the accounts of what appeared to be large numbers of children dying from the use of opium for cough suppression, as a 'comforter' and for sedation. The third was accounts in the press of what were described as Chinese 'opium dens' in London's East End (South 1994). South notes the irony of the idea of the Chinese as a corrupting influence given that Britain was the principal sponsor of the international trade in opium. There were also reasons associated with the increase in power of the medical profession to define certain behaviours as pathological. In particular, by the end of the century, excessive opium use was beginning to be seen as a form of addiction.

## The medicalization of drug use

For most of the nineteenth century, opiate use was considered a normal and largely unexceptional activity. During the last quarter of the century, opiate use became defined as a disease and within the scope of the medical profession. In both a practical and conceptual sense, opiate use was medicalized. According to Berridge and Edwards (1981: 242), 'opiates were taken away from the people and became the property of the doctors'. Addiction was viewed as a disease and the addict was defined as a patient. The proper response to habitual opiate use was treatment by medical specialists.

The redefinition came about over a number of years and involved political lobbying by various pressure groups with an interest in defining the nature of drug use. One of the earliest groups with an interest in drug use was the Pharmaceutical Society. The Pharmaceutical Society of Great Britain was established in 1841 and brought together the interests of chemists, druggists and apothecaries. At the time, pharmacists were in competition with shopkeepers and other retail outlets, such as market-stall holders and travelling vendors, and doctors who were allowed to dispense their own drugs. One of the aims of the Pharmaceutical Society was to challenge the competition and become the sole legal suppler of poisons and other drugs. They sought to argue that they were the only suitably qualified persons to sell poisons (Stimson and Oppenheimer 1982).

Their lobbying was successful and resulted in the first British Act of Parliament to regulate the sale of drugs. The 1851 Arsenic Act required that sales of arsenic were recorded and witnessed, and that the buyer was known to the seller. A record of the transaction was to be made in a book that both vendor and purchaser had to sign. However, the Act was only a partial victory for the pharmacists. Its provisions applied to arsenic only and to no other poisons or drugs. There was no restriction on who should keep a record of the sale and pharmacists were not given a monopoly on the administration of the procedure. Any trader could sell arsenic provided that a record was kept.

The passing of the 1851 Arsenic Act was followed by a period of lobbying in which the Pharmaceutical Society pressed for the sales of other drugs and poisons to be restricted (Stimson and Oppenheimer 1982). This lobbying was again successful and resulted in the passing of the 1868 Pharmacy Act. This Act covered 15 drugs and included morphine and opium (South 1994). The 1868 Pharmacy Act also went further than the 1851 Arsenic Act in that sales of restricted drugs were limited to pharmacists. Shop-keepers, grocers, general stores and other traders were no longer allowed to trade restricted drugs. The subsequent 1908 Poisons and Pharmacy Act placed further restrictions on the sale of opiates and preparations containing more than 1 per cent of morphine. As was the case with the 1868 Pharmacy Act, the purchaser had only to be known by the pharmacist, or be personally introduced, and to sign the poisons register. There were no other restrictions on the possession or sale of drugs and there was no need for a doctor's prescription to acquire them (Stimson and Oppenheimer 1982).

The medicalization of drug use gained greater momentum towards the end of the nineteenth century and extended beyond the sale and availability of drugs. Drug use became medicalized through changes in definition and through changes in methods of control. In terms of definition, there were a number of factors that helped generate changes in ways of conceptualizing drug use. There was growing concern about some of the more excessive forms of opium use, such as opium eating and the use of the new hypodermic syringe method of administration to inject morphine. The concept of morphine addiction also developed about this time in part as a result of the high prevalence of non-therapeutic morphine use among doctors. The medical profession became interested in the phenomenon and many academic articles were published on the topic. In particular, case histories of morphine addiction (also referred to as 'morphinism', 'morphia habit' and 'morphia habitue') became common in medical journals (Berridge and Edwards 1981). The medical view at the time was that morphine addiction was increasing and that this was in part a result of lax medical prescribing and self-administration among doctors. Women were said to be peculiarly susceptible to morphinism (Berridge and Edwards 1981).

In terms of control, there was some interest among doctors in seeking medical solutions. In the early nineteenth century, before opium and other drug use had been framed as a disease, little attention had been paid to the issue of treatment. With the development of the concept of drug use as a disease, there emerged new forms of treatment for dealing with the problem. One of the earliest approaches was 'rapid reduction' over two or three days (Berridge and Edwards 1981). The 'abrupt method' was so much the preferred method of treating addiction that it became known as the 'English treatment'. Later, semi-rapid and gradual methods of withdrawal were also introduced. Addiction was sometimes treated as if it were a form of poisoning and some treatment methods were similar to those used for treating a drug overdose (Berridge and Edwards 1981). Less severe forms of 'poisoning' were dealt with using an 'antidote'. These included potassium and sodium bromide, codeine, cocaine and cannabis. Some approaches drew more upon current moral views of drug addiction and focused instead on advocating self-control and self-help. These methods included hypnotism as a means of encouraging self-control and restoring conventional values. Towards the end of the century, many doctors favoured a combined approach of both medical treatment and moral enlightenment. Other approaches involved what Berridge and Edwards (1981: 163) refer to as 'physical antidotes'. These included removing decayed teeth, which may be the cause of morphine use, and wearing warmer clothes rather than using opium to keep out the cold. Physical changes that promoted health and hygiene were also recommended, including taking the air, exercise, Turkish baths and cycling.

While the nineteenth century witnessed the development of medicalization, the medical approach became consolidated with the emergence of the 'British System' during the second quarter of the twentieth century. The British System originated with the publication of the Rolleston Committee Report in 1926. The 1920 Dangerous Drugs Act permitted doctors to prescribe dangerous drugs for medical treatment only. This gave them the right to prescribe controlled drugs to addicts if they thought that it was medically beneficial. However, the Home Office became concerned about whether prescribing controlled drugs to addicts constituted proper medical treatment as defined under the 1920 Act. The issue of the right of doctors to prescribe addictive drugs was presented to a departmental committee under the chair of Sir Humphrey Rolleston, the British Minister of Health.

The Rolleston Committee's mandate was to consider and advise (among other things) as to the circumstances, if any, in which the supply of morphine and heroin (including preparations containing morphine and heroin) to persons suffering from addiction to those drugs may be regarded as medically advisable. The committee's report concluded that prescribing heroin and morphine to addicts was a legitimate medical treatment for addicts. The report thus reaffirmed the disease model of addiction and placed the treatment and control of addiction in the hands of the medical profession. The recommendations of the Rolleston Committee Report, which were incorporated into the *Dangerous Drugs Regulations* of 1926, formed the basis of British policy for the next four decades. It has been argued that the relative absence of a drugs problem during that period was a result of the decision to medicalize rather than criminalize drug use. However, the extent to which the Rolleston Committee recommendations and medicalization helped to contain the spread of addiction is unclear.

Evidence from prosecutions and convictions for drug offences relating to opium and Home Office statistics on the number of known addicts indicate that there was relatively limited use of dangerous drugs in Britain during the period from the 1930s to the 1950s (Spear 1969). However, the characteristics of the addicts during this period were markedly different to those of current addicts. Until the early 1960s, most known addicts were addicted to morphine and most addicts were either 'professional addicts' (e.g. doctors, dentists and pharmacists who had direct access to morphine) or 'therapeutic addicts' (e.g. people who became addicted due to morphine treatment for their illnesses). While the statistical evidence shows that the level of addiction in Britain was fairly stable during the years following the Rolleston Committee Report, it is unlikely that this was caused by the policy to medicalize rather than criminalize addiction. Medicalization was likely to increase rather than decrease the number of 'professional addicts' and would have had little effect on the number of 'therapeutic addicts'. It is also difficult to see how the 'British System' contained addiction during the 1930s, 1940s and 1950s, but failed to contain it during the 1960s.

The first significant challenge to medicalization came during the 1950s when it was discovered that marijuana was being used for recreational purposes by members of the general public (Stimson and Oppenheimer 1982). In June 1958, the Ministry of Health set up an interdepartmental committee, chaired by Sir Russell Brain, to reappraise the recommendations of the Rolleston Committee. The Brain Committee reaffirmed in its report of 1961 that addiction was a medical matter and continued to support the Rolleston Committee's recommendations. During the next few years, further changes occurred in the British drug scene. Young people from a wide range of social backgrounds began using amphetamines, LSD, marijuana, cocaine and heroin. In response, the government asked the Brain Committee to reconvene and reconsider its recommendations. The committee recognized the problem, but believed it to be the result of overprescribing by a small number of private doctors. The Brain Committee concluded that addiction was still a medical matter. However, it recommended restricting the prescribing practices of ordinary doctors and encouraged the development of specialized drug treatment centres. In a sense, this small step in restricting the prescribing powers of doctors marked a turning point and the beginning of a gradual decline in the influence of the medical profession in defining and controlling addiction and drug use.

## The criminalization of drug use

The nineteenth-century legislation on drugs mainly concerned domestic distribution and was consistent with the progress of medicalization. Their controls focused on the activities of pharmacists and doctors and the methods by which drugs were sold or prescribed in the course of treatment. In the early years of the twentieth century, drug legislation broadened and began to focus on international distribution and consumption. Its function was to begin the process of defining drug use as a crime to be controlled by legal penalty. However, the distinction between medicalization and criminalization was not clear-cut and for most of the twentieth century drug use was viewed as both a medical and a criminal problem.

There is some debate about the exact origins of criminalization of drug use in the UK. One view is that criminalization began in June 1916 when the Home Office became the first government department to take responsibility for matters relating to dangerous drugs (see generally Spear and Mott 2002). It has also been argued that criminalization began with the passing of the first Dangerous Drugs Act in 1920 and the later amendments and additions to the Act. However, others believe that British criminal justice policy on drug misuse began earlier than this through a number of international conventions and agreements that began to control the international distribution of drugs. Spear and Mott (2002) argue that the 'true origin' of British criminal policy on drugs was the International Opium Convention, signed by 12 nations, including Great Britain, at The Hague in January 1912. In fact, the earliest international conference was the Shanghai Conference in 1909, which resulted in the Shanghai Treaty that ruled that the use of opium should be limited to medical purposes. It was agreed that other uses of opium, such as research, should be controlled by a system of prohibition and regulation. The Hague Convention in 1912 was the second international conference on drug misuse and recommended that the manufacture, trade and use of opiates should be limited to medicinal use only. It was also proposed that opium dens should be closed and the possession and sale of opiates to unauthorized persons should become punishable offences (Fortson 2002).

The first substantive evidence of a British policy on drugs was the Defence of the Realm Act Regulation 40, which came into force in December 1915. The regulations originated in response to a concern about use of cocaine among members of the armed forces. The Regulation made the gift or sale of 'intoxicants' (defined as any sedative, narcotic or stimulant) to a member of the armed forces a criminal offence punishable by imprisonment of up to 6 months (Spear and Mott 2002). There were also other wartime concerns relating to smuggling cocaine and opium from British ports. A further step in the direction of criminal justice policy occurred in an agreement made by an interdepartmental meeting in June 1916 that the problems of drug misuse were more appropriately viewed as 'police matters' and the proper responsibility of the Home Office. In July 1916, the Home Office introduced through Parliament a series of drug controls under the Defence of the Realm Regulation 40B (DORA 40B). It became an offence for anyone except members of the medical, pharmaceutical and veterinary professions to possess cocaine (Stimson and Oppenheimer 1982). The regulations also introduced licensing laws that restricted opening times of public houses and regulated alcohol sales. In the view of some writers, the 1916 regulations were a turning point and marked the Home Office as the central body in control of drugs (South 1994).

While the 1916 regulations were important in defining the role of the Home Office as the centre of drug policy, not all writers are convinced that this amounts to the beginnings of a policy of criminalization. Berridge (1984) argues that Defence of the Realm Regulation 40B dealt with the exceptional and specific problems of drugs control during wartime and that the medical profession remained centre stage as the main agency of control. If this view is accepted, then the first attempts at criminalization outside of the wartime context could be attributed to the passing of the Dangerous Drugs Act 1920 and the Dangerous Drugs Regulations 1921. The Dangerous Drugs Act 1920 prohibited importation of raw opium, morphine and cocaine, and authorized the Home Secretary to regulate the manufacture, sale, distribution and possession of dangerous drugs. It was illegal to possess these substances unless they had been supplied or prescribed by a doctor (Stimson and Oppenheimer 1982). However, it should be noted that the provisions of the Dangerous Drugs Act 1920 were not wholly new. In effect, they brought into British domestic legislation the provisions of the Hague Convention of 1912 and ratified the principles of the wartime Defence of the Realm Regulation 40B.

Nevertheless, it is widely regarded that the passing of the Dangerous Drugs Act 1920 and the subsequent Dangerous Drugs Act 1923, which imposed heavier penalties and gave the police increased powers of search, were strong markers of a policy of criminalization. Stimson and Oppenheimer write:

> The Home Office, then, had successfully claimed the problem as a criminal and policing one. The 1920 and 1923 Acts aimed at the prohibition of supplies to addicts, and were directed at doctors as well as drug users. The ideas behind the Acts were rooted in a criminal rather than medical model of addiction, and the 'vice' conception of drug use dominated the newspaper reports of the period, with stories of 'peddlers' and 'dope fiends'.
>
> (Stimson and Oppenheimer 1982: 25)

Despite a few amendments to the legislation, which introduced a wider range of drug types under legislative control and strengthened various aspects of the control process, the next 40 years or so remained relatively quiet in terms of the progress of criminalization. In fact, the dominant method of regulation during that time was medical control and a return to a policy of medicalization, as discussed in the previous section. The laws generated in the 1920s and 1930s remained on the statute books and provided a legal context for the dominantly medical approach. However, there were very few prosecutions for drug offences and for most of this period the number of known addicts remained stable. In the late 1950s and early 1960s, this situation began to change. At the time of the first Brain Committee meeting in 1958, there was evidence of a small increase in the number of known addicts, but by the time of the second Brain Committee meeting in 1964, there were signs of a substantial change in the extent and nature of drug misuse in Britain. There was also evidence that a number of private doctors in London were prescribing heroin to street addicts. During the period 1955–1965, the number of addicts known to the Home Office almost trebled (Stimson and Oppeheimer 1982). In addition to these changes, there were also changes in the population of addicts. The age of new addicts began to decline, the preferred drug of addiction switched to heroin, and the proportion of therapeutic and professional addicts fell sharply (Mott 1991). One result of these changes was a burst of legislative activity, which began a period of revival of criminalization and decline of medicalization.

The earliest legislation focused on developments in two new drug problems. The first was the growth of cannabis misuse during the 1950s. The amount of cannabis seized by Customs and Excise and in police raids increased markedly during this period and for the first time cannabis exceeded opium as the main source of drug trafficking (Spear and Mott 2002). Cannabis use previously had been confined to small groups of people such as musicians, artists and bohemians. During the 1950s, its use became widespread. The second drug problem was the misuse of stimulant drugs such as amphetamines. During the early 1960s, prescribed 'pep pills' were widely misused as recreational stimulants, as slimming aids and to maintain addiction. The first legislative response was the Dangerous Drugs Act 1964, which made it illegal to cultivate cannabis or to allow premises to be used for the consumption of cannabis. The second legislative change was the Drugs (Prevention of Misuse) Act 1964, which focused on amphetamines. Under the existing law amphetamines could be possessed legally as long as they were obtained on prescription. It was not an offence to possess legally prescribed amphetamines. The Drugs (Prevention of Misuse) Act 1964 introduced the offence of illegal possession of amphetamines and made it an offence to import them without a licence.

Further provisions and restrictions were introduced in three related pieces of legislation: the Dangerous Drugs Act 1967, the Dangerous Drugs (Supply to Addicts) Regulations and the Dangerous Drugs (Notification of Addicts) Regulations. In effect, these Acts and Regulations implemented the main recommendations of the second Brain Committee report. One of the aims of the legislation was to limit what was felt to be 'irresponsible' prescribing practices among a small number of doctors. This included restricting prescribing to addicts of heroin and cocaine to doctors licensed by the Home Secretary and establishing a system of notification of addicts. Doctors who knew or believed that a new patient was addicted to any drug in Part 1 of the schedule to the Dangerous Drugs Act 1965 was required to notify details of the patient to the Chief Medical Officer at the Home Office (Spear and Mott 2002).

The legislation also made a number of important provisions for addicts, including the establishment of what has been referred to as the 'Clinic System' (Bennett 1988: 304). Specialist drug dependency units or clinics were to be established that could provide a centre of expertise in the treatment of addiction (South 1994). The first clinics were established in 1968 in London and shortly afterwards they were established in other parts of England and Wales. In the early years, many addict patients received a prescription for injectable heroin on a maintenance basis. However, the reluctance of the medical profession to engage in 'competitive prescribing' (undercutting the black market by providing legal sources of controlled drugs) and their natural abhorrence to treatment as a form of control resulted in a general reduction in maintenance prescribing within the clinic system. By the end of 1970s, most clinic consultants had switched to oral methadone on a reduction basis.

One of the most important pieces of legislation of the 1970s was the Misuse of Drugs Act 1971. This replaced much of the previous legislation, including the Drugs (Prevention of Misuse) Act 1964 and the Dangerous Drugs Acts of 1965 and 1967, and remains to the present day the main Act of Parliament concerning the supply and possession of illegal drugs. The Act maintained the system of notification of addicts and the existing regulations on the safe custody of drugs. In addition, it established the Advisory Council on the Misuse of Drugs, a statutory body which aimed to advise the government on drug policy and treatment. The Act is perhaps best known for its system of classification of drugs. Drugs were placed in three classes (Class A, B or C) depending on the perceived hazard of the drug and its associated penalty. The most hazardous drugs (including heroin and cocaine) were classified as Class A drugs and offences relating to these drugs (e.g. possession or supply) were to receive the harshest penalties.

## The prevention of drug use

Most of the work towards criminalizing drug misuse had been completed by the early 1980s. The Misuse of Drugs Act 1971 defined the criminal nature of drug misuse and the main principles of this Act (with revisions) continue to the present day. By the early 1980s, most of the work towards medicalizing drug misuse had also been completed. The high point of the medical conception of drug misuse passed sometime during the 1960s. Over the next 20 years or so, the main policy efforts turned to prevention.

In 1984, the Advisory Council on Misuse of Drugs (ACMD) published a report that recommended that future policy should concentrate on measures that reduced the risk of an individual engaging in drug misuse and reduced the harm associated with drug misuse (ACMD 1984). The report identified three main elements of prevention: reducing the supply of drugs, reducing the demand for drugs and reducing the harm resulting from drug misuse. These three elements formed the basis of government policy for the next two decades. While there was some overlap of these strategies and bearing in mind that government policy is typically a mix of past and current policies, the emphasis placed on each of these elements of prevention followed a rough chronological order. In the 1980s the focus was supply reduction, in the 1990s the focus was demand reduction, and in the 2000s the focus has shifted towards harm reduction.

## Reducing supply

Interest in supply reduction was in part stimulated by a rapid expansion in the availability of drugs in the UK (particularly heroin) during the late 1970s. Before this time, heroin misuse grew fairly slowly. However, by 1980, the national drug indicators showed a substantial increase in heroin misuse (Mott 1991). This was in part explained at the time by a change in sources of illegal heroin. During the 1960s, there was virtually no illegally imported heroin in the UK. The main source of heroin for misuse was pharmaceutical heroin diverted from legitimate prescriptions (Stimson 1987). By 1985, the government announced that virtually all heroin and cocaine, and most of the cannabis misused in the UK, was illegally imported (Home Office 1985). This was in part because the problem of illegal prescribing had been reduced and in part because of the sheer numbers of new users seeking drugs.

The new government policy published in the document *Tackling Drug Misuse: A Summary of the Government's Strategy* (Home Office 1985) marked a radical shift in thinking about drug misuse. It represented the end of the period of growth in criminalization and the end of the generation of new laws that defined illegal drugs. According to Stimson and Oppenheimer (1982), it also marked the end of medicalization and the period during which government policy gave prominence to doctors. Drug misuse was to be tackled on five fronts: (1) reducing supplies from abroad; (2) making enforcement even more effective; (3) maintaining effective deterrents and tight domestic controls; (4) developing prevention; and (5) improving treatment and rehabilitation. While this list covered most forms of prevention, the major focus of the policy (reflected in the order given to the five actions) was control of the supply of drugs.

The focus on supply lasted for the remainder of the 1980s. The strategy document was followed by a number of new laws that aimed to control the availability of drugs. These included the Controlled Drugs (Penalties) Act 1985, which increased the maximum penalty for trafficking offences to life imprisonment, and the Drug Trafficking Offences Act (DTOA) 1986, which made provision for the recovery of the profits of crime in relation to trafficking offences.

In 1990, the government published *UK Action on Drug Misuse: The Government's Strategy* (Home Office 1990). This was a summary of the action taken by the government to tackle drug misuse since the publication of the first strategy document, *Tackling Drug Misuse*. The report restated the government's five-point strategy, but using slightly different terms: (1) improving international cooperation to reduce supplies from abroad; (2) increasing the effectiveness of police and customs enforcement; (3) maintaining effective deterrents and tight domestic controls; (4) developing prevention publicity and education; and (5) improving treatment and rehabilitation. The focus on controlling supply that characterized the first report continued in this second report.

### Reducing demand

The shift in focus to reducing demand for drugs began towards the end of the period of the last Conservative government. In May 1995, the government published *Tackling Drugs Together: A Strategy for England 1995–1998* (Home Office 1995). In the introduction, the Prime Minister (John Major) noted that, while the strategy continued to recognize the need to reduce the supply of drugs, it also recognized 'the need for stronger action on reducing the demand for illegal drugs' (Home Office 1995: 1). This small shift in emphasis marked the beginning of a period of intense activity aimed at reducing demand.

Interest in demand reduction gained greater pace with the election of a new Labour government. In 1997, Tony Blair became Prime Minister and, shortly after the election, established the UK Anti-Drug Coordination Unit (UKADCU). In 1998, following an extensive review by the UKADCU, the government published a White Paper outlining their 10-year strategy for tackling drugs, *Tackling Drugs to Build a Better Britain* (Home Office 1998a). The new strategy had four elements: (1) to help young people resist drug misuse in order to achieve their full potential in society; (2) to protect our communities from drug-related antisocial and criminal behaviour; (3) to enable people with drug problems to overcome them and live healthy and crime-free lives; and (4) to stifle the availability of illegal drugs on our streets. The first element aimed to reduce demand by reducing the number of young people who begin drug use. The third element aimed to reduce demand by reducing the number of drug users who continued using.

The method of reducing demand by providing treatment for drug users is not new and was one of the features of the early clinic system that operated in the 1960s. However, this most recent version of treatment was strikingly different. Whereas the earlier version of treatment for drug misuse was based on voluntary provision, the new form of treatment was provided as part of a sentence or order made available by the criminal justice system. This new treatment strategy has been referred to as 'coercive treatment'.

The concept of 'coerced' treatment is broad and, in the extreme, can mean compulsion, as might be the case of administering certain forms of medical treatment to psychiatric patients in special hospitals. The concept of 'coerced' treatment in relation to drug treatment is less extreme. Hough (1996) summarizes three instances in which treatment for drug misuse might be viewed as 'coercive': (1) at sentence, offenders may often be faced with an 'offer they cannot refuse', in that failure to agree to treatment as part of a community sentence may well trigger a prison sentence; (2) where treatment is accepted as a condition of probation, defaulting on the condition may well result in breach proceedings (and imprisonment); and (3) even if treatment is not a formal condition of probation, continued drug misuse or offending could result in breach, as could results from drug testing (Hough 1996: 36).

'Coercive' treatment as a means of reducing demand was established under a number of Acts of Parliament passed in the late 1990s and early 2000s. Drug treatment and testing orders were introduced in the Crime and Disorder Act 1998. Courts were granted the powers to create an order requiring offenders to undergo treatment, either as part of another community order or as a sentence in its own right. It could last from 6 months to 3 years. Drug treatment and testing orders differed from probation orders to the extent that the sentencing court was required to check progress throughout. Compliance was to be checked at regular intervals by mandatory urine testing. Drug abstinence orders and drug abstinence requirements were introduced in the Criminal Justice and Court Services Act 2000. A drug abstinence order requires offenders to abstain from misusing heroin and crack/cocaine and to undergo regular drug testing under the supervision of qualified probation staff. The order applies to offenders aged over 18 who have committed certain 'trigger offences' and who are suspected of being a drug user. A drug abstinence order can be used when the court believes that the offender would benefit from continued monitoring of their drug misuse, and that any other community order is not justified. A drug abstinence requirement is similar to a drug abstinence order, but is attached to a community sentence.

### Reducing harm

Harm reduction is not a new concept and was one of the stated aims of the drug clinics established in 1968. Edwards (1969) noted at the time that, 'There are believed to be some patients who cannot – or cannot for the time being – function without the drug, but who on a regular maintenance dose can live a normal and useful life as a "stabilized addict"; such patients will be maintained on heroin rather than have their drug withdrawn' (p. 768). Several factors led to the reversal of these early harm-reduction policies during the 1970s. One factor was the observation that younger users were not necessarily becoming more stable on prescriptions of heroin. At the outset of the clinic system, heroin was prescribed mainly to small numbers of more stable, middle-aged, middle-class addicts. Another factor was the problem that during the 1970s the clinics were becoming silted up with long-term patients and the system became overloaded (Mitcheson 1994).

Harm reduction went out of fashion for a while in the UK during the early 1980s as concerns about heroin maintenance grew and new policy initiatives were developed. However, there was a return of interest during the late 1980s with the fear of HIV and AIDS among injecting drug users (Stimson and Lart 1991). This was reinforced by the Advisory Council on the Misuse of Drugs, which argued in its report at the end of the 1980s that AIDS was more of a threat than drug misuse (ACMD 1988). In response, a number of needle exchange schemes were established with the initial aim of reducing the spread of HIV infection among drug users. The development in needle exchange programmes was documented in the guidance notes of the first strategy document of the new Labour government. The notes welcomed the expansion of needle exchange programmes over the previous decade. They explained that their primary aim was to reduce the use of shared injecting equipment among users who injected and to increase the use of clean equipment among injectors who shared. The document noted that, 'In terms of HIV, this approach has been a considerable success' (Home Office 1998b: 32).

The guidance notes that accompanied *Tackling Drugs to Build a Better Britain 1998* (Home Office 1998b) also included a section that summarized the government's position on harm reduction. The paper accepted that there were harm-reducing benefits attached to maintenance prescribing and noted that, 'The controlled prescribing by doctors of drugs to help users deal effectively with withdrawal from heroin, tranquillisers or alcohol, and the longer term prescribing of substitute opiates as a suitable and safer alternative to street heroin, are well established practices in the UK' (p. 33). However, it noted that it had not been government policy to return to the British system of prescribing injectable heroin. Instead, the preference had been for substitute prescribing and the use of methadone rather than heroin to tackle heroin addiction. According to the Home Office (1998b), the main arguments for substitute prescribing are that 'it avoids leakage onto the black market and it provides consistency and continuity of practice' (p. 33).

The issue of heroin prescribing re-emerged within the general debate about harm-reduction in the *Updated Drug Strategy* (Home Office 2002). The document stated that the medical prescription of heroin would be available for all those who had a clinical need. It was argued that the policy aimed to break the cycle of drug misuse and crime by providing effective treatment and rehabilitation. The strategy was in part a response to a report by the Home Affairs Committee (2002), which recommended that a pilot programme of prescribing heroin should be conducted, targeted, in the first instance, at chronic heroin users who are prolific offenders. There are some differences between the earlier versions of heroin prescribing and the more recent proposal. Stimson and Metrebian (2003) argue that earlier approaches were based on reducing harm to individual users and broader public health concerns relating to the risk of HIV. The more recent discussion focuses more on prescribing heroin as a means of reducing drug-related crime.

Other recent harm-reducing projects include the 'safer clubbing' guide made available to club owners with information to reduce the numbers of drug-related deaths. The brochure includes tips on how to prevent drugs being brought into and used in clubs, as well as methods for ensuring that there are adequate supplies of drinking water, no overcrowding, proper air conditioning and ventilation. They also include the provisions of the Paraphernalia Act 2003, which extended the principles of needle-exchange schemes to include other drug use paraphernalia. It is now no longer an offence for doctors, pharmacists or drug workers to supply certain types of drug paraphernalia to drug users, such as filters, sterile water and swabs for cleaning injecting sites.

## Variations across countries

This chapter has focused so far on the legal and policy context of the UK. However, the methods used for understanding this context can be applied equally well to other countries. In particular, drugs policies can be divided into those that are 'tough' and crime oriented (focusing on criminal processing and punishment) and those that are 'lenient' and user oriented (focusing on treatment and harm reduction). Although, in practice, most national policies contain elements of both approaches, it is possible to provide a rough comparison of countries that are more or less 'tough' and those that are more or less 'lenient'. In the following section, we have identified two countries that are fairly lenient in their approach (The Netherlands and Switzerland) and two countries that are fairly tough (Sweden and the United States). The degree of 'toughness' has been determined from national policy documents and statements made about the aims of the policy and the types of interventions used.

### The Netherlands

The Netherlands can be thought of as being a relatively 'lenient' country in its approach to drug use. The details of this approach can be found in the drugs policy document, *National Drug Policy: The Netherlands* (Dolin 2001), in which it is noted that the Dutch system is rooted in the concept of harm reduction. This is described as a policy of minimization of the risks and hazards of drug use, rather than the suppression of drugs. It is also noted that the central aim of the policy is the prevention or alleviation of social and individual risks caused by drug use. Like most national policies, the Dutch system includes what are described as repressive measures (particularly in relation to drug trafficking) and general criminal justice responses. However, it is felt that in some areas (particularly in relation to demand reduction) criminal justice measures alone are inadequate and a different kind of response is required. The document mentioned above discusses the benefits of what is described as a policy of 'normalization' of drug use. Normalization is described as social control achieved through 'depolarization' and 'integration' of deviant behaviour, rather than isolation and removal. This is contrasted with the deterrence model, which, it is argued, tends to be based on exclusion. The Dutch approach is based on the principle that drug problems are 'normal' social problems and require 'normal' social responses.

The policy of The Netherlands might also be identified through the types of interventions implemented. A policy can be defined as 'lenient' or 'tough' through a number of indicators. These include the range and availability of treatment services to drug users, whether treatment is voluntary or coercive, the existence of maintenance prescribing of methadone or heroin, the presence of harm-reduction programmes, evidence of decriminalization or legalization, and the severity of maximum penalties for possession and supply of drugs. In the case of The Netherlands, interventions tend towards the 'lenient' side of the spectrum. The Netherlands has an easily accessible and widespread network of medical and social services at local and regional level. These include non-residential services (fieldwork, social counselling, therapy, methadone supply and rehabilitation), semi-residential services (day/night centres, day-care treatment, employment and recreation) and residential services (crises and detoxification drug dependence units and therapeutic communities). Treatment for problematic drug users is largely on a voluntary basis (Netherlands Institute of Mental Health and Addiction 1999). Methadone maintenance is available on demand. In 1998, several Dutch cities began experimenting with prescribing heroin in combination with methadone. The Netherlands also has a number of harm-reduction programmes, including a national syringe exchange programme covering 60 Dutch cities and towns (Drug Policy Alliance 2003a).

Simple possession of drugs in The Netherlands has been substantially decriminalized. The penalty for possession, preparation, sale, transportation or manufacture of Schedule II (soft) drugs, up to a quantity of 5 grams, is currently confiscation, with no further action taken. According to the Netherlands Ministry of Foreign Affairs (2002), the possession of small amounts of cannabis for personal use has been decriminalized. An operator or owner of a coffee shop may sell cannabis and avoid prosecution as long as certain criteria are met – that is, no more than 5 grams per person are sold in any one transaction and minors cannot enter the premises. Dutch policy in relation to alcohol also tends to be fairly lenient. The minimum legal age for the purchase of alcohol is 16 for beer and wine and 18 for spirits. Alcoholic beverages are for sale at liquor stores and supermarkets. However, supermarkets can only sell beer, wine and alcoholic beverages with a strength of up to 13 per cent alcohol (International Center for Alcohol Policy 2002). Drink-driving laws are enforced at a blood alcohol concentration of 0.5 mg/ml and above. However, the penalties for more serious drugs are more severe. The maximum penalty for possession of hard drugs for personal use is one year's imprisonment and/or a fine of €11,250. The maximum penalty for possession of hard drugs beyond personal use is imprisonment of 4 years and/or a fine of €45,000. The maximum penalty for sale of hard drugs (i.e. heroin, cocaine and ecstasy) is 8 years and/or a fine of €45,000.

## Switzerland

Switzerland also has adopted a more 'lenient' approach to drug misuse. According to the Swiss Federal Office of Public Health (2002) document, *Swiss Drugs Policy*, the main aims of the national drugs policy focuses on users rather than offences. The main aims reported in the document are: to reduce the number of new drug users and addicts; to increase the number of individuals who succeed in giving up drugs; to reduce damage to the health of drug addicts and their marginalization in society; and to protect society from the effects of the drug problem and combat criminality. The third aim suggests a harm minimization approach. It also refers to reduction of marginalization, which is similar to the normalization and integrative approach of The Netherlands discussed above. Hence, in terms of its aims, the Swiss drugs policy falls clearly on the 'lenient' side of the spectrum.

   This general lenient orientation can be found also in its choice of treatment and control responses. As mentioned above, a 'lenient' policy might be regarded as one which provides a good range of treatment services for drug users, focuses on voluntary rather than coercive provision, includes harm-reduction programmes, shows evidence of some decriminalization or legalization, and has modest (rather than severe) penalties for drug offences. According to the above document, Switzerland has a wide range of residential and outpatient treatment options. At the end of 1999, some 400 places were available in Swiss clinics or hospital wards, and there were a further 1750 places in residential therapeutic facilities. Switzerland also has over 200 community-based counselling centres whose task is to prevent drug abuse and to care for drug-dependent individuals. The report estimates that about half of the opiate addicts in Switzerland are receiving methadone treatment. In 1999, this amounted to about 16,000 of the estimated 30,000 opiate addicts. Methadone is available on what is described as an easy-access basis. Heroin prescribing has also been available since 1999. The dominant treatment philosophy is 'harm reduction'. The principle of this approach is that 'low-threshold facilities' are open to all drug users without imposing specific conditions of entry. These include easy access to syringes through pharmacies, contact centres, street workers and vending machines, drug-injecting rooms, employment and housing projects, and projects to assist drug-dependent women involved in prostitution.

There is some evidence of decriminalization or at least leniency in terms of enforcement. Intentional consumption of narcotics is punishable by detention or a fine. However, for minor offences involving non-narcotics, the appropriate authority may stay the proceedings, waive punishment or issue a reprimand. Preparing narcotics for personal use or for shared use at no charge is not punishable when the quantities involved are small. Marijuana is still technically illegal. However, stores specializing in the sale of 'hemp products' exist throughout the country. In 1999, the Federal Commission unanimously recommended that prohibition of possession should be removed from the statute books and provision should be made for marijuana to be purchased lawfully. This was approved by the Swiss Senate in December 2001 and approval by the House of Representatives is pending (Drug Policy Alliance 2003b). The alcohol laws are similar to those in The Netherlands. Advertising for alcoholic beverages is restricted. The minimum legal age to purchase spirits is 18, yet the minimum age for drinking alcohol in public places is controlled by each Canton, and ranges from 14 to 16 (International Center for Alcohol Policy 2002). The blood alcohol concentration permitted for drivers is slightly higher than The Netherlands at 0.8 mg/ml.

**Sweden**

Swedish drug policy might be regarded as falling at the 'tough' end of the spectrum. The main objective of Sweden's drug policy is to achieve a drug-free society (Swedish Ministry of Health and Social Affairs 2002). The policy document notes that Swedish drug policy is more restrictive than that of many of the other countries in Europe. Drug use is seen as a serious social problem and an 'external menace' to the country. One of the aims of the policy is to send the message that drugs are not tolerated in Swedish society. In particular, the policy aims to reduce the number of new recruits to drug abuse, to encourage drug abusers to give up the habit, and to reduce the supply of drugs.

In Sweden, it is possible to coerce people into drug treatment for a period of up to 6 months. The goal of treatment is to obtain complete abstention (Lafrenière 2002). There are a limited number of methadone substitution programmes in Stockholm, Uppsala, Malmö and Lund. However, the programmes are strictly regulated and are officially viewed as experimental only. There are strict conditions for participation, including the provision that the patient must be over 20 years of age and demonstrate at least 4 years of intravenous opiate abuse (Lafrenière 2002).

In Sweden, almost all forms of involvement with narcotics are prohibited in law (mainly the Narcotic Drugs Criminal Act). Drug offences include possession for personal use and supply. Hence, even personal consumption of drugs is prohibited in law. For minor drug offences (personal use or possession for personal use of cannabis up to 50 g/cocaine up to 0.5 g/heroin up to 0.39 g), the maximum penalty is a fine based on the offender's income or up to 6 months' imprisonment. For serious drug offences (possession or supply involving cannabis 2 kg or more/cocaine 51 g or more/heroin 25 g or more), the penalty is between 2 and 10 years' imprisonment (Lafrenière 2002). Consistent with the general tough enforcement policy on drugs, there has been no attempt at decriminalization of drug use. A survey conducted in 2000 revealed that 91 per cent of the Swedish public were against decriminalizing cannabis (Lafrenière 2002). Cannabis has not received the same pressure for decriminalization that has occurred in some other European countries. Instead, cannabis is viewed as a dangerous drug that leads to harder drugs and lifelong addiction (Drug Policy Alliance 2003b).

Alcohol laws in Sweden are equally strict. There remains a state monopoly on the sale of alcohol and it can only be supplied from approved outlets. Alcoholics can be forced into treatment for a period of up to 6 months in the same way that other drug addicts can be forced into treatment. The minimum legal age for the purchase of beer is 18. However, the minimum age for the purchase of all other alcoholic drinks is 20 (International Center for Alcohol Policy 2002). The blood alcohol concentration permitted for drivers is one of the lowest in Europe at 0.02 mg/ml (just over the level that can be produced naturally in the human body). In practice, this means that drivers cannot drink any alcohol and drive.

## United States

The US drugs policy might also be regarded as being at the 'tough' end of the spectrum. Its policy is based on the enforcement model and its main strategies are described as interdiction, arrest, prosecution and incarceration of users (Drug Policy Alliance 2003c). However, the current policy is slightly more wide-ranging than this and has three main priorities: 'stopping drug use before it starts' (e.g. drug prevention programmes in schools and student drug testing programmes), 'healing America's drug users' (e.g. more money for short-term treatment programmes and drug courts), and 'disrupting the market' (e.g. interrupting the flow of drug trafficking from Columbia) (The White House 2003). The United States also maintains a wide range of treatment services for drug users. These include methadone maintenance programmes, outpatient programmes, residential programmes, medical detoxification and prison-based treatment programmes. The National Survey of Substance Abuse Treatment Services (Department of Health and Human Services 2003) estimated from a one-day survey conducted in 2002 that a total of 13,720 facilities reported 1,136,287 clients receiving substance abuse treatment. The prescribing policy includes methadone maintenance and is available to an estimated 14 per cent of clients in the substance abuse system (Levine et al. 2004). However, the policy is more restrictive in terms of other aspects of treatment. The possession, distribution and sale of syringes are criminal offences in some parts of the country. The majority of States have passed laws allowing pharmacy sales of sterile syringes. However, it is reported that there are still major obstacles to obtaining sterile syringes in the United States (Drug Policy Alliance 2003d).

The maximum penalties for possession and supply in the United States tend to be punitive. Possession 'with intent' (i.e. possession of large amounts of illegal substances) and the supply or manufacture of large quantities of drugs carries a maximum penalty of life imprisonment (Drug Enforcement Agency 2002). Possession of small amounts ('a personal use amount') carries a maximum penalty of a $10,000 fine. There is also little evidence of decriminalization of drug laws. Some States have enacted what is referred to as 'treatment instead of incarceration' legislation. This mandates that anyone arrested for non-violent drug possession offences must receive drug treatment instead of jail for their first and second offence (Drug Policy Alliance 2003d). However, there is little support for the idea of decriminalizing cannabis or other 'soft drugs'. The national policy document reports that groups asserting the medical value of marijuana are 'making outlandish claims that deceive well-meaning citizens' (The White House 2003: 9).

The United States has a history of control over alcohol, typified most strongly in the years of prohibition during the early years of the twentieth century. Alcohol policy remains tough. The Federal Minimum Legal Drinking Age (MLDA) Laws make it illegal for any person who is less than 21 years old to purchase, possess or consume alcoholic beverages or to misrepresent their age to obtain such beverages. There is some variation in the MLDA Laws across States and some States allow persons under age 21 to possess and consume alcoholic beverages for religious purposes and at home. Most States have adopted some form of mandatory incarceration for impaired (through intoxication) driving and the blood alcohol concentration allowed for adult drivers varies from 0.08 to 0.1 mg/ml. The limit for those under 21 is a very strict 0.02 mg/ml.

## Conclusion

We have argued in this chapter that drug use is not inherently a deviant or criminal activity and for many years has been regarded as normal and acceptable. However, in more recent years various factors have come together that have encouraged both the medicalization and the criminalization of drug use. The process by which these changes have come about has been influenced in particular by the actions of pressure groups, religious and moral beliefs, technological developments (especially the hypodermic syringe and drug production systems), political expedients and developments in related social problems (such as concerns about public health and crime). The response to the problem has varied across countries. Some countries are more tolerant and focus on treatment provision, while other countries are less tolerant and focus on law enforcement. However, the similarities between countries are perhaps more notable than the differences. Most countries see drug use as a major social problem and most countries tackle drug use through a combination of supply-reduction, demand-reduction and harm-reduction policies.

## Further reading

The best book on the early history of opiate use in the UK is *Opium and the People* (Berridge and Edwards 1981). In particular, it provides a fascinating insight into the widespread use of heroin before it was defined as a problem. The book by Spear and Mott (2002), *Heroin Addiction, Care and Control*, provides an authoritative overview of the growth of heroin addiction and control in the UK throughout most of the twentieth century. Bing Spear was the chief drugs inspector at the Home Office and for many years knew every registered heroin addict by name (a skill he was forced to relinquish with the spread of opiate use in the 1960s). Current government policy is summarized on the Home Office website in various reports and other publications (http://www.homeoffice.gov.uk).

**chapter** three

# Extent of drug misuse

## Introduction

This chapter gives an overview of the extent of drug misuse and provides a context for the discussion covered in the remainder of the book. It focuses mainly on the UK, but includes references to other countries as appropriate. The chapter begins by looking at the types of drugs misused, the kinds of people who take them and the number of drug users in the population. It then examines the sources of supply of drugs entering the country, the types of drugs supplied and the nature of drug markets. Finally, the chapter considers some of the problems associated with drug misuse, including the problems of addiction and dependence, health problems, economic and social costs, and drug-related deaths.

The early part of the chapter makes a distinction between measures of the demand and supply for drugs. While the two concepts are similar, in that for every buyer there is a seller, the methods of measuring drug misuse often fall into one or other of these two categories. The section on demand discusses the nature and extent of the population of drug users. The section on supply discusses the origins and distribution of drugs.

## Demand for drugs

Information about the extent of drug use can be obtained by looking at general populations, offender populations and drug-user populations.

General populations are usually investigated by large (sometimes national) self-report surveys, offender populations are sometimes investigated by surveys or by official criminal justice data, and drug-user populations are usually investigated by small surveys of users in treatment or official treatment usage data. The following section will focus on drug use in the general and the offender population. Drug use among drug users will be discussed in later chapters.

### Drug use in the general population

One of the largest national surveys of crime and drug misuse among adults is the British Crime Survey. Since 1996, the British Crime Survey has included a module of questions on illicit drug use (Condon and Smith 2003). The surveys are conducted among a representative cross-section of private households in England and Wales approximately once every year. The results of the 2000 survey showed that 34 per cent of the population of adults (aged 16–59) had consumed at least one illegal drug at some time in their lives and 11 per cent had done so in the previous year. Similar percentages for drug use in the last year were given in the results of the 2002–2003 sweep of the British Crime Survey. This showed that 12 per cent of all 16- to 59-year-olds had used an illicit drug in the previous year. The authors of the report calculated that this equates to around 4 million illicit drug users in the general population (Condon and Smith 2003). Information on alcohol use can be found in other national surveys. One of the largest national surveys of the adult population is the General Household Survey. This is based on a representative sample of adults in England, Scotland and Wales. Results of the 2001 General Household Survey showed that approximately two-thirds of respondents (67 per cent) aged 16 and over reported having an alcoholic drink in the last week (Walker *et al.* 2002). The majority of these drank only infrequently. However, 17 per cent of the general population reported drinking alcohol on 5 or more days in the last week.

The second major source of information on drug use in the general population is school surveys. The National Centre for Social Research (NCSR) and the National Foundation for Educational Research (NFER) carry out a regular series of surveys of school children for the Department of Health. In 2003, questionnaires were distributed to over 10,000 pupils in 321 schools in England (NCSR/NFER 2004). The study found that 21 per cent of respondents aged 11–15 had used one or more drugs in the last year (almost twice that of the adult population). Over 80 per cent of respondents had drunk alcohol at some point in their lives and 25 per cent had drunk alcohol in the last year. Most young people admitted only occasional use. However, about 10 per cent reported drinking at least once a week on average. One of the longest running series of surveys is organized by the Schools Health Education Unit. The surveys have been conducted annually since 1986 and cover approximately 500 primary and secondary

**Table 3.1** Prevalence estimates of use of drugs in the last 12 months among various surveys

| Survey | Population | Age group | Drug type | Prevalence |
|---|---|---|---|---|
| BCS 2002/2003 | General | 16–59 years | Any illegal drug | 12% |
| NCSR/NFER 2003 | General | 11–15 years | Any illegal drug | 21% |
| YLS 1998/1999 | General | 12–30 years | Any illegal drug | 27% |
| Criminality Survey 2000 | Offender | 17–59 years | Any illegal drug | 73% |
| NEW-ADAM 1999/2000 | Offender | 17+ | Any illegal drug | 80% |
| | | | | |
| BCS 2002/2003 | General | 16–59 years | Cannabis | 11% |
| NCSR/NFER 2003 | General | 11–15 years | Cannabis | 13% |
| YLS 1998/1999 | General | 12–30 years | Cannabis | 22% |
| Criminality Survey 2000 | Offender | 17–59 years | Cannabis | 65% |
| NEW-ADAM 1999/2000 | Offender | 17+ | Cannabis | 70% |
| | | | | |
| BCS 2002/2003 | General | 16–59 years | Heroin | <1% |
| NCSR/NFER 2003 | General | 11–15 years | Heroin | 1% |
| YLS 1998/1999 | General | 12–30 years | Heroin | <1% |
| Criminality Survey 2000 | Offender | 17–59 years | Heroin | 31% |
| NEW-ADAM 1999/2000 | Offender | 17+ | Heroin | 32% |

*Notes:* BCS 2002/2003: British Crime Survey (Condon and Smith 2003); NCSR/NFER 2003: National Centre for Social Research and National Foundation for Educational Research (NCSR/NFER 2004); YLS 1998/1999: Youth Lifestyles Survey (Goulden and Sondhi 2001); Criminality Survey 2000: The Criminality Survey (Ramsay 2003b); NEW-ADAM 1999/2000: New English and Welsh Arrestee Drug Abuse Monitoring Programme (Holloway and Bennett 2004).

schools across the UK. The most recent report of these surveys conducted in 2002 was based on 37,150 school children aged between 8 and 18 years. The survey included questions on a wide range of issues relating to the health and behaviour of young people, including drug use. The latest figures show that about one in four pupils in year 10 had tried at least one drug in their lifetime (Balding 2002).

A third source of information on drug misuse in the general population is surveys of young people. One of the largest national surveys of young people, which includes information on drug use, is the Youth Lifestyles Survey (Goulden and Sondhi 2001). The 1998–1999 Youth Lifestyles Survey was a self-report study based on 4848 young people aged 12–30 living in England and Wales. The results of the survey showed even higher percentages of drug use among young people than shown in the above surveys of school children. In total, 43 per cent of all young people interviewed reported having used an illegal drug in their lifetime and 27 per cent said that they had used a drug in the last year (Pudney 2002).

Most of these surveys provide a breakdown of the types of drugs consumed. The most recent British Crime Survey showed that the most commonly used illegal drug among adults aged 16–59 was cannabis, used by 11 per cent of the population in the last year (Condon and Smith 2003). This amounts to approximately three million recent cannabis users in the adult general population (Condon and Smith 2003). About 2 per cent of the population had used amphetamines in the last year and about the same proportion had used ecstasy. Far fewer people had used heroin or crack (less than 1 per cent). Surveys of school children tend to show generally lower prevalence rates for each of the main drug types. The most recent NCSR/NFER survey of school children found that cannabis was the drug most likely to have been taken by 11- to 15-year-olds: 13 per cent reported using cannabis in the last year (about half the rate for young people), 8 per cent reported taking volatile substances and 4 per cent reported taking 'poppers'. One per cent had taken heroin in the last year and 1 per cent had taken crack (a similar proportion as shown in the other surveys). The proportion of young people (typically aged 12–30) using different drug types tends to be slightly higher. The 1998–1999 Youth Lifestyles Survey found that 22 per cent of respondents aged 12–30 reported using cannabis in the last year (compared with 11 per cent found in the adult population). Almost twice as many young people as adults reported using ecstasy in the last year (4 per cent of young people, compared with 2 per cent of adults). However, the proportion of young people in the general population using heroin or crack remains small at less than 1 per cent (Goulden and Sondhi 2001).

The surveys can also be used to determine who takes drugs. The British Crime Surveys show that drug use in the last year tends to decrease with age. Twenty-eight per cent of 16- to 24-year-olds reported using drugs in the last year, compared with 17 per cent of 25- to 34-year-olds and 5 per cent of 35- to 59-year-olds (Condon and Smith 2003). This relationship held for most drug types. Cannabis use in the last year tended to decrease with age (reducing from 26 per cent of 16- to 24-year-olds to 4 per cent of 35- to 59-year-olds). Amphetamine use and ecstasy use in the last year also tended to decrease with age, along with that of cocaine and crack. However, research on the relationship between age and alcohol use shows a slightly different pattern. The results from the 2001 General Household Survey showed that the prevalence of alcohol use in the last week followed an inverted 'U' shape with the lowest rates for the younger and older groups and the highest rates for the middle-aged groups (Walker *et al.* 2002).

In the general population, males are more likely than females to report using drugs. Figures for the 2000 sweep of the British Crime Survey show that 40 per cent of males reported ever using drugs compared with 28 per cent of females (a ratio of 1.4 to 1). When looking at drug use in the last year, this gap widens to 1.8 to 1 and in relation to drug use in the last month it widens further to 2.3 to 1 (Ramsay *et al.* 2001). A similar pattern emerges in relation to alcohol use. The results of the 2001 General Household Survey showed that the prevalence of alcohol use in the last week was 75 per cent for males compared with 59 per cent for females.

There is also some information available on variations in drug use by ethnic groups. General population surveys show that lifetime drug use is more prevalent among white groups than ethnic groups. The 2000 British Crime Survey showed that lifetime use of any drug was 34 per cent among white people compared with 28 per cent among black respondents, 15 per cent of Indians and 10 per cent of Pakistanis/Bangladeshis (Ramsay *et al.* 2001). However, self-reported drug use in the last year was highest among 'all black groups' (13 per cent), compared with 11 per cent for whites and 5 per cent for Indian/Pakistani/Bangladeshi respondents. Research on ethnicity and alcohol use has shown that minority ethnic groups are less likely than the general population to drink alcohol and, when they do, they consume smaller amounts (Erens and Laiho 2001). This research showed that 7 per cent of men in the general population were non-drinkers compared with 13 per cent of Afro-Caribbeans, 30 per cent of Chinese, 33 per cent of Indians, 91 per cent of Pakistanis and 96 per cent of Bangladeshis.

### Drug use in offender populations

It might be expected that there will be differences between drug use in the general population and in the offender population. It is widely believed that there is an association between drug use and crime (to be discussed in more detail later) and offenders might be viewed as generally a more deviant sub-set of the general population and more willing to try illegal substances. The results of empirical research tend to support these assumptions. The main source of information on drug use among offenders is from surveys of arrestees and surveys of prisoners.

The Criminality Survey conducted in prisons in England and Wales during April and May 2000 showed that 73 per cent of inmates had taken an illegal drug in the 12 months before imprisonment. Almost half (47 per cent) had used heroin or crack or cocaine in the same 12 month period (Ramsay 2003a). Similarly, high levels of drug use have been found in surveys of arrestees. The results of the first two years of the New English and Welsh Arrestee Drug Abuse Monitoring (NEW-ADAM) programme showed that 80 per cent of arrestees reported using an illegal drug in the last 12 months, compared with 12 per cent in the general population (Holloway and Bennett 2004). These differences are most marked for the more serious drugs. Thirty-two per cent of arrestees reported using heroin in the last year (compared with less than 1 per cent of the general population) and 29 per cent reported using crack cocaine (compared with less than 1 per cent of the general population). Twenty-five per cent of arrestees said that they had used amphetamines in the last year and 26 per cent said that they had used ecstasy.

The offender research also provides information on who takes drugs. The results of the Criminality Survey of prisoners show that drug use tended to decline with age (Liriano and Ramsay 2003). Eighty per cent of 17- to 24-year-olds reported cannabis use in the year before imprisonment, compared with 54 per cent of 25- to 59-year-olds. The pattern persisted for the more serious drugs, with the younger groups reporting the highest rates of cocaine, crack and heroin use and the older groups the lowest rates. The relationship between declining age and declining drug use was also found in the NEW-ADAM research. Holloway and Bennett (2004) found that the proportion of positive tests for any drug was highest among 20- to 24-year-olds (77 per cent) and lowest among the 30+ age group (60 per cent). There was some variation by type of drug. The percentage of positive tests for cannabis was highest for the youngest group and lowest for the oldest group. However, use of opiates and cocaine (as measured by percentage positive tests) followed an inverted 'U' shape, with the highest rates shown for the middle age group and the lowest rates for the youngest and oldest groups (although the differences were small).

One of the most striking differences between the general population surveys and the offender surveys is the effect of gender. General population surveys tend to show that males are much more likely than females to have used both minor and major drug types. However, the offender research tends to show either that there is little difference between the two sexes or that females are more likely than males to use drugs. The NEW-ADAM research found, for example, that female arrestees were more likely than male arrestees to test positive for any drug (46 per cent compared with 35 per cent). Females were also significantly more likely than males to test positive for Class A drugs (50 per cent compared with 36 per cent) and opiates and/or cocaine (49 per cent compared with 36 per cent) (Holloway and Bennett 2004). There was some variation by type of drug. Females were significantly more likely than males to test positive for opiates, methadone, cocaine, amphetamines and benzodiazepines. By contrast, males were significantly more likely than females to test positive for canna-bis (50 per cent compared with 36 per cent) and alcohol (24 per cent compared with 14 per cent) (Holloway and Bennett 2004). All prisoners interviewed in the Criminality Survey were male. Hence there were no breakdowns by gender. One possible explanation for the difference between general population and offender surveys in terms of female involvement in drug use is selection bias that might favour females. It is possible that female offenders who get through the selection process are even more deviant than their male counterparts and even more likely to be involved in drug misuse.

The results were more mixed in relation to ethnic minority status. The results of the NEW-ADAM surveys showed that there was no difference in the proportion of white and non-white arrestees testing positive for one or more drugs (69 per cent of each). However, significantly more white arrestees than non-white arrestees tested positive for multiple drugs, Class A drugs and opiates and/or cocaine (Holloway and Bennett 2004). Conversely, 52 per cent of non-white arrestees tested positive for cannabis compared with 48 per cent of white arrestees (although this difference was not statistically significant). Twenty-seven per cent of white arrestees compared with 21 per cent of non-white arrestees tested positive for cocaine (this difference was statistically significant) (Holloway and Bennett 2004). Similar results were obtained from the Criminality Survey. In general, white respondents were more likely than non-white respondents to report all types of drug use, with the exception of cannabis and crack (Liriano and Ramsay 2003).

### Sizing the market

The demand for drugs in a country can also be assessed by what is sometimes called 'sizing the market'. In effect, this means estimating the total expenditure on drugs by all drug users over a set period of time (usually a particularly year). A sizing exercise of this kind was conducted in the UK for the year 1998 by Bramley-Harker (2001). The study was based on the results obtained on drug use and expenditure from the 1998 NEW-ADAM programme (Bennett 2000). The sizing exercise aims to estimate the total number of regular users of different types of drugs and the total expenditure by those users on those drugs. The study concluded that the best estimate of the total value of the UK market in 1998 was £6.6 billion. This was slightly higher than another study completed by the Office for National Statistics (Groom *et al.* 1998), which gave an estimate of £4.2 billion for 1996. Hence, it might be assumed from this either that the true estimate is somewhere between these two figures or that it is increasing over time.

The study also broke down the estimates of total expenditure per year by drug type. It was estimated that a large proportion of the total expenditure on drugs resulted from expenditure on heroin (£2.3 billion) and crack (£1.8 billion). However, the total amount spent on cannabis (£1.6 billion) was only slightly less than that spent on crack. Far less was spent on cocaine (£0.35 billion), ecstasy (£0.29 billion) and amphetamines (£0.25 billion). The study also estimated the physical quantities of drugs consumed in the UK based on the known expenditure and known price of the various drug types. This showed that the total market per year in cannabis is approximately 486,000 kg, followed by heroin at 31,000 kg and crack at 18,000 kg. The total number of ecstasy tables consumed per year is about 27 million.

### Trends in demand

It is useful to distinguish trends in demand and trends in supply of drugs. While they are likely to move in a similar direction in the longer term, they might move differently in the short term. There is also a conceptual distinction between trends in the number of drug users and trends in the availability of drugs.

Trends in the demand for drug use can be examined by looking at trends in the general population and trends in the offender population. The main advantage to looking at trends in the general population is that they provide a baseline for drug misuse in the population as a whole. The main disadvantage is that the proportion of drug users in the general population is generally low and it is sometimes difficult to identify meaningful change. Consequently, it is sometimes more useful to look also at changes in the offender population. The main advantage of looking at the offender population is that they tend to be more heavily involved in drug use and it is easier to determine change in a larger proportion. It could also be argued that offenders are more likely to be at the forefront of trends in the use of drugs and might be the first to be involved in drug switching or exploring new drugs. The main disadvantage is that the trends might be different for this population compared with other populations.

### General population

According to the 2002–2003 British Crime Survey, there has been a steady increase over the last few years in the proportion of the adult population that uses drugs (see generally Ramsay *et al.* 2001; Aust *et al.* 2002; Condon and Smith 2003). However, these general trends mask more specific changes in the use of particular drug types. During the period 1994 to 2003, the proportion of the adult population using crack and cocaine increased. Conversely, the proportion using heroin decreased slightly (from 0.2% in 1994 to 0.1% in 2002–2003). The idea that crack and cocaine might be replacing heroin as a drug of choice among serious drug users is offered some support by this finding. The proportion of the adult population using cannabis and the proportion using ecstasy have also both increased. However, the proportions using amphetamines and LSD have decreased.

There are some notable changes in drug use over time among different age groups. Drug use among the younger section of the adult population (16- to 19-year-olds) has generally declined over the period 1994 to 2002–2003. In 1994, 34 per cent of this group reported using one or more drugs in the last year. In 2002–2003, this proportion fell to 27 per cent. This reduction was fairly consistent among drug types. Use of cannabis fell from 29 per cent in 1994 to 25 per cent in 2002–2003. Similarly, use of amphetamines fell from 10 per cent in 1994 to 3 per cent in 2002–2003. At the same time, use of heroin and cocaine remained more or less constant at a low level, while use of crack increased slightly. Hence, much of the increase in drug misuse in the general population over the last 10 years has occurred among the older adult groups.

The 2001 General Household Survey included questions on daily amount of alcohol drunk in the last week. Over the period 1998 to 2001, the research found that the proportions of adult men and women who had an alcoholic drink in the previous week did not change. However, there was evidence of an increase in the amount of alcohol consumed among women. During the period 1998 to 2001, the proportion of women who had drunk more than six units on at least one day in the previous week rose from 8 per cent in 1998 to 10 per cent in 2001 (Walker *et al.* 2002). A

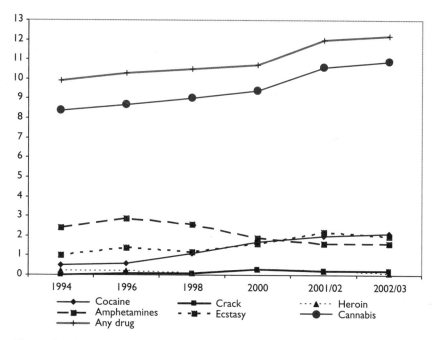

**Figure 3.1** Percentage of the adult population reporting using specific drugs in the last 12 months.
*Sources:* British Crime Surveys (Ramsay *et al.* 2001; Aust *et al.* 2002; Condon and Smith 2003).

similar finding emerged from the survey of school children conducted by the Schools Health Education Unit (Balding 2002). This showed that there was little change over the last 10 years or so in the proportion of children reporting drinking alcohol on at least one day in the last week. However, there has been a clear increase in the proportion that reported drinking more than 10 units of alcohol in the last week. The authors concluded that while there has been little change in the proportion of children who drink, those who do drink now drink more.

### Offender population

Some information on trends in drug use among the offender population can be obtained from the NEW-ADAM programme. Surveys of arrestees were conducted in sixteen custody suites across the UK in 1999–2000 and were repeated in the same custody suites in 2001–2002. The results of a comparison across this 2-year period show that the proportion of arrestees testing positive for any drug remained steady at 65 per cent (Holloway *et al.* 2004). However, there were some differences by drug type. The proportion of arrestees testing positive for opiates (including heroin) increased significantly from 25 per cent in 1999–2000 to 28 per cent in 2001–2002. A similar increase was shown for cocaine (including crack), which increased from 15 per cent to 23 per cent. These results are similar to those for the British Crime Survey, which showed a small increase in heroin use (not significant) and a large increase in crack and cocaine use in the adult general population during the period 1994 to 2000. However, in this case, the percentages are much larger and the changes more marked. The proportion of arrestees testing positive for amphetamines decreased significantly over this period from 9 per cent to 6 per cent. Again, this result is in line with those of the general population surveys, which show notable reductions in amphetamine misuse over this period.

### Summary

The section has looked at the patterns and changes in demand for illegal drugs over the last few years. It has shown that a minority of the general population and the majority of the offender population had recently consumed illegal drugs. The most common illegal drug used among both populations was cannabis. Younger people were more likely than older people to use recreational drugs and older people were more likely than younger people to use the more serious drugs. In the general population, males were more likely than females to use drugs, whereas in the criminal population females were as likely, or more likely, than males to use drugs (depending on the drug type). Over the last 10 years, the use of illegal drugs generally has increased among both the general and criminal populations. However, the use of some recreational drugs has tended to decline, whereas that of some serious drugs has tended to increase.

## Supply of drugs

Illicit drug use can be conceived as a drug market that balances the demand and the supply of drugs. Information about the extent of drug use can be found, therefore, by looking at either the demand or the supply of drugs. In this section, we look at drug markets and the supply of drugs.

### Drug markets

In any particular country, the overall drug market might be thought of as comprising a number of sub-markets. Pearson and Hobbs (2001) identify what they refer to as a four-tier classification of drug markets: importers, wholesalers, middle-market brokers and retail dealers. The whole process can be thought of as containing a fifth element: the source or country of production.

Looking first at the *source* of drugs entering the UK, the vast majority (over 90 per cent) of all heroin seized in the UK originates from opium produced in Afghanistan (Corkery 2002). According to National Criminal Intelligence Service (NCIS), Afghanistan accounts for around 70 per cent of global opium production. Specifically, Afghanistan produces opium for the heroin markets of Europe and South Asia, as well as Africa (NCIS 2003). However, opium destined for the North American market is usually grown in South America, mainly Colombia. Almost all of the world's cocaine is produced in Colombia, Peru and Bolivia. In 2002, it was reported that Colombia accounted for the vast majority, although the contribution of Peru was increasing (NCIS 2003). It is estimated that up to 80 per cent of all MDMA (ecstasy) consumed worldwide emanates from laboratories in The Netherlands and Belgium. However, there is some production in Poland, Germany and in Eastern Europe, including Romania (NCIS 2003). Corkery (2002) notes that most of the herbal cannabis in the world market originates in South America (e.g. Colombia), Jamaica and Africa. Morocco is the primary source of cannabis resin for the UK market.

The issue of *importation* concerns the methods by which drugs originating from the producer countries enter the consumer country. According to NCIS, most heroin enters the UK through ports in the south east of England, particularly Dover, Felixstowe and Harwich. The bulk arrives in freight vehicles, although some is transported by couriers in passenger vehicles or as baggage. The Channel Tunnel is a major route for importing heroin into the UK. Some heroin also enters the UK through the main UK airports, particularly those with connections to Turkey or Pakistan (NCIS 2003). Estimates by Her Majesty's Customs suggest that two-thirds of cocaine destined for the UK arrives by air, on scheduled flights, concealed in baggage or air cargo (Corkery 2002). According to NCIS, most cocaine is smuggled into the UK by couriers hired by organized criminal gangs of Caribbean origin. Ecstasy arrives in the UK through ferry ports, mainly in the south east, especially Dover, and the north east of England. The drugs are often concealed in private and heavy goods vehicles, in freight or are carried by passengers (NCIS 2003).

The first level of distribution in a country is sometimes referred to as *upper-level* distribution. There is widespread agreement in the research that upper-level dealing is mainly organized by criminal gangs. However, there is very little research on gangs of this kind (Pearson and Hobbs 2001). Nevertheless, it is widely believed that criminal drug gangs are typically based on specific nationalities. For example, it is thought that Turkish criminal groups dominate the European and UK heroin trade. However, gangs of other national groups also play a part in heroin distribution, including British Caucasian gangs, Asian gangs, Albanian gangs and West African gangs (NCIS 2003). The NCIS notes that many of the most significant British Caucasian groups are based in Merseyside, although some are based in Scotland and some in east London. Cocaine distribution into the country appears to be controlled mainly by British Caucasian, West Indian and Colombian gangs.

The next level is usually referred to as *middle-level* drug distribution. However, there is little agreement about how this should be defined. Pearson and Hobbs (2001) suggest that the middle-market drug broker is identified as occupying a strategic position that links the upper levels (importation and wholesale) and lower levels (retail) of the market. While at first sight this definition might seem simplistic, it actually works well in practice in identifying a unique section of the market. There is also very little research on middle-market drug distribution. However, there have been one or two recent studies that have helped shed light on this topic. Pearson and Hobbs (2001) describe the middle-market dealer as someone who buys in multi-kilo amounts heroin, cocaine and other substances from the importers and sells in part-kilo amounts or ounces at the retail level. Some middle-market dealers specialize only in recreational drugs. According to Pearson and Hobbs (2001), middle-market drug networks are typically small: just one or two people, who control finances and have established contacts and a small team of runners working for them who collect and deliver quantities of drugs. Some runners are employed on a weekly wage basis, while others are paid per transaction (Pearson and Hobbs 2001).

The bottom level of the supply chain is usually referred to as low-level or *retail-level* drug distribution. Pearson and Hobbs (2001) believe that there are three types of retail drug dealer: heroin dealers who sometimes also sell crack cocaine, cannabis dealers who sometimes sell pills, and pill dealers who sometimes sell cannabis. The third type of dealer is closely associated with the clubbing scene. Lupton *et al.* (2002) conducted a study of retail drug markets in deprived residential areas of England in 2000 and 2001. The authors thought that the markets could be divided into two broad types. The first type was long established and had a widespread reputation. It drew buyers from outside the area and included open as well as closed selling. These were found mainly in inner-city areas, with mixed housing type and mixed ethnicity and tenure. The second type had a less wide-spread reputation and served a smaller number of buyers mainly from the local area. It had mainly closed selling with established buyer and seller arrangements. These were found outside the city centre in areas with stable populations and were almost exclusively white. Most of the selling took place through a closed system involving mobile phones and personal drug deliveries (Lupton *et al.* 2002).

### Seizures

The number of drug seizures in a country is widely recognized as the best single indicator of the supply of drugs. However, it is acknowledged that the number of seizures is in part a reflection of law-enforcement activities and in part a reflection of the total amount of drugs available. The main source of information on drug seizures in the UK is the Home Office regular series of bulletins covering seizures of controlled drugs within the UK by police (including the British Transport Police), HM Customs and Excise and the National Crime Squad. HM Customs generally make fewer seizures than police forces, but tend to seize larger amounts. For example, in 2001, the police were responsible for 78 per cent of the total number of cocaine seizures, but only 36 per cent of the total amount of cocaine seized (Corkery and Airs 2003).

In the UK in 2001, there were 130,894 seizures of controlled drugs. Seventy-five per cent of these were seizures of cannabis, 14 per cent heroin, 8 per cent ecstasy, 5 per cent cocaine, 5 per cent amphetamines and 3 per cent crack (Corkery and Airs 2003). These findings reflect earlier results that show cannabis as the most common illegal drug in the UK. Overall, 29 per cent of seizures were in relation to Class A drugs (the most serious drugs), 76 per cent were of Class B drugs (middle of the range drugs) and 2 per cent were of Class C drugs (the least serious drugs) (Corkery and Airs 2003).

### Prosecutions for drug offences

Another common measure of drug misuse is the statistics on the number of offenders processed each year for drug offences. While these statistics mainly cover offences relating to drug possession, they also cover offences relating to the supply of drugs. The statistics for the year 2000 provide a category of offences called 'trafficking', which includes a range of supply-type offences including unlawful production of drugs, unlawful supply, possession with intent to supply unlawfully, and unlawful import or export. In 2000, a total of 104,000 people were found guilty, cautioned, given a fiscal fine, or dealt with by compounding for drug offences (Corkery 2002). Fourteen per cent of these were drug-trafficking offences (14,900 offences). The most common trafficking offence was possession with intent to supply (7296) (most of which were offences involving cannabis). The next most common was unlawful supply (5742), followed by unlawful production (1960) and unlawful import or export (1490). Approximately half of all drug offenders were aged 17–25 and 90 per cent of drug offenders were males. In terms of type of drug, the largest category of supply prosecutions concerned cannabis offences, followed by offences involving heroin, ecstasy, amphetamines and cocaine.

### Trends in supply

Data on drug seizures can also be used as a measure of trends in drug availability over time. In some respects, the problems associated with using these data (i.e. the fact that they are based on a combination of factors, including law-enforcement activity, number of users and number of drugs available) are less pronounced when measuring estimates over time, as the sources of error are likely to remain more or less stable over time. Over the last 10 years or so, the number of seizures has tended to increase (with a brief dip during 1998 to 2000). During the period 2000–2001, the total number of drug seizures continued to increase. During this period, seizures of heroin increased by 10 per cent, whereas seizures of cocaine and crack rose by 16 per cent and 33 per cent, respectively. Seizures of most other types of drugs also tended to increase, with the exception of amphetamines and LSD, seizures of which both went down. This trend is generally consistent with survey data on trends in demand, which showed increases in the use of heroin, crack and cocaine and decreases in the use of amphetamines and LSD. This similarity in results provides some support to the idea that changes in the number of drug seizures might reasonably reflect changes in drug use (despite the other compounding factors involved mentioned earlier).

Trends in supply can also be observed through trends in the processing of people for drug supply offences; however, again, the data will be affected by enforcement activity. Over the last 10 years, prosecutions for all supply (trafficking) offences have tended to increase. In relation to the three main drug supply offences (production, supply and possession with intent to supply), the increase peaked in 1998 and has since fallen back slightly. However, there is some variation in this trend by type of drug. The trend in the number of prosecutions for cocaine, crack and heroin has shown a steady increase over the last few years, with no evidence of a peak and fall back (although there was a slight drop in 2000 in relation to heroin). Instead, it appears that the main reasons for the recent decline in the total number of prosecutions for supply offences has been the reduction in prosecutions relating to cannabis. However, the decline is also evident among those drug types experiencing a decline in popularity, including amphetamines and LSD. There was no similar recent decline in prosecutions for offences relating to ecstasy, a drug experiencing a current increase in popularity. Hence, trends in prosecutions for drug supply offences more or less reflect other indicators of the demand and supply of drugs.

## Summary

This section has looked at the methods of supply and changes in rate of supply of illegal drugs. Most of the indicators discussed show a steady increase in involvement in heroin, crack and cocaine and a steady decrease in involvement in LSD and amphetamines. Broadly speaking, it could be said that there has been a switch in the last few years from 'recreational drugs' to 'hard drugs'. However, this misses the noticeable increase in ecstasy and cannabis. It is possible that these findings reflect trends in drug preference, which have resulted in 'drug switching' (e.g. crack and cocaine being preferred to amphetamines, and perhaps ecstasy and cannabis being preferred to LSD). They may also be a result of the changing age structure of the drug-using population, with the older users continuing to use cannabis and ecstasy (but not LSD and amphetamines), while, at the same time, new users are also taking up these drugs.

## Problems of drug misuse

The extent of drug misuse in society can also be measured by the problems caused by drug misuse. It is relevant to know something about the number of drug users and the number of drugs in circulation. However, it is also important to know something about the impact of these numbers on society. There are a number of major social problems associated with drug misuse (in addition to the problem of crime, which will be discussed in depth later). These include:

- addiction and dependence;
- health problems relating to injection and disease;
- the economic and social costs to the health service and criminal justice system;
- drug-related deaths.

### Addiction and dependence

Dependence on drugs can lead to the continuation and exacerbation of some of the other problems associated with drug misuse, such as health problems or the problems of crime. However, dependence can also be regarded as a problem in its own right. It makes desistance from drug use harder and can lead to drug misuse dominating individual user lifestyles. No recent information on drug dependence in the general population has been published in the British Crime Surveys. Similarly, drug dependence is not covered in the General Household Surveys. However, a survey conducted by the Office for National Statistics in 2000 reported psychiatric morbidity among adults in Great Britain (Singleton *et al.* 2001). The results of this survey showed that the lifetime prevalence of dependence in the general population for any drug was 4 per cent. Most people who were classified as dependent said that they were dependent on cannabis (3 per cent of the population) and most scored '1' on a 5-point scale of levels of dependence.

There is more information available on dependence in the offender population. Information on drug dependence in the offender population was collected as part of the NEW-ADAM surveys of arrestees. This information was collected because of concerns at the time that dependence on Class 'A' drugs was serving to prolong drug use and exacerbate the other problems associated with drug use, including the spread of disease through injection (discussed later) and crime. Arrestees who took part in the surveys were asked if they had ever or recently been dependent on drugs. Specifically, they were asked, 'Have you recently felt that you needed [a particular drug] or felt bad or ill when you did not have [a particular drug]?' The research defined arrestees whom reported recent dependency on one or more illicit drugs as 'problem drug users'. Using this definition,

the study found that 35 per cent of all interviewed arrestees could be
defined as problem drug users (Holloway and Bennett 2004). Sixty-two per
cent of all problem drug users were dependent on heroin (alone or in
combination with other drugs). Twenty-seven per cent said that they were
dependent on cannabis, 15 per cent reported dependency on crack and
3 per cent said that they were dependent on cocaine.

The study also compared differences between problem (or dependent)
drug users, 'non-problematic' drug users and non-users in terms of various
individual characteristics. The results showed that problem drug users
were more likely than other arrestees to be female, to be aged 20–29, to be
white, to have left school before the age of 17, and to be in current receipt
of social security benefits. There is also some information on the offender
population from surveys of prisoners. A survey of female prisoners conducted in 2001 included questions on drug use and dependency (Borrill
*et al.* 2003). The study found that almost half of the women interviewed
reported being dependent on at least one drug. The most common drugs
of dependence were heroin (33% of all inmates) and crack (24% of all
inmates). There were strong ethnic differences, with 60 per cent of all white
inmates being dependent on one or more drugs compared with 29 per cent
of all black or mixed-race women.

Information on alcohol dependency is more readily available. This
includes data on alcohol dependency in the general population. The results
of the General Household Survey for the year 2001 showed that 75 per
cent of men and 59 per cent of women had drunk at least one unit of
alcohol in the last week. The report defined safe use (having no significant
health risk) as regular consumption of three or four units a day for men
and two or three units a day for women. Using this definition, it was found
that 39 per cent of men and 22 per cent of women drank more than the safe
limit in the last week, and 21 per cent of men and 10 per cent of women
drank at least twice the safe limit. However, this does not mean that they
were dependent on alcohol. Information on alcohol dependence in the
general population is available from the Office for National Statistics
survey of psychiatric morbidity among 10,000 adults in Great Britain in
the year 2000. Seven per cent of adults were assessed as being dependent

**Table 3.2** Percentage of arrestees currently dependent on selected drug types
(*n* = 3135)

| Drug type | Per cent dependent |
| --- | --- |
| Any drug | 35% |
| Cannabis | 27% |
| Heroin | 62% |
| Crack | 15% |
| Cocaine | 3% |

*Source:* Holloway and Bennett (2004).

on alcohol. Men were more likely to show signs of dependence than women (12 per cent compared with 3 per cent), and younger people were more likely to have signs of dependence than older people (24 per cent of all 20- to 24-year-old males were deemed to be dependent on alcohol compared with 2 per cent of all 70- to 74-year-old males). However, in most cases the form of dependence was described as mild (Singleton *et al.* 2001).

### Health problems relating to injection

Many drug users, especially those dependent on heroin, choose to administer their drugs by intravenous injection. This is potentially a very harmful way of administering drugs. It carries various kinds of health risks to the user, including abscesses, blood clots, blood poisoning and the risk of overdose. It also carries various kinds of health risks to others, including cross-infection when equipment is shared, health problems relating to the disposal of used syringes, and the spread of diseases such as the HIV virus.

The prevalence of injecting drugs has been investigated in studies of the offender population. The results of the second developmental stage of the NEW-ADAM programme showed that about one-quarter (23 per cent) of all arrestees said that they had injected an illegal drug at some time in their lives. The most common drugs injected were heroin (18 per cent of all arrestees), amphetamines (12 per cent) and cocaine (11 per cent). The survey of female prisoners mentioned above also included questions on injecting drugs. Nearly a third (31 per cent) of the sample said that they had injected drugs at some time in their lives. The majority of inmates (90 per cent) who injected a drug said that they had injected heroin. White women were more likely to report injecting than black or mixed-race women. The prevalence of injecting in the drug user population has been investigated through the statistics collected as part of the Regional Drug Misuse Database of clients attending treatment facilities. According to the published statistics, 65 per cent of drug users had injected a drug. Men were more likely than women to have injected a drug and older users were more likely than younger users to have injected. The variation in levels of involvement in injecting across the three samples (23 per cent of arrestees, 31 per cent of prisoners and 65 per cent of drug users in treatment) is perhaps to be expected considering the nature of the samples.

One of the major problems with injection is the habit of drug users of sharing syringes. There are several reasons why users do this, including a shortage of syringes (heavy users might need three or more a day) and the social nicety of sharing something that is pleasurable to them. According to the results of the NEW-ADAM surveys, 6 per cent of all arrestees interviewed in 1999 said that they had shared injecting equipment at some point in their lives (Bennett 2000). This represented over a quarter (28 per cent) of all arrestees who injected. One-fifth of arrestees who had injected in the last 12 months said that they had shared their injecting equipment. The level of sharing is shown to be even higher among drug users in treatment.

The regular series of surveys conducted by the Department of Health (the Unlinked Anonymous Prevalence Monitoring Programme) based on drug users attending selected agencies in the UK includes some information on self-reported sharing of injecting equipment. The surveys showed that the prevalence of sharing needles and syringes among current injectors was stable for most of the 1990s at about 18 per cent (Department of Health 2002). However, since 1998 the proportion has increased to over 30 per cent. The level of sharing was highest among current injectors in London (41 per cent of current injectors). Data from the regional drug misuse database (a record of users presenting to drug misuse agencies) for the 6 months ending March 2001 found that just under half (49 per cent) of users who injected in that time had shared their equipment. The study found that women were more likely to share than men and younger users were more likely to share than older users (Department of Health 2002). Hence, the research shows that a notable proportion of injecting drug users (perhaps as much as half) share their needles or syringes.

Another problem of injection is drug-related infectious diseases. The Unlinked Anonymous Prevalence Monitoring Programme of drug users attending agencies in the UK in 2000 (Department of Health 2002) showed that in London 1 in 27 male and 1 in 34 female injecting drug users were HIV infected. In other parts of the UK, the rates were much lower (1 in 544 males and 1 in 331 females). Since 1995, the prevalence of HIV infection among injecting drug users has remained stable, which, according to the survey authors, indicates a continuing low rate of HIV transmission through injecting drug use. One of the most prevalent diseases among drug users is hepatitis B. The above report estimates that one in five drug users attending agencies in London in the year 2000 had hepatitis B.

## Economic and social costs

Drug misuse not only creates problems for the individual drug users, but also for the community and society as a whole. A study conducted on the social and economic costs of Class A drug use in England and Wales in 2000 estimated that the total economic costs were £3.5 billion and the total social costs were £12 billion. The economic costs equated to £1927 across all Class A drug users and £10,402 across all problem drug users. The social costs equated to £6564 across all Class A drug users and £35,456 across all problem drug users. The main economic and social costs identified in the study related to health costs, work-related costs, driving, crime, and other economic and social impacts. The main health costs associated with problem drug users are costs relating to treatment, hospital admissions, accident and emergency admissions, and community care. The work-related costs include unemployment and associated state benefits. The costs of crime fall on the criminal justice system and the victims of crime. Other economic and social costs include the impact of drug use on the children of drug users.

### Drug-related deaths

One of the most extreme problems associated with drug misuse is premature death. In 2002 in England and Wales, 1565 deaths were related to drug misuse. The definition of drug-related death used in the Office for National Statistics surveys is death where the underlying cause is poisoning, drug abuse or drug dependence and where any of the substances controlled under the Misuse of Drugs Act (1971) are involved (ONS 2004). In addition, there were 2685 deaths for which selected substances were mentioned on the death certificate. In 2002 in England and Wales, 790 deaths had heroin/morphine mentioned on the death certificate (heroin breaks down into morphine in the body) and 139 deaths had cocaine mentioned. In the same year, 93 deaths had amphetamines mentioned on the death certificate, 55 had ecstasy mentioned and 15 had cannabis mentioned. The UK showed a steady increase in drug deaths up until 2000. However, the proportion of heroin–morphine cases has increased more steeply (EMCDDA 2003). The Interim Analytical Report prepared by the Prime Minister's Strategy Unit estimated between 15,000 and 22,000 deaths per year were associated in some way with alcohol misuse (Department of Health 2003). Deaths related to alcohol use are also increasing among both men and women.

## Conclusion

The aim of the chapter has been to provide an overview of drug misuse in the population to identify its extent and its effect. The chapter has shown that in some senses drug use is pervasive in our society and covers many aspects of our lives. A notable proportion of the general population consumes illegal drugs and the majority consume alcohol. Fewer people consume these substances to excess. Nevertheless, in certain sub-sets of the population, especially the offender population, serious drug misuse is widespread. It has been estimated that at least 80 per cent of offenders take drugs and about one-third regularly use heroin, crack or cocaine. There is some evidence that serious drug misuse (involving heroin, crack or cocaine) is increasing in both the general population and the offender population. There is also some evidence that there is no shortage of supply of drugs in the country. Most of the indicators of supply show that the availability of drugs is at least keeping pace with the demand for them. The problems associated with drug misuse are also wide-ranging. These affect not only the drug user, through personal health risks, but also the wider community, through the economic and social costs involved in the consequences of drug misuse. The consequences of drug misuse on crime and criminal behaviour have not been discussed in this chapter, but will be dealt with in detail in the later chapters of the book.

# Further reading

A major source of information about drug use in the UK is the Home Office website, which can be found at http://www.homeoffice.gov.uk/rds/index.html. This site can be used to obtain the results of the British Crime Surveys on drug use in the general population and the NEW-ADAM surveys on drug use in the offender population. Another important general source of information is the DrugScope website, which can be found at http://www.drugscope.org.uk. This site can be used to obtain information on drug use in Europe, including the very useful European Monitoring Centre for Drugs and Drug Addiction (EMCDDA) reports.

# Types of drug misuse

## Introduction

The main aim of this chapter is to identify different types and patterns of drug misuse and consider the implications of these for understanding the consequences of drug misuse, including crime. The chapter will look at variations in drug use over time and across countries and the effects of different drug types on the user. It also looks at methods of administering drugs and the effect that these different methods of administration might have on the user. The chapter will also examine patterns of drug misuse, including multiple drug use. The final section examines motives for drug misuse.

### Types of drugs misused

Common sense suggests that the drugs–crime connection will vary over time and location as fashions in drug misuse vary. There cannot be a connection between cocaine use and crime in countries that have no cocaine misuse or at times when cocaine use is not fashionable. The choice of drug of misuse is important, therefore, in determining the nature of the association between drug misuse and crime at any particular time or place.

## Drug type classification

Drugs can be categorized in a number of different ways. These include *legal classification*, based on the severity of the penalties attached to breaches of drug laws, and *chemical classification*, based on whether the drug is derived from natural, semi-synthetic or synthetic sources. One of the most common methods of categorization is *pharmacological classification*, which is based on the effects of the drug on the user. Within this system, drugs are often classified into four groups: stimulants, depressants, analgesics and hallucinogens.

*Stimulants*, commonly known as 'uppers', activate the central nervous system. They increase wakefulness and physical activity and induce a feeling of euphoria and excitement. These include cocaine, crack and amphetamines. *Depressants*, or 'downers', depress the activity of the central nervous system and are used to relieve stress, induce sleep and allay anxiety. Alcohol is one of the most widely used depressants. Other depressants include benzodiazepines (e.g. temazepam and diazepam) and barbiturates. *Analgesics* mainly relieve pain, but sometimes have pleasurable side-effects, including a feeling of well-being or euphoria. They include opium, morphine, codeine, heroin and methadone. *Hallucinogens*, such as LSD, magic mushrooms and ecstasy, disrupt the interaction of the nerve cells and affect perceptions, sensations, thinking, self-awareness and emotions. They also cause visual, auditory and tactile hallucinations.

## Variations over time

It was shown in Chapter 3 that patterns in drug misuse tend to vary over time. There is some evidence, for example, that crack use is becoming less fashionable in the United States. Jacobs (1999) argues that the United States is coming to the end of the recent crack epidemic and explains how history has shown that, 'the decline of one drug often signals the incubation of another' (p. 556). There are some signs that heroin use might be becoming more fashionable in the United States. Recent surveys have shown that heroin use is increasing (National Institute of Justice 2003). It is unknown whether heroin will eventually overtake crack as the hard drug of choice in the United States (Jacobs 1999).

Conversely, there is some evidence that crack use is increasing in the UK. The New English and Welsh Arrestee Drug Abuse Monitoring (NEW-ADAM) Programme data show a significant increase in the proportion of arrestees testing positive for cocaine (including crack), from 15 per cent to 23 per cent over the period 1999 to 2001 (Holloway *et al.* 2004). The British Crime Survey (Ramsay *et al.* 2001) shows that between 1998 and 2000, there was a significant increase in the proportion of respondents reporting use of cocaine and crack in the last year. The British Crime Survey results indicate that heroin use has remained statistically unchanged in recent years. However, the results of the NEW-ADAM Programme show a significant increase in the proportion of positive tests for opiates (including heroin) in the last few years, from 25 per cent to 28 per cent (Holloway *et al.* 2004).

There are clear fashions in the use of drugs. In the 1990s, heroin use became so fashionable that it has been argued that it became 'normalized' (Pearson 1999; Parker *et al.* 2002). The concept of 'heroin chic' emerged in the fashion world in the 1990s, as the use of gaunt and glassy-eyed models became commonplace. The rave scene and all-night club culture, characterized by the use of ecstasy and amphetamines, also became fashionable. The 1990s were dubbed the 'decade of dance', 'a period during which the use of cannabis and other stimulant drugs became commonplace at dance venues' (Parker *et al.* 2001). Fashions in drug misuse can also be based on the appearance of new drugs on the streets. The most recent new drugs include ketamine, a drug normally used as an anaesthetic during surgery. Ketamine is currently being used on the dance scene in much the same way as ecstasy is used (Riley *et al.* 2001).

### Variations across countries

There are also variations in the type of drugs misused in different countries. The type of drug misuse is also likely to affect the nature of the drugs–crime connection. In Muslim countries, where Islam prohibits alcohol and drugs, the use of these substances is rare. Alcohol cannot be sold or consumed in Libya, Saudi Arabia and many other Middle Eastern countries. Some Middle Eastern countries, such as Bahrain and the United Arab Emirates, are more lenient and permit the limited sale of alcohol to visitors. Smart and Ogborne (2000) investigated drug use and drinking among students in 36 countries (mainly developed countries in Western Europe). Alcohol and cannabis were identified as the 'first-choice' drugs for students in all 36 countries. However, there was considerable variation across the countries in the proportions of students reporting alcohol use (from 32 per cent in Zimbabwe to 99 per cent in Wales) and cannabis use (from 1 per cent in Lithuania to 53 per cent in Scotland).

There are many other strong country differences in type of drug misuse. Results from the ADAM programme in South Africa showed that no arrestees tested positive for amphetamines, and only a very small proportion tested positive for opiates or cocaine (Parry *et al.* 2000). The main drug of choice after cannabis and alcohol was mandrax (or methaqualone). Taylor and Bennett (1999) compared ADAM data collected in the United States and England. The study was based on a comparison of five matched US sites with five English sites. The comparison showed that there were significantly higher prevalence rates of cocaine use in the United States than in England. By contrast, there was a significantly higher prevalence of marijuana, opiate, benzodiazepine and methadone use in England than in the United States. A report on the state of the drugs problem in the European Union and Norway in 2002, based on the results of national surveys on drug use, shows that the UK had the highest prevalence of amphetamine use in the last 12 months of all the countries. It also had one of the highest prevalence rates of cannabis and ecstasy use (only Ireland had a higher prevalence of cannabis use or ecstasy use). There are also cross-country differences in terms of the pattern of drug use. Ecstasy use in the UK, for example, is 'quite different from that in the USA' (Pearson 1999: 481). In the United States, ecstasy is reportedly used infrequently and on a contemplative basis. In the UK, ecstasy is used in the context of all-night dance events and there is evidence to show that some users indulge in binge use (Pearson 1999).

### Fashions in drug misuse and the link with crime

There are some countries that have almost no reported alcohol use (Saudi Arabia), heroin use (Taiwan) or crack use (South Africa) for religious, geographic or cultural reasons. In these countries, therefore, there cannot be a connection between these drugs and crime. However, there are also likely to be variations in the drugs–crime connection within countries depending on the prevalence of misuse of certain drug types over time and location. A study by Baumer *et al.* (1998) showed a clear connection between changes in type of drug misuse in the United States and changes in type of crime committed. Using data from the ADAM surveys, they showed a correlation between cities that reported recent increases in crack misuse and cities reporting recent increases in robbery. They also showed that cities reporting increases in crack misuse and robbery also showed decreases in residential burglary. They argued that crack use demanded more immediate funds for drugs and that robbery generated such funds more quickly than burglary.

## The effects of drug use

The effects of drug misuse are relevant to the study of the relationship between drugs and crime in a number of ways. At one level, drug misuse might have a direct or indirect effect on criminal behaviour. The pharmacological properties of the drug might directly evoke certain kinds of behaviour, including criminal behaviour (e.g. alcohol use might directly cause violence). The pharmacological properties of the drug might also indirectly generate criminal behaviour through some other mediating factor (e.g. alcohol use might cause violence, but only in particular crowded settings). At another level, drug misuse might affect crime through some of the longer-term and related consequences of drug use. These might include the development of addiction or other kinds of mental or physical condition.

### Short-term effects

The evidence for a direct or indirect link between the pharmacological effects of drugs and crime is still unclear. Kaplan *et al.* (2001) argue that the relationship between drug use and aggression is arguably one of the most investigated, but least understood, associations in the behavioural science literature. Fagan (1990) conducted a detailed review of the literature on the relationship between intoxication and aggression. He concludes that evidence of an association between use of illicit substances and aggressive behaviour is pervasive. However, the precise causal mechanisms by which aggression is influenced by intoxicants are still not well understood. Most alcohol or drug users do not resort to violence. There is only limited evidence that ingestion of substances is a direct, pharmacological cause of aggression. Bushman (1997) and Lipsey *et al.* (1997) conducted laboratory investigations and discovered that intoxication by alcohol was only related to aggression when an individual was provoked. Kaplan *et al.* (2001) argue that the social environment is a much more powerful contributor to the outcome of violent behaviour than are pharmacological factors. There is some evidence to support this view in research on the use of violence as retaliation in interactions between drug users and dealers in drug markets (Topalli *et al.* 2002). Collins and Messerschmidt (1993) found that 50 per cent of assaultive offenders in their study reported drinking at the time of their offences. However, 59 per cent of these did not think that drinking was relevant to the commission of their crimes. Moreover, not all research supports the idea that the short-term effects of drug use might increase the probability of criminal behaviour. Stimson and Oppenheimer (1982) noted that, on some occasions, the short-term effects of heroin use might reduce crime. Heroin can have a calming effect. One man interviewed by them while serving a prison sentence was convinced that he would have been a more violent person if he had not been addicted.

### Long-term effects

Aside from death, addiction is one of the most serious long-term effects of drug use. The term 'addiction' is derived from the Latin verb *addicere*, which referred to a Roman court action of binding a person to another. The term later came to mean attachment or devotion to an activity (Maddux and Desmond 2000). Swift *et al.* (2001) describe addiction as a state of chronic intoxication characterized by an overpowering desire, need or physical compulsion to continue taking more of the drug. This results in psychological and physical dependence, which leads to withdrawal syndrome when the drug is terminated. Not all drugs, however, are addictive.

Heroin, cocaine and crack are widely acknowledged to be profoundly addictive. In Great Britain, a total of 40,181 drug users sought treatment for their drug use in the 6 months ending 31 March 2001. Two-thirds of cases reported were opiate users (Office for National Statistics 2002).

However, heroin dependence is not inevitable and some users are able to take heroin for long periods on an occasional and non-problematic basis (Ashton 2002). Ashton believes that heroin has had a 'bad press' and that, unlike many narcotics, heroin is fairly 'benign'. He explains that there is little evidence to suggest that a lifetime of using pure heroin would lead to anything more than a strong tolerance to the drug. Pure unadulterated heroin does no damage to the body's organs. The real problems arise from other factors, such as adulterants in the drug, infected needles, the environment of the user and the methods of administration (Ashton 2002). Street heroin may have additives that do not properly dissolve in the body and that result in clogging of the blood vessels. This can cause infection or even death. The main physical effects of long-term heroin use (apart from the above) are loss of appetite, chronic constipation, irregular periods for women, sexual dysfunction, pneumonia and decreased resistance to infection.

The misuse of drugs can result in death. This can be a result of overdosing, poisoning or extreme physiological damage. Opiates and alcohol are most frequently implicated in drug-related deaths. Both drugs depress the central nervous system and, at a certain level of intoxication, the respiratory system will slow down and fail. Fatal overdoses of heroin can occur when users take their usual dose after a period of abstinence, during which time tolerance has faded. Fatalities can also occur when the drug is combined with use of other depressant drugs. Other misused drugs can cause death under certain or extreme conditions. Cocaine use can result in heart failure, ecstasy use can result in coma, amphetamine use can lead to a stroke, and alcohol consumption can lead to liver failure and brain damage (Jones and Millar 2000).

## Methods of administration

Some of the problems associated with drug misuse, including the problem of criminal behaviour, can be affected by the method by which the drug is administered. There are a variety of ways in which drugs can be consumed. Gossop *et al.* (2000) conducted interviews with 1053 clients entering treatment programmes across England. The interviewees reported four main routes of administration: injecting, smoking, snorting and swallowing. Less common methods of administration include 'muscling' (where the drug is injected into the muscle rather than the vein) and 'skin-popping' (where the drug is injected between the skin and fat layers). A drug may also be placed under the tongue and absorbed into the bloodstream through the mucous membranes in the mouth.

### Methods of administering different drug types

Many of the most widely used illicit drugs can be administered, or can be adapted for administration, by different routes (Gossop *et al.* 2000). Some drugs are closely associated with one particular method of administration (e.g. crack is generally smoked and alcohol is usually swallowed). Gossop *et al.* (2000) found that for some drugs (e.g. methadone and benzo-diazepines) one main route of administration was used, while for other drugs (e.g. heroin, amphetamines and cocaine powder) many methods were used. Heroin, for example, can be smoked (or chased), snorted, injected or swallowed. Some drug users administer drugs in unusual ways. Some arrestees interviewed as part of the NEW-ADAM programme reported that they had injected alcohol. Crack, which is usually smoked, was sometimes injected intravenously.

The major sources of information on national rates of different methods of administration are treatment studies. Statistics from the Regional Drug Misuse Databases for the period ending 31 March 2001 show that 54 per cent of heroin users reported injecting the drug. By contrast, just 12 per cent of cocaine users reported injecting the drug. Results from the NEW-ADAM programme show that nearly half (48 per cent) of all arrestees interviewed, who had reported using heroin in the last 3 days, had injected it (Holloway *et al.* 2004). The corresponding figures for amphet-amines, crack and cocaine were 19 per cent, 12 per cent and 9 per cent, respectively. Other research projects have provided information on methods of administration. Parker and Bottomley (1996), for example, found that smoking rock in a pipe or on foil was the most common mode of administration among the 63 crack cocaine users that they interviewed.

### Reasons for selecting particular methods

Certain methods of administration are more popular than others. There are a variety of reasons why users may select a particular method of administration. The chosen method may prove to be more effective in terms of either strength or speed of effect. The user may be under pressure from peers (social environment) to try a new method, or they may perceive the method to be safer or cheaper than other methods. Strang *et al.* (1997) explored the history of heroin smoking by 'chasing the dragon'. They describe how changes in the drug, changes in attitudes and changes in technology have contributed to changes in methods of administration. Curruthers and Loxley (2002) explain that a barrier to the promotion of smoking heroin is the composition of the available heroin. Smoking or chasing heroin in its salt form is inefficient and yields a considerably lower recovery rate than heroin in its base form. A user may not always employ the same method of administration. Patterns of drug-taking are sensitive to social, environmental and interpersonal influences, and patterns of administration are subject to variation over time (Gossop *et al.* 2000).

Curruthers and Loxley (2002) explain that, before 1978, initiation into heroin use was principally by injection, but, by 1985, heroin chasing had become the predominant mode of administration for early users.

### Geographic variation in methods of administration

Gossop *et al.* (2000) found that for all drugs, except benzodiazepines, there were regional differences in routes of administration. The authors identified a north–south split, with higher rates of heroin injecting in the Midlands and southern England. By contrast, in the north, heroin was most often taken by chasing the dragon (i.e. smoking). Regional differences were also found in the use of stimulants. Rates of cocaine injection were much higher in the north west of England than in other areas. Smoking was the predominant route of crack use in all regions, although injection of crack was found to be common in some regions. In the south west of England, as many as one in five crack users regularly injected the drug. In contrast, this practice was virtually absent among users in the north east (Gossop *et al.* 2000). A particularly high rate of amphetamine injecting was also found in the south west of England.

Curruthers and Loxley (2002) explored heroin injecting in Western Australia. They concluded that the cultural move towards smoking, snorting or chasing heroin in the UK, The Netherlands and in parts of the United States had not occurred in Australia. The 2002 annual report of the European Monitoring Centre for Drugs and Drug Addiction revealed that the proportion of heroin injectors varied markedly between countries, from 13 per cent in The Netherlands to 74 per cent in Greece. Taylor and Bennett (1999) compared ADAM-type data collected from five English cities with data collected from five comparable US cities. The biggest difference between the two countries was in the method of administering drugs. Among detainees in England, 16.3 per cent said they had injected amphetamines at some time in their life, compared with 1.7 per cent of those in the United States. By contrast, a significantly larger proportion of arrestees in the United States reported having injected cocaine at some point in their lives (11 per cent compared with 8 per cent). There were no significant differences between the two countries in terms of the proportion reporting injecting opiates (13 per cent in England versus 12 per cent in the United States).

### Method of administration and crime

The method of administration is directly linked to criminal behaviour when it is part of the definition of the criminal act. Injecting illegal drugs is acknowledged in the UK drugs legislation as increasing the seriousness of certain drug crimes. Class B drugs in 'injectable' form receive the same penalties as Class A drugs. The method of administration may be indirectly linked to criminal behaviour when it is associated with an increase in frequency or severity of crime.

Giannini *et al.* (1993) explored the relationship between the route of cocaine administration and levels of violence. Interviews with 101 cocaine users showed that freebase and intravenous routes were related to higher levels of violence than nasal insufflation. Ross *et al.* (1997) interviewed 312 heroin users about their use of benzodiazepines. They found that injectors scored significantly higher on a criminality scale than oral users, who in turn scored higher than non-users. Domier *et al.* (2000) compared injecting and non-injecting methamphetamine users in California. They found that injecting users committed more felonies and were on parole more often than other users. Matsumoto *et al.* (2002) explored the route of administration among amphetamine users and found that a significantly larger proportion of injectors than smokers had criminal records.

## Sources of drugs

The source of supply of drugs is relevant to the study of the drugs–crime connection in at least three ways: (1) the source of supply of drugs is a defining part of some drug offences; (2) misused drugs are often obtained from illegal sources; and (3) drug markets generate opportunities for criminal behaviour.

### Sources of supply as a defining part of drug offences

The Misuse of Drugs Act 1971 regulates the production, supply and possession of 'controlled' drugs. Offences under this Act include: possession of a controlled drug; possession with intent to supply a controlled drug; the production, cultivation and manufacture of a controlled drug; supplying another person with a controlled drug; offering to supply another person with a controlled drug; import or export of a controlled drug; and allowing premises you occupy or manage to be used for the consumption of controlled drugs. Hence, producing, cultivating, manufacturing and supplying controlled drugs are all illegal acts.

### Illegal sources of supply

Drugs can be obtained from three main sources: (1) legal sources (the 'white' market), such as over-the-counter drugs; (2) legally prescribed drugs sold illegally (the 'grey' market), such as drugs prescribed to one person and sold to another; and (3) illegally imported or distributed drugs (the 'black' market), such as drugs bought on the street from a drug supplier. The first source of supply is legal, but constitutes a form of drug misuse when the drug is used in a manner that is not recommended for therapeutic purposes. The second and third sources of supply are both illegal.

### Legal sources (the 'white' market)

There are many non-prescription medications for sale in chemist shops, supermarkets and other places that are misused by drug users. These usually include medications containing very small quantities of a controlled drug, such as opiates (e.g. some cough medicines and anti-diarrhoea mixtures). Alcohol would also come under the heading of over-the-counter drugs, as it can be legally purchased from licensed premises.

### Illegal sources (the 'grey' market)

Grey market drugs are those originally obtained on prescription from medical practitioners and re-sold for the purpose of drug misuse. The most common grey-market drug is methadone. This is usually prescribed to one user to relieve the discomfort of addiction and then sold to another user. However, other drug types are traded on the 'grey' market. These include opiates (such as codeine) that are often prescribed to treat pain, depressants prescribed to treat anxiety and sleep disorders, and stimulants prescribed to treat narcolepsy, attention-deficit, hyperactivity disorder and obesity (Fountain *et al.* 1997).

### Illegal sources (the 'black' market)

The black market refers to the illegal production and distribution of drugs for sale for non-medicinal purposes. Black market drugs typically include those imported into a country illegally. However, black market drugs may also include drugs legally produced in a particular country, but illegally diverted to the black market by theft or other criminal means. These might include drugs stolen *en route* to a pharmacy or stolen as part of a pharmacy burglary.

## Drug markets and crime

Drug markets provide opportunities for crime and generate various forms of criminal behaviour. Street violence, in particular, is often associated with drug dealing and drug markets. Lupton *et al.* (2002) identified, in their UK study, three ways in which drug markets generate violence: to enforce payment of drug debts, to resolve competition between dealers, and to sanction informants. They noted that the threat or use of violence to enforce drug debt was common practice in all of the eight drug markets studied. A study of twenty recently robbed, active drug dealers in St Louis, Missouri argued that violence in drug markets is a form of informal social control (Topalli *et al.* 2002). Drug dealers cannot call the police if they have been victims of a crime. This results in direct retaliation in the form of violence. The advantage of direct retaliation, they argue, is that it fulfils the main aims of formal justice, namely retribution (in the form of vengeance), deterrence (in the form of reputation maintenance) and compensation (in the form of loss recovery).

Violence can also be the outcome of preventative action taken by drug dealers and their customers. A random sample of half of all arrestees interviewed as part of the NEW-ADAM programme was asked if they had owned or got hold of a gun in the last 12 months. Approximately one-quarter of arrestees who said that they had owned or got hold of a gun in the last year said that one of the reasons for doing so was connected with drugs. The majority of these mentioned self-protection as one of the reasons for owning or getting hold of a gun. When probed, they said that drug dealers frequently carried guns, carrying guns was part of the drug-dealing lifestyle, drug dealers sometimes sold guns, and guns were sometimes offered in exchange for drugs (Bennett and Holloway 2004).

## Patterns of drug use

There is some variation among drug users in their drug use patterns. This applies to use of individual drug types as well as drug type combinations. Single drug users may have different preferences and may consume their drug of choice infrequently (e.g. recreational use) or regularly (e.g. heavy use). Multiple drug users may use a variety of drug types and may combine them over time, sequentially or concurrently. Patterns of drug use are likely to be important in shaping the drugs–crime connection.

### Patterns of individual drug use

Research has shown that certain drug types tend to be consumed in particular ways. LSD, for example, is associated mainly with experimental use, while ecstasy is closely associated with recreational use. Heroin and crack are typically associated with habitual or addictive use.

Hammersley et al. (1999) explored patterns of ecstasy use among 229 drug users recruited from the 'dance scene' in Glasgow. The results showed that ecstasy was rarely taken on a daily basis. The heaviest use group took the drug, on average, about once a week. Some users consumed ecstasy in a 'stable' pattern, taking the same amount of the drug at regular intervals. Other users adopted an 'erratic' pattern, sometimes taking more and other times less. No users were stable in a dependent fashion on high daily doses. The most problematic pattern found was that of the heavy erratic user (20 per cent had binged at least twice and one in four of these was a heavy erratic user).

Parker et al. (2002) present evidence on cannabis use from the North West England Longitudinal Survey of young adults. Of the 465 participants interviewed in year 9, 70 per cent had used cannabis in their lifetime, 47 per cent had used the drug in the last 12 months, and 26 per cent had used cannabis in the last month. Of the past month users, 5 per cent were daily users. Perkonigg et al. (1999) conducted a longitudinal study of patterns of cannabis use among a sample of German adolescents. They found that nearly 50 per cent of the baseline users who had tried cannabis once reported never having used the drug again. However, the probability of stopping cannabis use was found to decrease fairly consistently with increased frequency of use at the baseline survey.

The results of the NEW-ADAM programme indicate that LSD is rarely used on a regular basis among the arrestee population (perhaps indicative of experimental use only). While approximately 50 per cent of arrestees reported 'ever' using LSD, less than 10 per cent reported using the drug in the last 12 months, less than 3 per cent reported using LSD in the 30 days, and just 1 per cent said that they had used the drug in the last 3 days (Bennett 2000).

Heroin is highly addictive and its use therefore tends to be habitual. Data from the NEW-ADAM programme shows that a large proportion of heroin users are high-rate users of heroin. More than three-quarters (80 per cent) of arrestees who said that they had used heroin in the last 30 days had used the drug on 15 or more days during that period (i.e. every other day). Nevertheless, one-fifth of the sample of heroin users were not high-rate users. Eight per cent were classified as medium-rate users and 12 per cent were low-rate users (Holloway and Bennett 2004). Bennett and Wright (1986) examined the drug-taking careers of 135 opioid users. Contrary to popular belief at the time, there was little evidence of quick escalation to daily use and addiction once the first opioid had been taken. The majority of addicts reported that it took them over a year to become addicted. On reaching daily use, addicts continued to show signs of control and choice in their drug taking.

Cocaine use appears to be less habitual than crack use. In a survey of 300 young offenders, Hammersley *et al.* (2003) identified differences in the pattern of cocaine and crack use. While only one-tenth of those who had ever used cocaine were heavy users (i.e. 25–365 days in the last year), more than one-quarter of those who had used crack were heavy users. Inciardi *et al.* (1994) interviewed 699 crack and other cocaine users in Miami, Florida who had used crack or cocaine in the last 90 days. More than three-quarters of crack users used the drug either daily or several times a week. By contrast, less than a fifth of cocaine snorters and 10 per cent of cocaine injectors used the drug either daily or several times a week.

## Patterns of multiple drug use

Polydrug use can take a variety of different forms and can include the use of different drug types on different occasions (e.g. cannabis one day, ecstasy the next), the use of two or more drug types consecutively (e.g. cocaine followed by alcohol), and the use of two or more drug types concurrently (e.g. heroin and cocaine simultaneously ['speedballing']).

Hammersley *et al.* (1999) looked at the types of drugs used during ecstasy binges among 'dance-goers' in Glasgow. Overall, cannabis and amphetamines were the most popular other drugs combined with ecstasy, closely followed by LSD. Overall, there is a clear preference for the co-use of hallucinogens and stimulants. Riley *et al.* (2001) found that two-thirds of participants in a sample of Edinburgh 'rave-goers' reported mixing drugs. All mixes included the use of ecstasy or amphetamines in combination with one or more other drugs. Ecstasy and amphetamines was the most prevalent mix. Pedersen and Skrondal (1999) found that ecstasy use was often intermingled with the use of cannabis and amphetamines.

Parker and Bottomley (1996) compared the polydrug use of 63 crack users with that of 20 heroin users. They found that crack cocaine users developed a repertoire around their rock use, based on alcohol, cannabis, heroin and methadone. However, the heroin sample was far more conservative. Where half the rock sample used cannabis every week, only just over a quarter of the heroin sample followed suit. One in 19 of the heroin sample used cocaine during a 7-day period, whereas 37 of the 63 rock users consumed heroin. Fitzgerald and Chilvers (2002) looked at multiple drug use combinations in their sample of Australian detainees. While 79 per cent of arrestees who tested positive for cocaine also tested positive for opiates, only 12 per cent of those who tested positive for opiates also tested positive for cocaine.

A number of studies have generated empirical typologies of drug users. Wilkinson *et al.* (1987) investigated a sample of 256 individuals assessed for a drug abuse treatment programme. Ninety per cent of the sample had used four or more of eight classes of drug during the last year. Using cluster analysis, they identified five clusters of drug use: (1) predominantly alcohol; (2) high use of alcohol, depressants and recreational drugs; (3) predominantly depressant drugs; (4) mainly recreational drugs; and (5) very high use of solvents.

Braucht *et al.* (1978) also used cluster analysis to develop an empirical typology of multiple drug abuse among clients receiving treatment in seven drug programmes in Denver, Colorado. Fifteen drug types were studied and each client was questioned about their current and past use of each type. The analysis identified four multiple drug use clusters: (1) cocaine, other opiates, methaqualone and illegal methadone; (2) inhalants, codeine and non-narcotic analgesics; (3) marijuana, amphetamines and hallucinogens; and (4) minor tranquillizers and barbiturates.

## Patterns of individual drug use and crime

Research shows that the rate of drug use is important in explaining the prevalence and incidence of offending. The economic necessity argument hypothesizes that, as drug use increases, so too does involvement in income-generating crime (as a means of funding the elevated rate of drug consumption). Chaiken and Chaiken (1990) reviewed the literature on drug use and crime and observed that 'it is not drug abuse *per se*, but the amount or frequency of drug use, that is strongly related to crime commission rates' (p. 230). Fergusson *et al.* (2002) examined the associations between frequency of cannabis use and psychosocial outcomes in adolescence and young adulthood. They used data from a 21-year longitudinal survey of a birth cohort of 1265 New Zealand children. The researchers found that weekly users of cannabis were at a significantly greater risk than other users of committing property or violent crimes.

Hammersley *et al.* (1989) explored the relationship between crime and opioid use in a sample of 151 Scottish prisoners and non-prisoners. The interviewees were divided into five drug-using groups: (1) alcohol only; (2) cannabis and alcohol; (3) other drugs, but not opioids; (4) moderate opioids; and (5) heavy opioids. Significant differences were found between the different drug-using groups. Heavy opioid users committed crimes significantly more frequently than did moderate opioid users, non-opioid polydrug users, cannabis users or alcohol users. However, moderate opioid users did not commit crimes significantly more frequently than the other groups. As part of a study of Australian prisoners, Dobinson and Ward (1984) explored the prevalence and rate of offending among three types of heroin user. The results showed that there was a significant difference between regular, heavy and very heavy users in terms of the proportion involved in break-and-enter and stealing offences. The likelihood of committing burglaries was found to increase between regular and heavy use (from 69 per cent to 92 per cent), but to decrease once very heavy use had been reached (from 92 per cent to 57 per cent). Best *et al.* (2001) investigated patterns of criminal activity and drug use among 100 new entrants to a drug treatment service in south London. They concluded that the strongest predictor of the total number of crimes committed in the last month was the total quantity of heroin used in the last month.

## Patterns of multiple drug use and crime

Chaiken and Chaiken (1990: 203) note that 'individual predatory crime commission frequencies are typically two or three times higher among offenders when they use multiple drug types than they are for the same offenders when they are in drug treatment or abstain from drug abuse'. Holloway and Bennett (2004) explored levels of offending among arrestees interviewed as part of the NEW-ADAM programme. Arrestees were divided into nine groups based on the types of drug consumed in the last 12 months. The prevalence of offending was highest among those groups of arrestees who said that they had used heroin in combination with crack and/or cocaine. Eighty-five per cent of arrestees who had used heroin, cocaine *and* crack had committed one or more property crimes during that period. By contrast, 40 per cent of arrestees who had used drugs other than heroin, cocaine or crack in the last 12 months had committed one or more property crimes in that period. The group with the lowest proportion of offenders was the group of arrestees who had not used illicit drugs in the last 12 months (17 per cent). The NEW-ADAM data also showed that the 'rate' of offending was highest among arrestees who had used heroin, cocaine *and* crack in the last 12 months.

## Motives for drug use

A number of problems are associated with the use of the term 'motives' that should be mentioned from the outset. The first is that the meaning of the concept of 'motive' is unclear and can cover a number of motivating factors, including perceived needs and presumed causes. Presumed causes can also be wide-ranging and include factors operating in the immediate present and in the distant past. The second is that motives for drug misuse might not be the 'real' reasons for drug misuse. Motives are complex constructs that have multiple purposes, including justifying and neutralizing behaviour as well as imputing meaning and understanding to behaviour (Taylor 1972).

The term 'motives' is used here to refer to users' stated reasons for drug use. Motives can be given for starting drug use, continuing drug use and desisting from drug use.

### Motives for starting

Many of the studies that have investigated motives for initiating drug misuse discuss the reasons for first drug use or the reasons for beginning drug misuse in general. The most common reasons given for starting drug use are curiosity of the influence of friends. De Micheli and Formigoni (2002) found among their sample of 213 Brazilian adolescents aged 11–19 years that the main reasons for initial use of drugs were the influence of friends, pleasure seeking and curiosity. Ong (1989) concluded that peers or friends had an important influence on the decision to try drugs for the first time. Fewer studies have investigated the reasons for initiating particular drug types. In a study of early drug use among high-school children in the United States, Johnston (1998) found that the most common motives for marijuana use were what he called celebratory reasons. These included 'to feel good', 'to get high' and 'to have a good time with friends'. The most common motives for recent use of cocaine were 'to experiment'. Motives for initial alcohol use include what are sometimes referred as 'psychological' reasons. Towberman and McDonald (1993) found that initial use was sometime prompted by negative feelings and sensations such as loneliness, neglect and depression. Bennett and Wright (1986) found that the most common reason for starting heroin use was curiosity.

### Motives for continuing

Dobinson and Ward (1984) interviewed 225 prisoners detained for property crimes in eight Australian prisons. Of the prisoners who had used heroin, the majority (69 per cent) reported that they used the drug because they liked the euphoria that it induced. Other important reasons were the influence of peers (27 per cent), pressures (22 per cent), boredom/kicks (13 per cent), availability (3 per cent) and 'other' (1 per cent). A further 9 per cent said that they did not know what their reasons were. As part of the North West Longitudinal Study, Parker *et al.* (1998) asked their sample of adolescents what their main reasons were for drinking alcohol. In year 1 and year 2 (ages 14 and 15 respectively), the majority (approximately two-thirds) of respondents said that their main reason for drinking was to celebrate special occasions such as birthdays and weddings. Other popular explanations emphasized the social aspects of drinking, with between 40 and 50 per cent of respondents describing drinking as being 'fun' and making them 'less shy'. In year 3 (aged 16), the key reason for drinking was related to the place in which alcohol was consumed. Two-thirds of respondents said that their main reason for drinking was because they liked pubs and clubs. Qualitative interviews were also conducted among a sample of 17-year-olds. The seven main reasons for drinking given by this older group were: 'to socialize' (58 per cent), 'for enjoyment' (29 per cent), 'liking the taste' (26 per cent), 'to relax' (25 per cent), 'to get merry or drunk' (23 per cent), 'to have a good time' (17 per cent) and 'to increase confidence/reduce inhibitions' (13 per cent).

## Motives for stopping

Winick (1962) suggests that users may stop because they can no longer face the challenges posed by drug use. Parker *et al.* (1998) noted that some users give up because of a bad drug experience, often with LSD or MDMA. Johnston (1998) explored self-reported reasons for quitting drug use using data from the Monitoring the Future Study. Among the marijuana quitters, the most frequently reported reason for quitting (mentioned by more than 60 per cent of quitters) was that they did not want to get high. Parental disapproval was another common explanation for quitting, as too was 'not enjoyable' and fear of psychological and physical damage. Fear of addiction and concern that marijuana use might lead to use of stronger drugs were reported by more than 40 per cent of respondents. Among cocaine quitters, the most frequently reported reasons for quitting were fear of addiction and fear of physical and psychological damage. Loss of ambition and the expense were cited as reasons for quitting by nearly 80 per cent of all quitters. In their study of Australian prisoners, Dobinson and Ward (1984) explored reasons why the heroin users had stopped using heroin. Of the 53 users who had abstained from using heroin, the majority (57 per cent) reported that the main reason for doing so was that they were 'fed up', 'sick with the lifestyle', 'pressure' or 'influence of others', and a change in the individual's environment. Waldorf *et al.* (1991) explored motives for quitting cocaine use among 106 quitters. The most frequently mentioned reason was health problems; nearly half cited this reason as instrumental in their decision to quit. The second most frequently cited reason was financial problems, mentioned by two in five, and problems at work and pressure from a spouse or lover, cited by one in three.

### Crime as a motive for alcohol and drug use

Arrestees interviewed in the first year of the NEW-ADAM programme were asked about their offending behaviour and illicit drug taking over various periods of time (ever, last 12 months, last 30 days, last 3 days). Those arrestees who had committed one or more acquisitive crimes and used one or more illicit drugs within the last 12 months were asked if they believed that there was a connection between their drug use and offending. Twelve per cent of respondents said that they used the money generated from crime to buy drugs. Hammersley *et al.* (2003) asked their sample of young offenders about the nature of the relationship between drug use and offending. Of the 269 who provided answers, 25 per cent agreed or strongly agreed that sometimes they had taken alcohol or drugs to get the courage to commit crimes. Parker's (1996) study of 66 probationers showed that crime sometimes motivated drug use. One respondent said that he took amphetamines to keep him awake all night so that he could keep alert while stealing cars and took tranquillizers in the day to help bring him down and allow him to sleep. It was also reported that 20 per cent of self-defined problem drinkers in the sample and 7 per cent of other drinkers said that they drank alcohol to give them the courage to commit crime. Bennett and Wright (1986) also found that crime was a motivator for alcohol use in terms of giving potential offenders the courage to commit offences and in terms of the use of pubs as meeting places prior to the commission of an offence.

## Conclusion

This chapter has provided some basic information on the nature and variation in drug use in order to inform the more detailed discussion on the drugs–crime connection in the later chapters. It has shown that there is some considerable variation in the types of drugs used, the effects of different drugs, the effects of different methods of administering drugs, sources of supply of drugs, patterns of drug use and motives for drug use. Each of these factors may play a role in determining the nature of the association between drug misuse and crime. Crack will not be connected to crime in countries where there is no crack misuse. Drugs that are used infrequently (such as LSD) are unlikely to be connected with crimes that are committed frequently (e.g. shoplifting). Drug markets are unlikely to be a source of violence among users who obtain their drugs solely from medical practitioners. While these variations might seem obvious in the context of the

current discussion, they sometimes become lost in the context of discussions about the statistical association and causal connection between drug
use and crime.

## Further reading

A useful overview of patterns of drug misuse in the UK can be found in the various
publications by Parker and others (e.g. Parker *et al.* 1998, 2001). The special
edition of the *British Journal of Criminology* (1999, Volume 39(4)) on drugs and
the paper by Pearson in that volume are also worth looking at. A slightly older
book, but one that is still relevant, is *Heroin Addiction: Treatment and Control*, by
Stimson and Oppenheimer (1982). The DrugScope report, *UK Drug Report on
Trends in 2001*, provides an excellent summary of recent patterns of drug misuse in
the UK and is available at http://www.drugscope.org.uk/druginfo/drugreport.asp.
The related report from the European Monitoring Centre for Drugs and Drug
Addiction (2003) is also an excellent source of information on patterns of drug use
from a wider perspective.

# Explaining the drugs–crime connection

## Introduction

This chapter introduces the main theories that have attempted to explain the connection between drug/alcohol use and crime. These include theories that explain ways in which drug use might cause crime and crime might cause drug use. We will discuss the various meanings of causality and the ways in which these could be applied to the drugs–crime connection. It is argued that the drugs–crime link can be understood at the level of individual criminal or drug-using *careers* and also at the level of specific criminal or drug-using *events*. The main aim of the chapter is to provide a theoretical baseline from which to evaluate the findings of empirical research presented in the following chapters.

## Terminology

The term 'theory' is used here broadly to include both formal theories and informal explanations. The formal theories comprise one or more hypotheses that specify the relationship between drugs and crime in a rigorous and testable form. Informal explanations include generalized statements and broad summaries that concern either qualitative or quantitative aspects of the relationship in a less rigorous form.

## Types of explanation

The connection between drug use and crime has been discussed in the literature mainly in terms of statistical associations and causal connections.

### Statistical associations

A statistical association between drugs and crime tells us that when you find one of the variables you tend to find the other (Kenny 1979). Research on the drugs–crime connection has frequently shown a strong correlation between drug use and criminal behaviour (Harrison and Gfroerer 1992). French *et al.* (2000) suggest that research studies have established that the use of illicit drugs is strongly related to the commission of criminal acts. Yacoubian and Kane (1998) similarly argue that the relationship between illicit drug use and criminal activity has been repeatedly demonstrated over the past few decades and that there is considerable evidence to suggest that drug use is associated with criminality. However, they go on to argue that the debate continues as to whether drugs are contributing factors, correlates or determinants of criminality.

### Causal connections

A causal connection means something more than a statistical association. Goode (1997) points out that the fact that drugs and crime are frequently found together does not in itself demonstrate their causal connection. One simple definition is that a cause is something that produces an effect (Skog 1992). Kenny (1979) notes that a causal statement has two components: a cause and an effect. While these might sound rather simplistic statements, they establish the important principle that the cause must precede the effect and the effect must be a product of the cause. In other words, drug use would only cause crime if crime were one of the effects of drug use. There are fairly well-established essential criteria for establishing a causal connection. Moser and Kalton (1993) explain that there are three types of evidence that are relevant in assessing causality: (1) there must be an association between the contributory variables; (2) the connection must show that the cause occurs before the effect; and (3) the connection between the variables must not disappear when the influences of other variables are taken into account.

Kraemer *et al.* (1997) list the main elements of correlational and causal relationships: (a) if two variables measured together are correlated, they are concomitants from which no direction or effect can be determined; (b) if one of the variables precedes the other, it can be considered a risk factor; (c) if changing a risk factor brings about a change in the outcome, then it can be inferred that it is among the causes of that outcome.

## Types of connection

Perhaps one connection between drug use and crime that should not be overlooked is that the possession, manufacture and distribution of certain classified drugs are crimes in themselves (US Department of Justice 1994). However, in most respects the discussion about the connection between drugs and crime concerns whether one causes the other.

### Causal models

There are a number of ways in which drugs and crime might be connected. These are sometimes referred to as causal models. The number of models presented varies between authors. The most common number is four models (White 1990). These are often described as:

- the 'drug-use-causes-crime' model;
- the 'crime-causes-drug-use' model;
- the 'reciprocal' model; and
- the 'common-cause' model.

Some writers include a fifth model sometimes referred to as the coincidence model (Pernanen 1982).

The first two models – the drug-use-causes-crime model and the crime-causes-drug-use model – are the most simple to understand. Brownstein and Crossland (2002) note that they both have their supporters. At the most basic level, the models state that drug use leads to crime or crime leads to drug use. These authors note their appealing simplicity and point out that some government policies and programmes have been developed on the basis of these models. However, even these most basic models have some conceptual complexities. One possible variant is whether the relationship is direct or indirect. A direct relationship is one in which drug use leads directly to crime with no intervening variables. The clearest example of this would be the case of someone consuming alcohol and then violently attacking the person next to them. The consumption of alcohol could be seen as directly generating the violent attack. An indirect relationship is one in which drug use leads to crime through an intervening variable. This might be the case when the consumption of alcohol leads to a violent attack as a result of crowded conditions in a pub setting.

The third model – the reciprocal model – is a more complex model and argues that drug use sometimes causes crime and crime sometimes causes drug use. This model is based on the idea that the relationship between drug use and crime is bi-directional. There are also some conceptual complexities associated with this model. It could be argued that it is not an additional model at all, but a restatement of the first two models. The only difference is that the reciprocal model mentions the possible co-existence of two or more models, whereas the first two do not. A counter-argument is that the reciprocal model is a unique model because the bi-directional process is in itself causal. Menard *et al.* (2001) argue that drug use and crime are causally linked and mutually reinforcing. Illegal behaviour might lead to the initiation of drug use and serious drug use might lead to the continuity of illegal behaviour.

The fourth model – the common-cause model – proposes that drug use does not cause crime, and that crime does not cause drug use. Instead, they are both caused by a third or common variable. While also appearing to be straightforward, there is some lack of clarity in the literature about whether this constitutes a causal model or a spuriousness model. It could be argued that it is a causal model when looking at all the variables involved because it defines both the causal and non-causal connections among them. Conversely, it could be argued that it is a non-causal model when looking just at drugs and crime. In this case, the model appears to be making an unambiguous statement that drug use and crime are not caus-ally connected. It argues that the connection is not causal because it fails in terms of ruling out rival hypotheses. In fact, the common-cause model could be viewed as a rival hypothesis. It shows that crime is not an effect of drug use and that drug use is not an effect of crime. The relationship between drug use and crime is, therefore, spurious.

The fifth model – the coincidence model – could also be described as a spuriousness model. This model purports that drug use and crime are not causally connected. Instead, they exist within a nexus of correlated vari-ables and problematic behaviours. Pernanen (1982) provides an example of the pub setting in which alcohol is consumed and crimes are planned or committed. However, they all occur in a complex setting in which alcohol use cannot be independently connected to the occurrence of crime. The conceptual problems relating to the coincidence model, within the typ-ology of models, is that it is a second form of spuriousness model and that it is similar in some ways to the common-cause model. White (1990) argues that the common-cause model and the coincidence model are both spuriousness models. However, they are both useful in that they describe two different mechanisms. In the case of the common-cause model, the link between drug use and crime is caused by a third explanatory variable. In the case of the coincidence model, there is no clear causal connection between any of the variables.

### Onset and intensification

An important issue that is not made entirely clear in the literature is what precisely theories of the drugs–crime connection are trying to explain. The major confusion concerns whether the theories are attempting to explain the onset or the intensification of drug use and crime. Hammersley *et al.* (1989) assert that the literature has confused two kinds of cause that are logically distinct. They describe the first cause as the 'developmental' cause, where drug use leads users into crime for the first time or where crime leads an offender into using drugs for the first time. The second type of cause (which might be referred to as the 'intensification' cause) is described as occurring once both drug use and offending are established and concerns the way in which the need for drugs might cause crime, or the proceeds of crime might cause drug use. This conceptual lack of clarity will become more apparent when the particular theories and explanations are discussed. There are some theories, such as pharmacological and economic theories, that can explain both onset and continuation of both drug use and crime.

### Distal and proximal causes

There is some choice in the types of factors that can be used to generate explanations. The factors can be events occurring in the distant past or they can be events occurring right at the moment of the behaviour being explained. Events occurring in the distant past are sometimes referred to as 'distal' causes, whereas events occurring in the situation of the behaviour are sometimes referred to as 'proximal' causes (Ekblom 1999). The problem of time-scale might appear similar to the problem of onset and intensification. However, the problem of the use of distal or proximal factors in the explanation can apply to both. For example, both genetic factors and current situational factors might be used to explain the onset of drug use and crime. Similarly, both genetic factors and current situational factors can be used to explain how drug use might amplify crime once the criminal career has commenced. This problem will also become more apparent later when looking at the individual theories. Theories relating to the drug-use-causes-crime and crime-causes-drug-use models tend to be based on proximal factors, whereas theories relating to the common-cause model tend to be based on distal factors.

### Risk and protective factors

Another conceptual problem concerns assumptions about the direction of the effect. It is commonly believed that drug use causes or intensifies crime or that crime causes or intensifies drug use. White (1990) explains that this view has been the cornerstone of US drug policies. Brownstein and Crossland (2002), as mentioned above, have noted that many policies and programmes have been developed on the basis of the direct cause model. This is also true of British drug policy. A key aim of the government's updated drug strategy is to reduce crime by reducing the availability and use of illicit substances (Home Office 2002). However, it is possible that any causal relationship between drug use and crime need not necessarily be in the direction of drug use causing more crime or crime causing more drug use. Instead, the use of certain drug types might be negatively correlated with crime. Drug use might cause a reduction in crime or crime might cause a reduction in drug use. Using heroin, for example, might ameliorate aggressive impulses and might make the users physically unable to commit certain crimes. In other words, drug use might be either a risk factor or a protective factor for crime, depending on other conditions.

## Types of measures

The drugs–crime connection has been investigated in the literature using a wide range of measures of drug use and crime. It is likely that the nature of the relationship is affected by the type of measures used.

### Measures of drug use

Gandossy et al. (1980) argued over 20 years ago that research on drug use and crime has inadequately defined the independent variables (the 'cause' variables) and dependent variables (the 'effect' variables). The type of drug user and the categories of crime under investigation need to be carefully specified so that the relationship between specific drugs and specific crimes can be determined. However, research on the relationship between drug misuse and crime has been dominated by generalized measures of drug misuse (e.g. use of any illicit drug) and generalized measures of crime, usually either property crime or violent crime. Parker and Auerhahn (1998) make the same point when they complain that a fairly common problem within theoretical and empirical investigations is the tendency to lump all illicit drugs together, as if all drugs were the same. In contrast, there are also a large number of studies that have investigated the relationship between drug use and crime through just one drug type. South (1994) reports that the majority of criminological studies since the 1960s have focused on heroin. MacCoun et al. (2002) assert that almost the entire experimental literature on the relationship between drug use and aggression has focused on alcohol use.

There are several reasons for looking at the links between a number of different forms of drugs and crime. Drugs vary substantially in terms of their pharmacological properties, their addictive qualities and their costs (Farabee et al. 2001a). Goode (1997), for example, explains that narcotic and cannabis use may depress or reduce violent behaviour because of their 'soothing, calming, soporific effect', while cocaine and amphetamine use might increase violent behaviour because of their tendency to 'stimulate overall activity, alertness, edginess, suspicion, paranoia and behavioural fixations'. Hence, it is unlikely that the impact of different kinds of drugs on criminal behaviour would be identical.

### Measures of crime

The concerns described above relating to measures of drug use also can be directed at measures of crime. Research on the association between drug misuse and crime has tended to use fairly generalized measures of criminal behaviour. These include arrest rates or number of convictions for any crimes (e.g. Gossop and Roy 1977). However, criminal behaviour varies substantially in its nature and motivation. Some forms of criminal behaviour might have clear theoretical links with drug misuse (such as certain kinds of acquisitive crime) and others might have fewer plausible connections (such as certain kinds of expressive crime). A similar problem

**80** Understanding drugs, alcohol and crime

exists when studies focus on just one or two selected crime types. There may be variations in the nature of the links between drug use and specific crime types, such that results relating to one type of offence might not be the same as results relating to another type of offence. Some studies have used fairly uncommon offences that almost certainly could not be extrapolated to all crimes. White and Gorman (2000) explain this point in more detail: 'In some studies, crime refers to murder, rape, robbery, theft, and burglary – acts that fall within most people's definitions. In other studies, however, crime refers to relatively trivial acts, such as taking a few dollars from one's parents (this is especially true of studies of juveniles . . .)' (p. 159). There is a growing consensus that the investigation of the drugs–crime connection might be better served by studying disaggregated forms of both drug misuse and crime (Farabee *et al.* 2001a). In practice, this means looking at a range of drug types and a range of crime types. Only then will it be possible to identify both themes and variations in the drugs–crime connection.

The remainder of the chapter presents the main theories of the nature of the relationship between drugs and crime. These have been organized around the main causal models described above: (1) drug use causes crime, (2) crime causes drug use, (3) the reciprocal model, (4) the common-cause model and (5) the coincidence model.

## Drug misuse causes crime

One of the most common explanations of the drugs–crime relationship is that drug use causes crime. While there is some support for this view, there is some variation in the published accounts about the way in which drug use might cause crime. There are at least three broad categories of explanation: psychopharmacological explanations, economic explanations and drug-lifestyle explanations.

### Psychopharmacological explanations

Psychopharmacological explanations concern the way in which the chemical properties of drugs interact with the human organism to produce specific behavioural outcomes. These can be divided into explanations that focus on direct effects (no intermediary factors implicated) and indirect effects (intermediary factors implicated).

#### Direct effects
Goode argues that all psychopharmacological explanations are direct cause explanations.

The psychopharmacological model says that drugs cause violence because of their direct effects. As a result of taking a specific drug, this model argues, users become irritable, excitable, impatient, and irrational and, hence, are much more likely to engage in criminal behavior.

(Goode 1997)

Goldstein (1985) also describes the psychopharmacological model as a direct effect model and argues that 'some individuals, as a result of short or long term ingestion of specific substances, may become excitable, irrational, and may exhibit violent behavior' (p. 494). Brochu (2001) also notes that certain drugs 'act on specific areas of the nervous system, including the frontal lobe and the limbic system, where the centres of aggressiveness and impulsiveness are located'.

While these kinds of explanation are often classified as 'direct effect' explanations, the links between consumption of a drug and the commission of a crime are unlikely to be instantaneous. In most cases, it can be assumed that there is some kind of intermediary mechanism at work. However, the main distinction between direct and indirect effect explanations used in the drugs-and-crime literature is that the former (direct effect) requires only the psychopharmacological process involved, whereas the latter (indirect effect) requires one or more external variables to complete the causal process. Hence, this convention is used here. Direct effects are defined as those that are based on psychopharmacological processes alone. Indirect effects are those based on psychopharmacological processes plus the influence of one or more external variables.

Psychopharmacological explanations of the links between drug use and crime have tended to focus on the links between drugs and violent crime. There are several ways in which psychopharmacological processes might lead directly to crime. White and Gorman (2000: 170) list 'disinhibition, cognitive-perceptual distortions, attention deficits, bad judgment, and neuro-chemical change' as potential drugs–organism interactions that might cause violent behaviour. They also note that chronic intoxication may also contribute to subsequent aggression and crime due to 'withdrawal, sleep deprivation, nutritional deficits, impairment of neuropsychological functioning, or enhancement of psychopathologic personality disorders'. Brochu (1994) notes that the association between intoxication and violence might be ascribed to disinhibition, which he describes as a process whereby intoxication with a psychoactive substance overpowers internal restraints and gives free rein to socially repressed criminal tendencies. Goode (1997) also describes (as mentioned earlier) the direct pharmacological effects of cocaine and amphetamines on violent behaviour, 'as a result of these drugs' tendency to stimulate overall activity, alertness, edginess, suspicion, paranoia, and behavioral fixations'.

### Indirect effects
In practice, the psychopharmacological effects of drugs on crime are likely to operate indirectly through one or more mediating or moderating

factors. These are likely to be social or environmental elements of the situation in which drug use or crime takes place. Parker and Auerhahn (1998) report that one of the strongest findings from their own review of the literature on the links between alcohol and violence was the overwhelming importance of context in the relationship between substance use and violent behaviour. They conclude that 'the social environment is a much more powerful contributor to the outcome of violent behavior than are pharmacological factors associated with any of the substances reviewed here' (p. 306). MacCoun *et al.* (2002) state a similarly strong position in relation to violent crime: 'It may be that no drug is sufficient to produce aggression in isolation from psychological and situational moderators' (p. 6). They go on to list some common situational factors that may provide a link between the psychopharmacological effects of drugs on crime.

> Relevant moderators include: situational stressors and frustrators; expectancy effects (personal and cultural beliefs about the effect of the drug on behaviour, and local norms about tolerable versus unacceptable conduct when under the influence); disinhibition; impaired cognitive functioning (self-control, decision-making ability, reduced attention to situational cues, reduced self-attention); social threats to self-identity or self-esteem.
>
> (MacCoun *et al.* 2002: 6)

White and Gorman (2000) also add to the list of situational factors relevant to the relationship between alcohol use and aggression. They argue that this link is affected by factors relating to subject characteristics (e.g. gender, aggressive tendencies, cognitive abilities), social conditions (e.g. provocation, response, peer pressure, normative standards) and the characteristics of the drugs consumed (e.g. type and dosage).

A less common psychopharmacological connection that links the effects of drugs and the effects of situational factors can be found in the concept of victim-precipitation. This explanation suggests that crime is caused by the psychopharmacological effect of drug use on the victim rather than on the perpetrator. Goldstein (1985) argues that psychopharmacological violence may include drug use by either offender or victim. In other words, drug use may contribute to a person behaving violently or it may contribute to a person becoming a victim of violence. Previous research indicates relatively high frequencies of alcohol consumption in rape victims. Public intoxication may invite a robbery or mugging. One study found that rapes in which only the victim was intoxicated were more likely to be linked to physical injury (Goldstein 1985).

### Risk and protective factors

For the most part, psychopharmacological explanations have focused on the ways in which drug use causes or intensifies criminal behaviour. However, there is also evidence that the psychopharmacological effects of some drug types can have the opposite effect and prevent or reduce offending. The National Commission on Marihuana and Drug Abuse (1972) reported that, 'In sum, the weight of the evidence is that marihuana does not cause violent or aggressive behaviour; if anything, marihuana generally serves to inhibit the expression of such behavior' (p. 6). Goode (1997) speculated that, 'Judging by their direct or pharmacological effects, it might seem reasonable that narcotics would depress or reduce violent behavior because of their soothing, calming, soporific effect'. Stimson and Oppenheimer (1982) noted that heroin, like cannabis, can have a calming effect: 'One man interviewed while he was serving a prison sentence for a violent offence, was convinced that he would have been a more violent person if he had not been addicted' (p. 118). Maruna (2001) found from interviews with a group of ex-offenders that '[s]everal interviewees described scaling down their criminal pursuits after realizing that they were addicted to heroin (the threat of withdrawing from heroin in a jail cell without bathroom facilities was an enormous threat to persons addicted to heroin)' (p. 64).

## Economic explanations

Economic explanations are based mainly on the relationship between habitual drug use (such as heroin, crack and cocaine use) and income-generating crime (such as theft, burglary, robbery and fraud). The most common economic model is referred to as the 'enslavement' or 'economic necessity' model (Goldstein 1985). Goode provides a useful summary of the 'enslavement' viewpoint:

> Addicts and abusers become 'enslaved', unable to control their use of the drug; they spend so much money on it that they are unable to support their habit by working at a regular, legitimate job. Consequently, they must engage in crime; they have no choice in the matter.
>
> (Goode 1997)

Brochu provides more detail on the economic forces that might make crime an economic necessity:

> For illicit substances, the most significant relationship between drugs and crime starts with the economic dimension associated with purchasing certain drugs. Heroin, cocaine and similar drugs can produce dependence in some users. Someone who has become dependent on one of these products generally uses it several times a day to prevent the onset of physiological or psychological withdrawal. As a result of such habituation, the substance becomes terribly costly for the addict. Hence, the criminal activity of some users who can no longer control their habit can be attributed to a need for money due to dependence on drugs that are brought and sold on the black market at prices that are too high for their income from licit sources.
>
> (Brochu 2001)

### Onset and intensification

It has been argued that the enslavement model can be applied both to onset and intensification of drug use. Goode (1997) believes that the enslavement model is based on the view that addiction comes first and crime follows as a consequence: 'addicts turn to crime because of their addiction. In the absence of addiction, those persons who are now enslaved to a drug would not commit moneymaking crimes'. Lindesmith (1968) makes a similar point and argues that, 'while it is true that some addicts are criminals prior to addiction, many, perhaps most of them, turn to crime only when the high price of the drug and the danger and inconvenience of maintaining a supply force them to do so'. However, it is also possible that those addicts mentioned by Lindesmith who were criminals prior to addiction might intensify their offending behaviour following addiction as a result of economic pressures. In these cases, drug use might not have caused the onset of criminal behaviour, but might have generated the economic necessity to continue offending once addicted.

### Property and violent crimes

The economic necessity argument is based on the idea that drug users will seek to commit crimes to pay for their drug use. Hence, most writers describe the connection between drug use and various forms of property crime, including theft, shoplifting, burglary, handling, fraud and drug supply offences (Bennett 2000). However, there is a growing body of literature on the links between drug use and violent crime.

In some cases, such as street robbery, property crime may also involve violence. There are a number of reasons why drug users might choose violent property crimes as a source of income for drugs. One reason is the problem of raising money for drugs in the middle of the night. Opportunities for residential burglary might be limited because most dwellings are likely to be occupied. Opportunities for shoplifting are also likely to be limited and burglaries against non-dwellings (such as shops) are made more difficult by the security devices protecting these properties at night. Baumer et al. (1998) argue that habitual drug users (especially crack users) are likely at night to prefer street robbery. They argue that robbery usually nets cash directly and is more easily perpetrated during the hours of darkness when the streets are less crowded. Preble and Casey (1969) also argue that an important advantage of crimes against the person is that these offences yield cash which does not have to be sold at a discount, as does stolen property. It is easily concealed and can be easily exchanged directly for heroin. However, there are some disadvantages to obtaining money for drugs from robbery. Goldstein (1985) believes that most heroin users will avoid violent acquisitive crime if viable non-violent alternatives exist. This is because violent crime is more dangerous and carries with it a threat of imprisonment if caught. However, he also notes that on some occasions drug users may resort to violence because of the social context in which economic crime is perpetrated. These include 'the perpetrator's own nervousness, the victim's reaction, weaponry (or the lack of it) carried by either offender or victim, the intercession of bystanders, and so on' (p. 496).

### Mediating and moderating factors

The economic necessity argument is not intended to be a deterministic model of the relationship between drug use and crime. It would be expected that in some circumstances neither habitual drug use nor economic necessity would inevitably lead to crime. Brochu (2001), for example, acknowledges that economic explanations do not apply to all users and that the relationship may be affected by moderating factors. He notes that not all heroin and cocaine users become pathologically addicted and not all fund their habits from crime. Some will find ways to use less, take less expensive substitutes, or stop using for a while. Hunt (1991), for example, argues that whether users of illicit psychoactive substances engage in criminal activity will depend on: (a) the size of their income relative to the price of the product; (b) how frequently they use drugs and how involved they are in the drug lifestyle; and (c) their criminal history. Other writers have discussed the ways in which drug users fund their drugs and have noted that crime may be just one or even a minor way in which drug use can be financed. Preble and Casey (1969) note the role of drug dealing, money from family and friends, and payment in kind as alternative means of funding drug use.

### Drug lifestyle explanations

The third type of explanation is sometimes referred to as a 'lifestyle' explanation. Lifestyle explanations are also known as 'systemic' explanations in that crime is viewed as an intrinsic (or systemic) part of a broader lifestyle context. Lifestyle explanations can be used to explain both causal and non-causal (or spurious) connections between drug use and crime. In this current section, they are used in a causal sense. To clarify this distinction, they are referred to as 'drug lifestyle' explanations, as they show how certain aspects of the lifestyle of drug users can cause crime. These can be contrasted with 'crime lifestyle' explanations that explain how certain aspects of the lifestyle of criminals can cause drug use.

Goldstein (1985) notes that the lifestyle or systemic model reached prominence during the 1980s. The theory focused, in particular, on the relationship between drug-using lifestyles and violence. He argues that the system of drug distribution and use is inherently connected with violent crime. Systemic violence includes: disputes over territory between rival dealers; assaults and homicides committed within dealing hierarchies; enforcement of normative codes; robberies of drug dealers; violent retaliation by the dealers; elimination of informers; punishment for selling adulterated drugs; and punishment for failing to pay debts. These points are elaborated by Goode:

The systemic model argues that drug abusers are more likely to be violent than the rest of us because drug abuse is densely woven into a lifestyle that is, by its very nature, violent. This is especially the case when we consider drug selling in addition to the use and abuse of illegal drugs. One cannot be a drug dealer, especially in the inner city, without facing the possibility of violence; it is a world that is saturated with violence.

(Goode 1997)

Some writers have focused less on violence and noted the wider links between drug use and criminality. A fact sheet produced by the US Department of Justice (1994), for example, states that drug use and crime are both common aspects of a deviant lifestyle. As drug users often do not participate in the legitimate economy, the likelihood that they will become involved in illegal activity is increased. They will also be exposed to situations that encourage crime. Other writers have noted the link between deviant lifestyles and crime at the community level. White and Gorman (2000) note that drug markets can create community disorganization and affect the norms and behaviours of individuals living in the community. Drug use and drug dealing may bring about community decline, which, in turn, might bring about an increase in criminality.

## Crime causes drug misuse

While there are many theories purporting to explain how drug use causes crime, far fewer theories have been offered to explain how crime causes drug use. The few theories that have been suggested can be divided roughly into the same three groups: psychopharmacological explanations, economic explanations and criminal lifestyle explanations.

### Psychopharmacological explanations

There are a number of ways in which crime can be linked to the psycho-pharmacological effects of drugs. One common explanation is that drugs are used as part of the celebration of a successful crime. Menard *et al.* (2001) suggest that criminals use drugs as a form of 'chemical recreation' to celebrate the successful commission of a crime, in the same way that people use alcohol to celebrate birthdays and other special occasions. The main process that links crime to drug use is through their perceived pleasurable effects. Crime, therefore, may provide both the motivation for 'chemical recreation' (celebration of success) and the resources for it (money to buy drugs and alcohol). A similar point has been made by Wright and Decker (1997) in their study of street robbers in St Louis, Missouri, in which they note the importance of the sub-cultural value of 'life as a party'. While the primary motivation to commit street robbery was a perceived need for money, one of the products of this money was the purchase of drugs as a means of 'keeping the party going'.

Another common link found in the literature between crime and drug use is the instrumental use of drugs to facilitate the commission of crime. Offenders may sometimes use drugs to enable them to commit crime. Brochu (2001) describes how a person who has planned a crime might sometimes use drugs to give them the courage to carry out the plan. It is possible to view this theory as an example of drug use causing crime, as the offence might not have been committed without the drug use. However, in terms of the decision-making process, the decision to commit an offence comes first and the decision to take drugs follows. A variant on this approach has been applied to the commission of violent crime. Brochu (2001) argues that individuals who have antisocial predispositions may attempt to use substance abuse as a socially permissible means (by informal cultural standards) of expressing their aggressive tendencies. Thus, they may use drugs in a functional way to carry out a crime that they had previously planned. An example of this might be the use of alcohol by 'football hooligans' before a match that they had already decided would end in a fight.

### Economic explanations

Economic explanations of the way in which crime causes drug use centre around the belief that surplus funds obtained from crime can be spent on drugs. This explanation is similar to some of the psychopharmacological explanations of the links between crime and drug use. However, economic explanations focus more on funding drug use than on 'chemical recreation'.

Collins *et al.* (1985), for example, note: 'rather than the need for a drug compelling an individual to commit robbery, the income generated from a robbery might provide the individual with extra money to secure drugs and . . . place the individual in an environment that supports drug use' (cited in White and Gorman 2000: 174). Bennett (2000) showed that some arrestees interviewed as part of the New English and Welsh Arrestee Drug Abuse Monitoring (NEW-ADAM) programme reported that their drug use and offending behaviour were connected because drugs just happened to be one of the things that they bought from the money obtained through crime. Speckart and Anglin (1985) describe this view in more detail: 'narcotics use is precipitated by large amounts of available funds of the criminal who elects to spend such income on illicit or deviant recreation, such as heroin use, instead of other commodities. Essentially, in this view, heroin use is the outcome or result of a crime spree' (p. 269).

### Criminal lifestyle explanations

Criminal lifestyle explanations are based on the idea that drug use is a systemic part of the criminal lifestyle. This view is different from the drug lifestyle explanations, which view crime as a systemic part of drug lifestyles. Goode (1997), for example, notes that 'the criminal model argues that it is not addicts who turn to crime but criminals who turn to drugs'. This view is based on the idea that criminality comes first and that drug use follows. According to Goode:

> Addiction has nothing to do with their criminal behavior; they are not enslaved to a drug so much as participants of a criminal lifestyle. Their drug use is a reflection or an indicator of that lifestyle; it is a later phase of a deviant tendency or career. Take away the drugs and they would still commit a great deal of crime.
>
> (Goode 1997)

White and Gorman (2000) also suggest that 'several aspects of the professional criminal lifestyle are conducive to heavy drinking and drug use, such as working periodically, partying between jobs, being unmarried, and being geographically mobile' (p. 174). A variation on this argument is that some offenders use drugs in an effort to excuse their offending behaviour. MacCoun *et al.* (2002), for example, state: 'Arrested and incarcerated offenders report that they committed their offenses to raise money to purchase drugs. Of course, this might be a convenient rationalization or excuse for antisocial behavior. Should we believe them?' (p. 10). Brochu (2001) makes a similar point when he says, 'others, influenced by the symbolic and cultural association attached to certain substances, may see intoxication as a convenient excuse or as exoneration for a socially unacceptable act'.

## Reciprocal model

The reciprocal model maintains that both drug use causes crime and crime causes drug use. In other words, it is based on the assumption that the causal order is bi-directional. On one occasion, drug use might cause crime and on another crime might cause drug use. It has been argued that reciprocal models have been under-explored in the criminological literature. Thornberry (1987), for example, advocates greater use of reciprocal models in research on the origins of crime and delinquency. He argues that too little attention has been paid to the possibility that delinquency may be a cause of many social problems associated with it, such as poor family communication, inadequate school achievement and drug abuse.

Some writers have taken this line of thinking further by considering the factors that might determine the causal connection. White and Gorman

(2000) describe how 'opportunity' and 'need' moderate the direction of the causal relationship between drug use and crime. They explain, 'when an addict has an easy opportunity to commit robbery, he or she will commit it and then buy drugs with the money gained, not out of a compulsion but rather as a consumer expenditure. Conversely, when the need for drugs is great, users will commit crimes to get money to buy drugs' (p. 175). Hough (1996) applies this general principle to prostitution. He argues that there may be a dynamic between prostitution and drug dependence whereby prostitution can be a method of financing drug use and drug use can be a palliative to prostitution.

The issue of the nature of the dependent variable continues in relation to the reciprocal model. It is possible that the bi-directional nature of drug use and crime might relate to both onset and intensification. Some researchers have reported that the direction of the relationship varies during the course of the addiction career. Menard *et al.* (2001) report that illegal behaviour might lead to initiation of substance use, whereas serious illicit substance use (e.g. heroin, crack or cocaine) might lead to continuity of illegal behaviour. Once both substance use and crime have been initiated, serious drug users are more likely than recreational drug users to continue their illegal behaviour. Other writers have extended the idea of variations in the drugs–crime connection over time by looking at different relationships over different phases of the drug-using career. Faupel and Klockars (1987) suggest that during the 'occasional user' phase, drug use and crime are not causally connected. During the period of early stable use, criminal income facilitates drug use. By the time that the user has reached the 'street addict' phase, drug use causes crime.

## Common-cause model

The common-cause model holds that drug use does not cause crime, and that crime does not cause drug use. Instead, they are both caused by a common factor. A variety of common factors have been identified in the literature as possible causes of both drug use and crime. These have been grouped below into three broad categories: psychological, social and environmental.

### Psychological explanations

Psychological explanations describe how factors relating to the mind and behaviour of the individual cause both drug use and crime. White and Gorman (2000) give some examples of the kinds of psychological and other factors that have been implicated in the literature: 'The common-cause model postulates that substance use and crime do not have a direct causal link. Rather, they are related because they share common causes (such as genetic or temperamental traits, antisocial personality disorder, [and] parental alcoholism)' (p. 175).

Psychological factors can be viewed as either distal or proximal causes. Many explanations focus on the role of psychological factors as distal causes. These are viewed as factors operating in the past that predispose people to act in certain ways. Gottfredson and Hirschi (1990), for example, assert that crime does not cause drug use and that drug use does not cause crime. Instead, the cause of both is low self-control. Some writers have discussed ways in which psychological factors might be viewed as proximal causes of both crime and drug use. Goode (1997), for example, explains that the type of person who uses psychoactive substances is also the type of person who commits criminal offences. Both drugs and crime provide immediate, easy and certain short-term pleasures. In particular, they satisfy a hedonistic desire for danger, risk and excitement.

### Social explanations

Social explanations are concerned with social relationships and the way in which these might influence both drug use and crime. An important common cause is the role played by peer pressure. Elliott et al. (1989) argue that the most important influence on both substance use and illegal behaviour is the extent of involvement with friends who are engaged in illegal behaviour (including illicit drug use). White (1990) concluded from the results of a detailed review of the literature that 'Peer group influences are the best predictors of delinquency and drug use' (p. 240).

Another common-cause explanation concerns the role of sub-cultural factors. The National Commission on Marihuana and Drug Abuse (1972) concluded that there is no evidence that marihuana use causes crime. Instead, the evidence suggests that cultural variables account for much of the apparent statistical correlation. Wright and Decker (1997) drew attention to the role played by 'street culture' in explaining drugs-related violence. Another group of social explanations note the common-cause role played by either drug or crime lifestyles. It is argued that certain aspects of a broader deviant lifestyle can result in both drug use and crime (Walters 1994).

### Environmental explanations

Environmental explanations describe how factors within the environment cause both drug use and criminal behaviour. These include both the physical environment and situational factors operating at the time of commission of specific offences.

One of the oldest common-cause theories of the links between drug use and crime is social disorganization theory developed at the University of Chicago during the 1920s and 1930s (Shaw and McKay 1942). White and Gorman (2000) apply the principles of social disorganization theory to the problem of explaining drugs and crime. They argue that rates of violent crime and exposure to drugs are both higher in neighbourhoods that are poor, densely populated, racially segregated and composed of a transient population. More recent environmental theories of the kind developed by Wilson (1987) and others show that social exclusion, social disadvantage and a lack of social capital can be important mechanisms linking structural characteristics to crime and illicit drug use.

Aspects of the physical and social environment can also play a role in generating the situational factors that link drug use and crime. Parker and Auerhahn (1998) argue that environmental factors are a more powerful predictor of violent behaviour among young drug users than pharmacological factors. Crime rates and alcohol use might both be high, for example, in situations in which young people consume alcohol, such as at clubs, bars and entertainment areas (Fagan 1993). Proponents of the routine activities perspective argue that bars are crime hot spots because they bring together motivated offenders and suitable targets in the absence of effective guardianship (Roncek and Maier 1991)

## Coincidence models

The coincidence model maintains that drug use and crime are not causally related to each other or to a common factor. Instead, they are related spuriously and co-exist with other conjunctive factors in the same situation. According to Apospori *et al.* (1995: 213): 'the coincident model posits that delinquency and drug use among adolescents are nothing more than coincidental, simultaneous occurrences (non-causal and nonreciprocal) within a cluster of other youth problem behaviors that occur as a result of experimentation during adolescence'.

Pernanen (1982) makes a distinction between the coincidence model and the common-cause model. He states that some models explain the association 'by invoking a third variable or cluster of variables which, through cultural clustering or structural force, are associated with alcohol use' (p. 37). However, he notes that 'The most important difference between these models and common-cause models is that conjunctive factors do not determine the probability of alcohol use events' (ibid.).

There are many types of coincidental factor that might link alcohol use and criminal behaviour. Pernanen (1982) lists conjunctive factors that might occur in a situation in which alcohol is consumed: (a) time-out features of drinking occasions, (b) the setting of alcohol use (e.g. presence of males in the drinking setting), (c) the higher probability of interaction in alcohol use situations, and (d) criminal contacts made and/or crimes planned in public drinking places. While these factors co-exist, it cannot be said that they are causally related. Bennett and Wright (1984b) explain the links between alcohol use and burglary using the coincidence model: 'In the pub setting people of the same age meet and talk under more relaxed rules of social interaction which might provide an opportunity to talk about and decide upon committing offences (such as planning a burglary)' (cited in Bennett 1990: 833).

## Conclusion

Brownstein and Crossland (2002) argue that there is no lack of theories on the drugs–crime connection. The current chapter provides some support for this view. The main problem is not so much finding theories, but in making sense of them. At one level, they provide many conflicting and contradictory positions. Some writers have argued that drug use causes crime, while others have argued that crime causes drug use. There are some researchers who believe that the relationship between drug use and crime is causal, while others believe that it is spurious. There is a view that drug use increases crime and another view that drug use decreases crime. In some senses, it could not be more complex and divided. However, within these opposing positions are threads of continuity. There are no logical problems involved in explaining the relationship between drug use and crime using both distal factors operating in the past and proximal factors operating at the situation of the event. There is no inconsistency in the idea that drug use might sometimes cause crime and crime might sometimes cause drug use. The distinction between causal processes at onset of drug use and at continuation of drug use is helpful and clarifies the different processes involved. It is also logically possible that drug use sometimes increases crime and sometimes decreases it, depending on context. The challenge for the future is to integrate these disparate elements into a comprehensive theory of the drugs–crime connection.

## Further reading

There is no single publication that brings together theories and explanations of the drugs–crime connection. However, it would be worth looking at general titles on the drugs–crime connection, which usually include sections on theories and explanations. These include Tonry and Wilson (1990), Hough (1996), Inciardi (1981) and Walters (1994).

# chapter six

# The statistical association: just coincidence?

## Introduction

The statistical association between drug use and crime concerns the extent to which drug use and crime are found together. In other words, it concerns the question, 'When you find drug use, do you also tend to find crime?' It can be determined by looking at the proportion of drug users who commit crimes or the proportion of criminals who use drugs. It can also be determined by looking at the rate at which drug users commit crimes and criminals use drugs. The phrase makes no assumptions about whether the association is causal. Drug use might cause crime and crime might cause drug use. However, they both might be caused by other factors or the association might be a result of a non-causal overlap of problematic behaviours.

The chapter is divided into five main sections. The first looks at the results of previous reviews of the literature on the drugs–crime connection. The second considers studies that have investigated the relationship between involvement in drug use and involvement in crime. The third looks at the relationship between frequency of drug use and frequency of crime. The fourth looks at research that has attempted to disaggregate the relationship by looking at the connection between specific types of drug use and specific types of crime. The fifth section looks at the relationship between multiple drug use and crime.

## Previous reviews

It is widely believed that drug use and crime are in some way associated. However, there have been few detailed reviews of the drugs and crime literature to determine empirical support for this view. Existing reviews have tended to produce mixed conclusions.

Gandossy *et al.* (1980) conducted one of the first thorough reviews of the literature on the connection between drug use and crime. This was a comprehensive survey of the English language literature, covering studies from America, Australia, Canada and Europe. The study provided some breakdowns of the relationship in terms of type of drug used and type of offence committed. The review of the links between narcotics (mainly heroin) and crime concluded:

> it was difficult to avoid concluding that addicts engage in substantial amounts of income-generating crimes. This is true when analyzing the charges against drug-using arrestees, convictions of addicts in prisons, arrest records of treatment populations, or the observations of street addicts.
>
> (Gandossy *et al.* 1980: 52)

When looking at other drug types, the conclusions were less clear. In relation to amphetamine use and crime, the authors conclude that the research produced contradictory findings. One reason for this was the variation among the sample types selected. Studies based on amphetamine users who had a substantial prior record of criminal involvement were more likely to show a drugs–crime connection than studies based on amphetamine users who were white, middle-class college students. One study found that amphetamine users were more likely than comparison groups to be arrested for homicide and rape. Another study linked amphetamine use with violent behaviour. Studies of the relationship between barbiturates and crime also provide mixed findings. Some studies show that barbiturates inhibit violent behaviour, while others argue that they enable violence and aggression.

Gandossy *et al.* (1980) also provided a useful breakdown of the results in terms of user or offender characteristics. In relation to gender, they concluded that women addicts were less likely to be arrested than men, they were convicted and incarcerated less often and for shorter periods, and they committed fewer violent offences. They also tended to engage in different kinds of offences to male addicts. The most common means of support for women addicts was prostitution and drugs sales. One study cited showed that 40 per cent of women addicts relied on prostitution as their main source of financial support.

Hough (1996) also found some support for a relationship between drug use and crime in his review of British research on the drugs–crime connection. He concluded that it is clear that drug misuse makes a significant contribution to the overall total number of crimes committed in England and Wales. However, he was reticent in saying much more than this and concluded that, 'current knowledge about the volume and cost of drug-related crime is so patchy that all we can say with certainty is that problem drug misuse is responsible for a significant minority of crime in England and Wales' (Hough 1996: 19). He estimated that the number of 'drug-driven' crimes committed by dependent heroin users 'probably numbers in the hundreds of thousands, but it could run to a million or more' (ibid.).

Chaiken and Chaiken (1990) were more sceptical of the existence of a general association between drug use and crime. In their review of the literature on the relationship between drug use and predatory crime (i.e. instrumental offences committed for material gain), they found no evidence of a simple or unified association between drug use and participation in crime. They concluded that, when behaviours of large groups of people are studied in aggregate, there is no coherent general pattern associating drug misuse and predatory crime. They also concluded that, for the majority of drug types other than heroin and cocaine, drug use was unrelated to the commission of predatory crimes. They also noted that, even in relation to heroin and cocaine, there was no clear evidence of a relationship between consumption and offending. The only consistent evidence of an association between drug use and predatory crime was that offenders who were daily users of heroin or cocaine, and offenders who used multiple types of drugs, committed crimes at significantly higher rates than did the less drug-involved offenders. They go on to ask, therefore, 'Where, then, lies the strong relationship between drug misuse and criminality?' (Chaiken and Chaiken 1990: 212).

## Involvement in drug use and involvement in crime

We begin the search for a relationship between drug use and crime by looking at studies that have investigated whether people who take drugs are more likely to commit crime or whether people who commit crime are more likely to use drugs. The research mainly considers the simultaneous existence of drug use and crime over a fixed period of time (usually in the last 12 months). It does not consider the rate of offending or the rate of drug use, which will be discussed in the next section.

Research on the relationship between involvement in drug use and crime has tended to ask two broad questions:

1 Are drug users more likely than non-drug users to commit crime?
2 Are criminals more likely than non-criminals to use drugs?

Drug users have typically been taken from the general population or treatment samples and criminals have usually been taken from the general population, arrestees or from the prison population.

Q. Are drug users more likely than non-drug users to commit crimes?

Studies based on users in treatment tend to find that drug users are more likely than comparable samples of non-users to commit crimes. Hunt *et al.* (1984) conducted interviews with 368 methadone maintenance clients and 142 narcotics users not in treatment in the United States. The results showed that heroin users were more likely than non-users to report having committed property crimes and drug dealing crimes in the last week (or the last two weeks for the methadone sample). In a study of adolescent drug users admitted to therapeutic community drug treatment programmes in the United States, Hawke *et al.* (2000) found that amphetamine users were significantly more likely than non-users to have committed property crimes and drug supply offences at some point in their lives. Amphetamine users were also more likely than non-users to have engaged in prostitution offences. Kokkevi *et al.* (1993) found, in a study of drug users in Greece, that arrest and conviction rates were higher among drug users than among a control sample of non-users. Two-thirds of the drug users reported two or more previous arrests, compared with 15 per cent of the control group of non-users.

Studies based on users in the community also tend to show that drug users are more likely than non-users to commit crimes. Nurco *et al.* (1993) compared changes in the severity of criminal behaviour among three groups – a group of narcotic addicts, a control group who had never been addicted selected from peers of the addicts, and a group who had never been addicted drawn from the community at large. The narcotic addicts were more likely to report involvement in crime at ages 12–14 than the non-addict peer group and the non-addict control group. In total, 74 per cent of the narcotic addicts, compared with 50 per cent of the non-addicted peers and 31 per cent of the non-addict controls, reported involvement in crime. Turpeinen (2001) used a sample of 119 drug-experimenting school children in Finland to explore the association between intravenous drug use and offending behaviour later in life. Individuals who had used opiates intravenously in adolescence were compared with individuals who had not injected opiates. The results showed that those who had used opiates intravenously were significantly more likely than those who had not to have been in prison in the 20-year follow-up period. The same was also true for those who had used amphetamines intravenously during adolescence.

The results of our own systematic review of the literature on the association between drug use and crime included ten studies that provided information on the prevalence of offending among drug users. As part of the analysis, up to three research findings were extracted from each study (some studies had ten or more findings covering different combinations of drug use and offending). The results showed that all ten studies had at least one finding that showed that drug users were more likely than non-drug users (or less involved drug users) to report offending. In total, 25 of the 26 selected findings from these studies showed higher levels of involvement in crime among drug users than non-drug users (Holloway and Bennett in prep.).

Q. Are criminals more likely than non-criminals to use drugs?

The relationship between involvement in drug use and crime can also be determined by looking at samples of arrested or convicted offenders, or samples of offenders in the general population. Goulden and Sondhi (2001) conducted a study of young people in the general population as part of the second wave (1998–1999) of the Youth Lifestyles Survey. The sample comprised 4848 young people aged 12–30 living in England and Wales. The study showed that significantly more offenders than non-offenders in the general population had used drugs in the last year. Approximately half of the offenders reported using an illicit drug in the last year compared with one in seven non-offenders. The authors concluded, 'The differences in prevalence rates between the offender populations and non-offenders were strongly statistically significant and there was a clear relationship between rate and type of offending and drug use' (Goulden and Sondhi 2001: 18).

Potterat *et al.* (1998) explored the prevalence of illegal drug use among 237 prostitutes and 407 comparison women. Drug use was more commonly reported by prostitutes than comparisons (86% versus 23%). Kuhns *et al.* (1992) looked at the prevalence of illegal drug use among 53 female prostitutes and 47 female arrestees who were not prostitutes. The results showed that significantly more prostitutes had tried drugs, had used drugs with greater frequency and had begun drug/alcohol use at younger ages. A similar study by Yacoubian *et al.* (2001) compared 182 female arrestees charged with prostitution offences with over 3000 female arrestees charged with other non-prostitution offences. Seventy-eight per cent of prostitutes tested positive for at least one drug, compared with 51 per cent of non-prostitutes (the difference was statistically significant). Hser *et al.* (1998) explored drug use and correlates among sexually transmitted disease patients, emergency room patients and arrestees. Eighty-three per cent of individuals in the jail sample had used some form of drug in their lifetime, compared with 63 per cent of those in the emergency room group and 67 per cent of those in the sexually transmitted diseases group.

## Summary

The research is almost unanimous in its finding that drug users are more likely than non-drug users to be criminals and that criminals are more likely than non-criminals to be drug users. However, this research is based almost wholly on the proportions of one group found in the other group. To measure the connection more accurately, further information is needed on the details of the relationship. Research on the correlation between rates of drug use and rates of crime help in this respect.

## Frequency of drug use and frequency of crime

Another approach is to look at studies that have examined whether people who take drugs at a high rate are more likely to commit crimes (or commit them at a high rate) and whether people who commit crime at a high rate are more likely to use drugs (or to use them at a high rate). The main point of this research is to determine whether there is a correlation between frequency of drug use and frequency of crime.

Research on the extent of drug use and crime has addressed two pairs of questions:

1  Are high-rate drug users more likely than low-rate drug users to commit crimes?
2  Are high-rate drug users more likely than low-rate drug users to commit crimes at a high rate?
3  Are high-rate criminals more likely than low-rate criminals to use drugs?
4  Are high-rate criminals more likely than low-rate criminals to use drugs at a high rate?

**Q.  Are high-rate drug users more likely than low-rate users to commit crimes?** The frequency or extent of drug misuse is measured in the research literature in a number of ways, including dependent or non-dependent use, chronic or non-chronic use, and daily or non-daily use.

French *et al.* (2000) looked at the relationship between chronic drug use and crime using data from the 1993 and 1995 National Household Surveys on Drug Abuse. The sample was divided into three groups based on whether they were chronic drug users, non-chronic users or non-drug users. Chronic drug users included those users who had used one or more illicit drugs at least weekly. Non-chronic users were those who had used an illicit drug during the last year, but who did not meet the definition of a chronic user. Measures of criminal activity were based on numbers of arrests. The results showed that 19 per cent of male chronic users committed a property crime compared with 16 per cent of non-chronic users and 4 per cent of non-drug users.

Cross *et al.* (2001) investigated the association between drug use and crime using a sample of 602 African-Americans who were current users or sellers of cocaine powder, crack or heroin. The sample was recruited from randomly selected blocks in the Central Harlem area of New York City and was divided into groups on the basis of frequency of drug use. The authors investigated the proportion of frequent heroin and crack users and the proportion of non-frequent users of these drugs who had committed non-drug illegal crimes. The results revealed that frequent users of heroin, crack or cocaine were more likely than non-frequent users to have committed crimes in the past month. In another study, Shewan *et al.* (1998) investigated patterns of heroin use among a non-treatment sample of 74

opiate users in Glasgow and concluded that there were no significant differences between light, moderate and heavy heroin users in terms of their
involvement in crime.

Hence, two of the three studies that examined frequency of drug use and
criminal involvement indicated that more frequent drug users were more
likely than less frequent drug users to be involved in crime.

### Q. Are high-rate drug users more likely than low-rate users to commit crimes at a high rate?

The previous sub-section looked at whether high-rate drug users were
more likely to be involved in crime. This sub-section examines the rate of
crime. Best *et al.* (2001), for example, explored patterns of criminal activity
and drug use among a cohort of 100 new entrants to a drug treatment
service in south London. They found that entrants who reported daily
heroin use committed a higher mean number of acquisitive crimes in the
previous month than those who were not using heroin on a daily basis
(40.5 compared with 17.1). Similarly, daily heroin users reported a higher
total number of offences in the previous month than those not using heroin
on a daily basis. Regular crack users reported committing significantly
more acquisitive crimes than the occasional users. A regression analysis
revealed that the strongest predictor of total crimes committed in last
month was total quantity of heroin consumed in the last month.

Hammersley *et al.* (1989) conducted a self-report survey of an offender
sample (Scottish prisoners) and a drug-user sample (clients of a number of
drug treatment centres). They collected data on 16 types of drug, which
they collapsed into a 'drug-level' scale based on type of drug misused and
rate of use (alcohol use at the lower end of the scale and high-rate opioid
use at the top end of the scale). They also asked questions on 21 classes of
crime, which they collapsed into four crime types ('theft', 'fraud', 'delinquency and violence' and 'drug dealing'). They found that as 'drug level'
increased, various measures of rates of criminal behaviour increased.
However, the relationship only held true for 'theft' and 'drug dealing'.
There was no association between rates of drug misuse and rates of
'delinquency and violence' or 'fraud'.

Chaiken and Chaiken (1990) reviewed the results of nine studies that
included measures of rates of drug misuse and crime. From this review,
they drew a number of conclusions about the drugs–crime connection in
relation to rates. First, they concluded that the strongest connections
between frequent drug misuse and frequent criminal behaviour occurred in
relation to heroin and cocaine misuse. They argued that persistent use of
drugs other than heroin and cocaine appeared to be unrelated to persistence in committing predatory crimes. Second, they note that 'it is not drug
abuse *per se*, but the amount or frequency of drug misuse that is strongly
related to crime commission rates' (Chaiken and Chaiken 1990: 230).
They provide evidence from other studies to show that, while low-rate
heroin users show somewhat inflated rates of criminal behaviour over

non-users, the most substantial increases occur when users reach daily rates.

Our own systematic review included two further studies on the frequency of drug use and the frequency of crime and both showed that high-rate drug users committed crimes more frequently than low-rate drug users (Holloway and Bennett in prep.). Hence, the research evidence currently available points to a conclusion that the higher the rate of drug use, the higher the rate of offending. In particular, this group of studies points to an association between daily rates of use of heroin and cocaine and high offending rates.

### Q. Are high-rate criminals more likely than low-rate criminals to use drugs?

The previous two sub-sections focused on the frequency of drug use and its relation to criminality. This sub-section looks at the frequency of criminality and its relation to drug use. There are generally fewer studies that have investigated this relationship. However, those that have suggest a correlation between frequency of offending and involvement in drug use.

Hammersley *et al.* (2003) conducted interviews with nearly 300 clients of Youth Offending Teams across England and Wales. Using cluster analysis, three groups were identified on the basis of prevalence of offending in the last 12 months: frequent offenders, medium offenders and less frequent offenders. These three groups were compared in terms of the proportions reporting use of 14 drug types in their lifetime and in the last 12 months. In relation to 12 of the 14 drug types, the prevalence of drug use was highest among the most frequent offenders and lowest among the less frequent offenders. The prevalence of cannabis and heroin use, however, was greater among medium-rate offenders than frequent offenders.

Goulden and Sondhi (2001) used data from the Youth Lifestyles Survey to determine whether the prevalence of drug use varied by different types of offender. They found that frequent offenders had higher prevalence rates than infrequent offenders. Non-offenders had the lowest prevalence rates of drug used. Despite the small numbers, the findings of this research provide some evidence that high-rate offenders are more likely than low-rate offenders to use drugs.

### Q. Are high-rate criminals more likely than low-rate criminals to use drugs at a high rate?

This sub-section considers whether high-rate offenders also use drugs at a high rate. There are also few studies that have addressed this particular issue. Stewart *et al.* (2000) looked at the rate of heroin, cocaine and methadone use among individuals who had committed crimes at a high rate ($n = 103$), a low rate ($n = 438$) or not at all ($n = 534$) during the 90 days before treatment intake. The results showed that the rates of heroin and cocaine use were significantly higher among high-rate offenders than among non-offenders. The rate of methadone use, however, did not differ significantly between the two groups. Thus, the study provides some evidence in support of the view that offenders heavily involved in crime also tend to be heavily involved in drug use.

The report of the first two years of the New English and Welsh Arrestee Drug Abuse Monitoring (NEW-ADAM) programme also looked at the relationship between rates of offending and rates of drug use (Holloway and Bennett 2004). To allow comment on the progress of the government's anti-drug strategy, the research developed a measure of 'drug-misusing repeat offenders'. These were arrestees who recently had used heroin, crack or cocaine and who committed an average of two or more offences a month. These were then compared with other arrestees. The results showed that drug-misusing repeat offenders were significantly more likely to be receiving treatment for drug misuse (a measure of extent of drug misuse) than drug-misusing offenders who offended at a lower rate.

## Summary

The results of this section are similar to those of the previous section. High-rate drug users are more likely to be offenders and to offend at a high rate. High-rate offenders are more likely to be drug users and to use drugs at a high rate. Overall, the results of both sections provide strong evidence that drug use in general and crime in general are associated.

## Disaggregating the drugs–crime relationship

The results presented so far have focused mainly on the prevalence and incidence of offending and drug use. Little has been said about the details of the relationship and whether certain types of drug use or certain kinds of drug user are associated with certain types of crime. There are a number of reasons mentioned in the literature why the relationship between drug misuse and crime might vary by type of drug and type of crime. Drugs vary substantially in terms of their pharmacological properties, their addictive qualities and their costs (Farabee et al. 2001a). Hence, it is unlikely that their impact on criminal behaviour would be identical. Similarly, criminal behaviour varies substantially in its nature and motivation. Some forms of criminal behaviour have clear theoretical links with drug misuse (such as certain kinds of acquisitive crime) and others have fewer plausible connections (such as certain kinds of expressive crime).

There are also several reasons mentioned why the relationship between drug use and crime might vary by type of drug user and type of offender. Female drug users might have different needs and abilities to male drug users. For example, it has often been noted that female drug users dependent on drugs such as heroin, crack and cocaine might turn to prostitution as a means of financing their habit. There is also some evidence that different types of offender might prefer different types of drugs. For example, it is widely believed that black offenders are more likely than white offenders to use cannabis and cocaine.

This section investigates some of the variations among studies that have disaggregated the relationship between drug misuse and crime. We first examine different types of drug and different types of offence, and then go on to examine different types of drug user and different types of offender.

### Types of drug and types of crime

This sub-section looks at two questions that can be asked about types of drugs and types of crime:

1  Are certain types of drugs associated with certain types of crime?
2  Are certain types of drugs associated with high rates of crime?

**Q. Are certain types of drugs associated with certain types of crime?**
A number of studies have used disaggregated measures to investigate the connection between types of drug and types of crime. Makkai *et al.* (2000) used disaggregated measures in their analysis of data collected as part of the Drug Use Monitoring in Australia (DUMA) programme to investigate the relationship between drug misuse and the prevalence of offending. The study included urinalysis and interviews with arrestees to provide a break-down of six types of drug misuse and eight categories of criminal behaviour. The results showed some variations in the relationship between offence types and drug types. Property offenders were more likely to test positive for opiates (55 per cent) than those charged with drug offences (38 per cent) or violent offences (32 per cent). Arrestees charged with drug offences were more likely to test positive for cannabis (76 per cent) than property offenders (52 per cent) or violent offenders (46 per cent).

Another study based on the DUMA data provided a fuller set of results on the drugs–crime relationship and used different methods of analysis (Makkai 2001). The study included urinalysis and interview data from four sites over a one-year period in 1999. The results also showed some variation in the relationship depending on drug type and crime type. Over-all, testing positive for any kind of drug resulted in a greater likelihood of being charged with a property offence and (with one exception) a drug offence. Arrestees who tested positive for opiates were 4.2 times more likely to be charged with a property offence than those who tested negative for opiates. However, testing positive for any kind of drug resulted in a lower likelihood of being charged with a violent offence (with one excep-tion). The exception was that arrestees testing positive for cocaine were 2.4 times more likely to be charged with a violent offence.

The results of the NEW-ADAM programme showed that the relation-ship between drug misuse and offending was much stronger when looking at drug use and involvement in crime rather than drug use and rates of crime (Bennett and Holloway in press). Cannabis and diazepam use made a significant contribution to explaining participation in eight of the ten offence types investigated, amphetamines participation in five types, and ecstasy participation in three types. Use of crack explained participation in nine of the ten offence types. However, use of heroin explained participation in relation to only three offence types: shoplifting, burglary non-dwelling, and theft person. The greatest difference was in relation to shoplifting. Heroin users were almost five times more likely than non-heroin users to have committed shoplifting in the last 12 months.

### Q. Are certain types of drugs associated with high rates of crime?

Some studies have used disaggregated measures to investigate the relationship between drug misuse and the incidence or rate of offending. Johnston *et al.* (1978) used data from a national longitudinal high-school survey conducted in the United States to correlate rates of use of seven drug types with rates of 15 types of criminal behaviour. The results showed that virtually all drug measures correlated positively with measures of property crime. However, the relationship was strongest for minor theft, shoplifting and trespassing. The drug least strongly associated with rates of criminal behaviour (in relation to almost all delinquency items) was marijuana.

As part of a self-report survey of prisoners in eight institutions in Australia, Dobinson and Ward (1984) collected information on rates of use of eight categories of drugs and rates of commission of ten offence types in the period prior to arrest. They found a significant positive correlation between rate of heroin use and rate of armed robbery. However, they found no significant association between rate of heroin use and rate of burglary, larceny, fraud, receiving or other kinds of robbery.

In a review of the literature, Chaiken and Chaiken (1990) provided evidence for a link between certain drug types and rates of crime. They found that the strongest links between drug use and frequency of crime occurred in relation to heroin and cocaine misuse. They found little other evidence of a connection in relation to other drug types and concluded that persistent use of drugs other than heroin and cocaine appears to be unrelated to persistence in committing predatory crimes.

The results of the first two years of the NEW-ADAM programme showed that the relationship between rates of drug use and rates of crime were limited and specific (Holloway and Bennett 2004). In terms of rate of offending, the bi-variate analysis showed that use of heroin, crack and cocaine was linked to higher rates of offending in relation to four of the ten offence types (shoplifting, burglary non-dwelling, handling and drug supply offences). However, when these variables were combined in a logistic regression analysis, the results showed more modest associations between heroin use and shoplifting, and between crack use and fraud, handling and drug supply offences. No other connections were significant. Hence, the study concluded that the association between drug misuse and crime appears to be primarily a product of a small number of relationships between specific types of drug and specific types of crime.

### Types of drug user and types of offender

It was mentioned earlier that the drugs–crime connection might vary by type of drug user and type of offender. It is possible, for example, that certain individual characteristics of drug users or offenders are more frequently linked to certain kinds of drug use or crime. This sub-section looks at two questions about variations among drug users and variations among offenders:

1 Are certain types of drug user associated with certain types of offences?
2 Are certain types of criminals associated with certain types of drug use?

**Q. Are certain types of drug user associated with certain types of offences?**
Few studies have broken down the drugs–crime connection by demographic characteristics. Gandossy et al. (1980) concluded in their review of the literature that the types of crime committed by women addicts were substantially different from those committed by men. Usually women addicts engage in prostitution, drug sales and shoplifting to support their habits, whereas men addicts are more heavily involved in burglary and robbery in addition to drug sales and shoplifting (Gandossy et al. 1980). French et al. (2000), mentioned earlier in relation to their analysis of the 1993 and 1995 National Household Surveys on Drug Abuse, provide evidence that suggests that certain kinds of female drug users might be more involved in certain kinds of offending than male drug users. In the 1993 survey, 25 per cent of women chronic drug users were arrested for a property crime in the previous year, compared with the 1995 survey in which 19 per cent of male chronic drug users were arrested for property crime in the last year. However, the rates were slightly lower among females than males in relation to the non-chronic and non-drug users.

**Q. Are certain types of criminals associated with certain types of drug use?**
As before, very few studies have investigated the drugs–crime connection in terms of demographic characteristics. Hser et al. (1994) investigated the prevalence of drug use among arrestees in Los Angeles County and estimated (but do not provide any figures to support the estimate) that a larger proportion of female than male arrestees detained for income-generating offences tested positive for cocaine, heroin, any drug and intravenous drug use. Goulden and Sondhi (2001) also examined differences between the sexes in terms of the prevalence of drug use among different types of offenders in a general population survey of young people. They concluded that the prevalence of drug use in the last year was reasonably similar for male and female minor offenders, with the exception that male offenders were more likely to report use of magic mushrooms and female offenders were more likely to use solvents. However, when looking at more serious and/or persistent offenders, the proportion of males reporting drug use was higher than that of females in all categories, with statistically significant differences in use of ecstasy, magic mushrooms and 'poppers'. In their

survey of pre-arrest drug use among a sample of 1751 sentenced prisoners in England, Maden *et al.* (1992) investigated differences in drug use based on ethnic status. The results showed that black prisoners were more likely to report pre-arrest cannabis use (54 per cent) than white prisoners (34 per cent). Black prisoners were also more likely than white prisoners to use cocaine. However, white prisoners were more likely than black prisoners to report use of 'hard' drugs, drug dependence and injecting.

### Summary

Overall, the research shows that the drugs–crime connection is character-ized by some very specific connections between particular drugs and par-ticular offences. The drugs most strongly implicated in the connection are heroin and crack (and, to a lesser extent, powder cocaine). The crimes most strongly implicated are shoplifting, general theft and drug dealing. Fur-thermore, there is some evidence that the drugs–crime connection might vary by type of drug user and type of offender. Female drug users might be more likely than males to be involved in prostitution and property offences.

## Multiple drug use and crime

Research on the connection between drug misuse and crime has tended to focus on either aggregated measures of drug misuse and criminal behaviour or specific types of drugs and specific types of offences. Less attention has been paid to the extent to which combinations of drug misuse might be connected to crime. Perhaps as a result of this there also has been little attempt to develop theory relating to the link between multiple drug use and crime. However, there are a number of less formal explanations in the literature concerning the nature of the connection (see generally Bennett and Holloway 2004). The most common explanations of the links between multiple drug use and crime are:

- economic explanations;
- psychopharmacological explanations; and
- lifestyle explanations.

### Economic explanations

Economic theories of the association between drug use and crime are based on the idea that greater involvement in drug use leads to greater expend-iture on drugs and greater involvement in acquisitive crime to pay for these drugs. Some writers have attempted to explain the relationship between multiple drug use and crime in this way. Leri *et al.* (2003) argue that opioid users who also use cocaine will have drug habits that are even more expensive, which, in turn, might lead some of them to engage in income-generating crime. They also note that opioid addicts sometimes use amphetamines to sustain the activity level needed to 'hustle' the necessary funds to pay for their opioid habit. Chaiken and Chaiken (1990) report that a large body of research shows that high-rate offenders who commit predatory crimes are also likely to use many different types of drugs. The main principle of economic theory is that regular drug use is expensive and some users will seek funds for their drug use from illegal sources. This argument is usually made in relation to heroin addiction and the costs of habitual drug use (Brochu 2001). However, the theory can be applied to any costly form of drug use. Users of multiple drugs (especially when two or more of them are expensive drugs) may face additional financial pressures to commit acquisitive crime.

### Psychopharmacological explanations

Psychopharmacological explanations are based on the idea that drugs can have a direct or indirect effect on behaviour as a result of their chemical properties. These explanations are typically directed at drug use and violent crime and in most cases refer to the effects of individual drugs. However, some writers have discussed the interactive, protective or additive effects of multiple drugs on the nature or rate of criminal behaviour. Hammersley and Morrison (1987) believe that multiple drugs used simultaneously may increase intoxication. One reason for this is that drug combinations might create unique metabolites that are absent when the drugs are used individually. These metabolites may have greater toxicity than those formed when the drugs are used individually. Pennings *et al.* (2002) argue that there has been much theorizing about the possible mechanism by which the alcohol and cocaine combination might lead to greater violence than from either drug alone. These include the idea that alcohol and cocaine each elevate extraneuronal dopamine and serotonin concentrations, which may lead to deficits in impulse control and to violent behaviour.

### Lifestyle explanations

Lifestyle explanations of the links between drug use and crime are sometimes referred to as 'systemic' explanations in that crime is seen as an intrinsic (or systemic) part of the drug-using lifestyle. These have sometimes included references to multiple drug use. Leri *et al.* (2003) noted that addicts may also use other drugs as part of their general deviant lifestyle, which involves raising funds and purchasing illegal drugs. Lifestyle explanations are also sometimes referred to as 'spuriousness' explanations in that there may be no direct causal connection between drug use (or multiple drug use) and crime. Instead, they both co-exist within the same lifestyle context. One explanation for the co-existence of multiple drug use and crime is that habitual drug users are often at an advanced stage in their progression through a range of drug types. It has been argued that drug types are not necessarily dropped and replaced with new drug types as the progression continues. Instead, drugs used at earlier stages in the development might be carried through to the later stages (Clayton 1986). Hence, one possible explanation of the link between multiple drug use and crime is that drug-using criminals are sometimes users at an advanced stage in their drug-use career who have amassed a wide repertoire of drug types.

The research on multiple drug use and crime can be divided into three main groups:

- studies on the prevalence of multiple drug use and crime;
- studies on the number of drug types used and crime; and
- studies on specific combinations of drug types and crime.

### Prevalence of multiple drug use and crime

Some studies have looked at the prevalence of criminal behaviour among multiple drug users based on data derived from general population surveys. Chaiken and Chaiken (1990) recalculated Elliott and Huizinga's (1984) data from the US National Youth Survey to show that crime commission rates per year were between 10 and 20 times higher among multiple drug users (who used alcohol, marijuana and other drugs four or more times each) than among non-users. Other studies have investigated the various measures of criminal behaviour among multiple drug users within criminal populations. Some of the most detailed findings on multiple drug use and crime have come from studies based on arrestee surveys. Smith and Polsenberg (1992) found, in a study based on adult arrestee data for the District of Columbia, that 81 per cent of arrestees testing positive for two or more drugs had a previous criminal record, compared with 71 per cent of those who tested positive for one drug and 52 per cent of those who tested positive for no drugs. Makkai (2001) reported from a study of arrestees in Australia that the odds of being charged with a property offence were three times greater among those who tested positive for two or more drugs than those who tested positive for one or no drugs.

### Number of drug types used and crime

It is fairly rare for studies to report the connection between a precise number of drug types used and measures of crime. Smith and Polsenberg (1992) explored the relationship between the number of positive tests for different drug types among a sample of arrestees and the average number of prior arrests. They found that the average number of prior arrests increased with the number of positive tests. Those who tested positive for no drug type recorded an average of 1.95 prior arrests, those who tested positive for just one drug type had an average of 2.75 prior arrests, and those who tested positive for two or more drug types had an average of 4.64 prior arrests. Bennett (2000) used data from the second developmental stage of the NEW-ADAM programme in the UK to explore the relationship between number of drug types used and self-reported offending. Arrestees who used one drug type in the last 12 months reported an average of 26 acquisitive offences during the last 12 months. Arrestees who used two drug types reported an average of 95 offences and those who used three or more drug types reported an average of 176 offences. Hammersley *et al.* (1989), however, found no association among drug users in Scotland when they attempted to predict crime from drug use variables. They found that the number of drug types used ever was not a significant predictor of any of the five types of crime under investigation.

## Combinations of drug types used and crime

There has also been little research on the relationship between specific patterns of multiple drug use and crime. The available research to date has tended to focus on the effect of different combinations of heroin, crack and cocaine, plus subsidiary drugs, on crime. Among a sample of arrestees in Los Angeles, Shaw *et al.* (1999) found that those who had used cocaine only or crack only in their lifetimes had lower prevalence rates of criminal activities (10 per cent and 14 per cent, respectively) than those who used both cocaine and crack (16 per cent among those who used cocaine first and 24 per cent among those who used crack first). Other research has confirmed the effect on crime of combining heroin, crack and cocaine. Among a sample of incarcerated females, Sanchez *et al.* (1985) found that those who used heroin and cocaine in the last year had higher mean rates of drug and prostitution offences than users of heroin only. In a study of entrants into publicly funded drug abuse treatment programmes in six US cities, Collins *et al.* (1985) found that daily users of both heroin and cocaine reported higher levels of illegal income in the last year than those who reported daily use of heroin only or cocaine only. Based on arrestee research in the UK, Bennett (2000) confirmed this finding by showing that arrestees who reported both heroin use and cocaine/crack use in the last 3 days had higher annual illegal incomes than those using heroin without cocaine/crack or cocaine/crack without heroin.

## Summary

The research shows that there is a correlation between the number of drug types used and offending. Multiple drug users are more likely than single drug users to report offending. Multiple drug users who offend tend to report more offences than single drug users who offend. Multiple drug users who use a large number of drug types tend to report a greater number of offences than multiple drug users who used a small number of drug types. Multiple drug users who include heroin, crack and/or cocaine in their drug combinations tend to commit more offences than multiple drug users who use only recreational drugs.

## Conclusion

Research on the statistical association between drug use and crime operates at different levels. At the least detailed level, studies have focused on aggregate measures of drug use and crime. This research generally shows a strong statistical relationship between drug use and crime.

Greater insight into the relationship can be found in the results of studies using disaggregated data. This research has shown that the general relationship found in the aggregate level studies is largely the result of a limited number of connections between certain drug types and certain crimes. In particular, the drugs–crime connection appears to be primarily a product of the relationship between heroin and crack and a small number of acquisitive property crimes, including shoplifting and drug dealing. However, this does not mean that there are no other connections. It is likely that there are other, highly specific connections between certain kinds of drug use and certain kinds of crime. There is some evidence, for example, that drug use is correlated with violence (especially in the context of drug dealing). There is also evidence of some specific connections between prostitution-related offences and drug use.

Further insight into the drugs–crime connection can be obtained from research that has looked in greater depth into the relationship between specific drug type combinations and crime. There is some evidence that drug use and crime are not only linked by the use of particular drug types, but by the use of particular drugs in combination with other drugs. There is evidence to show that the use of cocaine might not be linked to crime when it is used in isolation of other major types, but is linked to crime when used in conjunction with other serious drug types (notably heroin and crack).

Overall, the chapter shows that there is substantial research evidence linking drug use and crime. However, there is less research evidence on the detail of this relationship. Hence, further research should be conducted that can help refine what is known about the details of the drugs–crime connection and identify not only consistencies but variations in the relationship. These include differences among different types of individual (e.g. differences in terms of socio-economic status, background or lifestyle), different settings (e.g. street users versus home users) and drug combinations (e.g. the effects of concurrent or consecutive use).

## Further reading

The review by Gandossy *et al.* (1980) is still one of the best reviews of the literature on this topic and is well worth consulting despite the absence of more recent research. The shorter review by Chaiken and Chaiken (1990) is also still one of the best and is also worth reading.

# chapter seven

# The causal connection:
# more than coincidence?

## Introduction

It was shown in the previous chapter that drug use and crime were often found together. Drug users (especially those who consumed heroin or crack) were also likely to commit crimes and offenders (especially those who committed shoplifting, general theft and drug supply offences) were also likely to consume drugs. However, this does not mean that the two are necessarily causally connected. They might be found together because they are both caused by other factors or co-exist within a nexus of problematic behaviours. This chapter examines the extent to which drug use causes crime or crime causes drug use.

The causal connection between drug use and crime has been investigated in the research literature in three main ways:

- 'age-of-onset' studies that investigate whether drug use preceded crime or crime preceded drug use in time;
- 'changes-over-time' studies that investigate the relationship between changes in involvement in drug use on crime and changes in involvement in crime on drug use; and
- 'qualitative' studies that investigate the causal connection by asking drug users and offenders their views on whether the two are connected.

The results presented below draw on our own systematic review of the literature on the causal connection between drug use and crime (Holloway and Bennett in prep.).

## 'Age-of-onset' studies

'Age-of-onset' studies help address the problem of whether the onset of drug use causes the onset of crime or vice versa. In terms of causality, the specific causal link is addressed of whether drug use can cause the onset of a career in crime or crime the onset of a career in drug use. 'Age-of-onset' studies have been based on samples of drugs users, offenders and the general population.

### Drug users

In our own review of the literature on the causal connection between drug use and crime, we found 13 'age-of-onset' studies based on samples of drug users (Holloway and Bennett in prep.). Nearly all of them reported findings on the age of first drug use (usually first recreational drug use) and the age of first crime. Similarly, most of these studies reported findings on the age of first use of heroin, crack or cocaine and age of first crime. The results of the studies vary considerably depending on whether drug use concerns first 'any drug' use (usually recreational drugs) or first 'hard' drug use (usually heroin, crack or cocaine).

The results of studies on the connection between first drug use (usually a recreational drug) and crime tend to show that drug use preceded crime. Byqvist (1999), for example, found in a study of drug users receiving treatment in Sweden that the age of first drug use occurred at an average age of 15 years, while the age of first recorded crime occurred at 18.4 years of age. McCoy et al. (1995) found from interviews with crack users in residential treatment in Miami that the average age of first crime was several years older than the average age of first drug use. However, interviews as part of the same study with crack users on the street showed that first drug use and first crime occurred at the same age (14 years).

Four studies looked specifically at the age of onset of cannabis use and compared this with age of first crime. All of these studies found that drug use either preceded crime or the two came together. Inciardi and Surratt (2001), for example interviewed 708 cocaine-dependent women in Miami, Florida and found that the average age of first cannabis use was 15 years compared with an age of first crime of 18 years. Another study looked specifically at age of first solvent use and age of first crime (Inciardi and Pottieger 1986). This study, based on 286 female narcotic users, found that the average age of first solvent-inhalant use was 13.9 years, compared with an average age of first crime of 15.7 years.

Hence, the results suggest that age of first drug use typically precedes age of first criminal offence. The studies show little variation from this overall conclusion in terms of type of first drug. None of the studies, for example, found that age of onset of criminal behaviour preceded age of onset of first drug use. There was also little variation in terms of type of first crime. Most studies investigated used aggregate measures of 'any crime'. One study investigated the relationship between onset of cannabis and onset of prostitution (Inciardi 1995) and showed that the onset of drug use preceded the onset of the offence by many years. Two studies used, as a measure of crime, official measures, including age first arrested and age first criminal record. Kokkevi et al. (1993), for example, looked at first drug use in relation to first arrest in a study of male drug users and found that first reported arrest occurred an average of many years after first drug use (average arrest was 21.2 years and average first drug was 16.2 years). The older age of onset for criminal behaviour is very likely the effect of using officially recorded crime rather than self-admissions as a measure of offending.

The results of studies on the connection between first 'hard' drug use and crime show quite different findings. Few of these studies found that first hard drug use (usually first use of heroin, crack or cocaine) preceded crime. The majority of the studies reviewed found that the onset of crime preceded the onset of hard drugs. Most of them looked at the relationship between age of first heroin use and age of first crime. Almost all found that crime preceded heroin use. Inciardi and Pottieger (1986), for example, in their study of female narcotic users in Miami, found that the average age of first heroin use was 17.5 years, whereas the age of first crime was 15.7 years. Most of the studies investigated age of onset of cocaine and seven found that crime preceded drug use. The average age of onset of cocaine use ranged from 16 to 22 years and the average age of onset of offending ranged from 14 to 19 years. Datesman (1987), for example, found among a sample of 153 female heroin users that the average age of first cocaine use was 19 years and the average age of first crime was 15 years. Some of the studies explored age of onset of crack use and crime. All of them found that the average age of onset of crime preceded the average age of onset of crack use by a number of years. The average age of first crack use ranged from 20 to 24 years and the average age of first crime ranged from 14 to 19 years (depending on the crime type).

Hence, most of these studies found that the onset of 'hard' drugs occurred somewhat later than the onset of crime. However, three studies found that the age of onset for heroin, crack or cocaine was younger than the age of onset for criminal behaviour. These were the study by Inciardi (1995), which focused on age of onset of prostitution (which tends to be older than the age of onset for 'any' crime), the study by Hall et al. (1993), which focused on recorded crimes (which tend to occur at an older age than self-reported crime), and the study by Kokkevi et al. (1993), which focused on arrests (which, like recorded crimes, tend to occur at an older age than self-reported crime).

## Offenders

It is worth investigating separately the relationship between onset of drug use and crime for samples of drug users and samples of offenders. It is possible that samples of drug users drawn from treatment sources or from communities with particular drug problems might be different from drug users drawn from criminal justice populations.

Seven studies used samples of offenders in their investigation of the causal connection between onset of drug use and criminal behaviour. The majority of the studies found that first drug use (usually recreational drug use) came before crime, one found that they came together at the same age, and three studies found that crime preceded any first drug use. The distribution of results is somewhat different to the drug user sample studies, which showed more conclusively that recreational drug use preceded crime. However, the results are in broadly the same direction in that only a minority of the studies claim that crime came before recreational drug use.

There is also some evidence from the research that the type of sample and the type of measures used may have some effect on the results. The study by Inciardi and Pottieger (1991), for example, based on a sample of crime-involved youths on the streets of Miami, found that the average age of first cannabis use was more or less the same age as age of first crime (both occurring about age 10). However, the comparatively young age of onset for both drug use and criminal behaviour was reported as being a possible result of the fact that the subjects were seriously delinquent (i.e. they had committed a minimum of ten FBI index offences or 100 lesser crimes within the last 12 months). It is possible that studies that draw their samples from among seriously delinquent populations will find that the age of onset of criminal behaviour is low and in some cases precedes first drug use.

Five studies investigated the relationship between age of onset of 'hard' drug use and onset of crime. All five studies looked at heroin use and crime and four of the five found that crime preceded heroin use. The single study that found that heroin use preceded crime was the study by Biron *et al.* (1995). This study was based on a sample of 94 incarcerated women in Quebec prisons who reported an unusually late mean age of onset in crime of 22.2 years. Three studies looked at the age of onset of cocaine use and crime and two of the three concluded that crime came first. The odd one out was again the study by Biron *et al.* (1995).

Hence, the results of studies based on offenders are broadly in agreement with studies based on drug users. However, there is a clear confounding effect from the nature of the sample. Samples based on drug users in treatment are likely to include the most seriously involved drug users, some of whom might have started drug use at an early age. Samples based on offenders in prison are likely to include the most seriously involved offenders, who also might have started their criminal behaviour at an early age. However, despite the tendency for the results to be skewed in different directions as a result of the sample source, there remains a clear tendency in the findings to show that first drug use tends to precede first crime and first hard drug use tends to follow first crime.

### General population

One way of resolving the inherent bias of study design is to select samples from the general population. Unfortunately, we could find only one study that addressed the age of onset of drug use and crime. The study by Pudney (2003) used data from the Youth Lifestyles Survey to investigate sequences of initiation to drugs and crime in the UK. A sample of 3901 youths was questioned about their current and past behaviour. The respondents were also asked about the commission of two groups of offences: minor crimes (including criminal damage, arson, theft, dealing in stolen goods, cheque and credit card offences, fraud and public fighting) and serious crimes (theft of vehicles, robbery, breaking and entering, and assault). The results show that the onset of criminal behaviour occurred before the use of illicit drugs with the exception of solvents (14.5 years compared with 14.1 years). Pudney concludes that there is 'a tendency towards a chain of events beginning with petty crime and truancy, and only later developing into drug use'. He goes on to suggest that if 'we were prepared to assume that this tendency has causal significance, then we might conclude that a policy addressing truancy and other problems at school might be more effective than a policy attacking drug use directly' (p. 187).

### Summary

In summary, the majority of studies described above show that criminal behaviour precedes the onset of harder drug use (such as heroin, crack and cocaine). This result was found across a number of countries, among samples of males and females, among drug users, offenders and members of the general population. This result lends support for the idea that crime causes drug use. The majority of studies described above also show that recreational drug use (such as cannabis and solvents) precedes the onset of criminal behaviour. This lends support for the idea that drug use causes crime.

   The two sets of findings appear at first sight to be in opposition. However, the mechanism by which the two might be connected has not yet been discussed. It is possible that neither connection is causal. Instead, they both might be the products of natural age variations in the onset of various kinds of problematic behaviours. It is also possible that, if they are causal, the mechanisms are different. Recreational drug use might lead to minor crimes perhaps as a result of judgement impairment or by providing the courage to commit minor crimes. At a slightly older age, crime (perhaps slightly more serious crime) might lead to hard drug use as a result of involvement in wider criminal sub-cultures and access to drug dealers. Further detail about the nature of the connection and the different kinds of causal connection are discussed in the following sections.

## 'Changes-over-time' studies

'Changes-over-time' studies are able to provide greater insight than 'age-of-onset' studies into the continuing relationship between drug use and crime following the onset of drug use and crime. They have the same advantage as 'age-of-onset' studies in that they are longitudinal in design and can address the issues of causal order (whether changes in drug use precede changes in crime or vice versa). They have the additional advantage that they typically include multiple measurement points and can analyse changes in both rates of drug use and crime over time. In other words, they can determine whether, for example, crime increased following an increase in drug use and also whether it decreased when drug use decreased. In this sense, they can offer some of the best quantitative evidence available on the causal connection between drug use and crime.

We found eight studies that explored the drugs–crime connection by investigating changes in drug use and crime over time. Four of these used samples based on drug users, three used samples of offenders and one used a sample drawn from the general population.

### Drug users

Most of the studies of drug users looked at the effect of changes in drug use on changes in crime. They also tended to focus on the effects of changes in use of 'hard drugs' such as heroin or crack cocaine rather than the effects of recreational drugs. They all showed that increases in drug use were followed by increases in the prevalence or incidence of crime.

The only research to look at changes in prevalence of offending was that of Jarvis and Parker (1989). In their study of 46 London-based heroin users, they found that the prevalence of offending (i.e. the proportion of individuals with convictions) increased from 56 per cent in the pre-heroin period to 83 per cent in the period when they were using heroin. The remaining studies in the group investigated the links between drug use and the rate of offending. Hanlon et al. (1990) interviewed a sample of 132 narcotic addicts in the United States about various periods of addiction and non-addiction during their drug-using careers. They found that the mean number of days per year spent offending in the last period of addiction was more than double the number of offences committed in the last period of non-addiction. Anglin and Speckart (1986) looked at groups of males undergoing methadone maintenance treatment in the United States. They found that in the 12-month period prior to addiction, the subjects reported a mean of 2.3 crime days per month, whereas in the 12-month period after addiction, they reported a mean of 9.0 crime days per month.

The above results relate to aggregate measures of drug use and crime. It is possible that changes in drug use are associated with changes in certain kinds of crime but not others. The nature of this association might provide clues about the causal processes at work. One of the studies provided breakdowns of the findings in terms of type of offences committed. Hanlon *et al.* (1990), discussed above, presented data on the mean rates of different crime types during periods of addiction and non-addiction. The greatest increase in offending over the last period of addiction occurred in relation to 'theft offences', 'con games/forgery' and 'drug distribution'. There was little change in the rate of 'violent offences' or 'other offences'. Unfortunately, none of the studies provided a suitable breakdown of the results by demographic characteristics.

## Offenders

Studies based on offenders also tend to focus on the effect of changes in drug use on crime rather than changes in crime on drug use. All three studies investigated found that changes in drug use were associated with changes in crime.

Ball *et al.* (1981) examined changes in drug use and crime among a sample of 243 opiate addicts drawn from police files in the United States. All subjects had one or more addiction periods, with an average addiction period of 2 years. The results showed that there were substantially more mean crime-days during periods of addiction than during periods of abstinence (248 days per year compared with 40.8 days per year). The authors concluded that 'criminality decreased markedly during the months or years that these addicts were not dependent on heroin and other opiates' (Ball *et al.* 1981: 60). In a study of 354 male heroin addicts living in the Baltimore metropolitan area, Ball *et al.* (1983) also found that the mean number of days spent committing crime was substantially lower in the non-addicted periods than in the addicted period. Nurco *et al.* (1984) found in a similar study that the mean number of crime-days per year was significantly lower during periods of addiction than periods of non-addiction (62 during the last period of non-addiction and 280 in the last period of addiction).

All three studies provided a breakdown of the results by type of crime. Nurco *et al.* (1984) found increases in the rate of crime among all crime types. However, the biggest percentage increase in mean crime-days per year occurred in relation to theft offences (excluding violent offences, which increased from 0 to 6). Ball *et al.* (1981) also found that the largest increases in crime during periods of addiction occurred in relation to theft and drug-dealing offences. Only one of the three studies looked at the effect of demographic factors on the drugs–crime relationship. Ball *et al.* (1981) found that race and age were both correlated with mean number of crime-days when addicted (black and older addicts had higher mean rates than their counterparts). However, neither was correlated with mean number of crime-days when non-addicted.

### General population

Studies based on members of the general population have the greatest potential to reduce the effects of bias from sample selection. Unfortunately, there have been very few general population 'changes-over-time' studies. One such study conducted by Mason and Windle (2002) investigated the relationship between self-reported substance use and delinquency through a four-wave panel data survey of more than 1000 high school students in the United States. A primary aim of the study was to examine what the authors described as the reciprocal relations between changing patterns of adolescent substance use and delinquency over time. One interesting feature of this study is that it included an analysis of the relationship between both changes in crime on changes in drug use and changes in drug use on changes in crime. The authors found that both sets of measures were closely correlated. They concluded that 'changes in delinquency were positively associated with subsequent changes in substance use . . . [and] . . . that level of substance use at Time 1 predicted increased delinquency at Time 2' (Mason and Windle 2002: 72). They conclude that these findings provide some support for the view that adolescent drug use and delinquency are reciprocally related and potentially reinforcing. The main problem with the study as far as the current discussion is concerned is that the measure of substance use included only minor drug types (including cigarette, alcohol and marijuana use) and minor crime types (including fights, property damage and theft from a store). The study is also problematic in that the measurements of change were made during a period of what might be naturally occurring change in both drug use and crime during adolescence.

### Summary

Overall, this small group of studies provides some evidence that drug use and crime might be causally connected. In general, these studies find that increases in drug use are associated with increases in crime and, to a more limited extent, that increases in crime are associated with increases in drug use. However, this general conclusion is based on some very specific findings that relate primarily to periods of addiction and non-addiction to heroin. Few of these studies disaggregate the findings to show the effects of different drugs on different crimes or to show the effect of different user characteristics.

Clearly, this is an important method of analysis and more research needs to be done in this area to help break down the results further into different measures of types of drug use and crime and different measures of types of drug user. The method has the power to address both the statistical association between drug use and crime and their temporal order. However, the research still addresses the issue of causality indirectly. To understand how drugs and crime are linked, it is necessary to know something more about the likely mechanisms involved. One method of understanding the details of the link and the specific processes involved is to ask the offenders.

## Qualitative research

In addition to many studies that have investigated the quantitative connection between drug use and crime, there is a growing body of research examining qualitative aspects of the relationship through interviews with drug users or offenders. These sometimes include direct statements from the respondents about the processes by which drug use and crime are connected. The following sub-sections divide these responses into the main theoretical models linking drug use and crime:

- drug use causes crime;
- crime causes drug use;
- crime and drug use are reciprocal; and
- there is no causal connection between the two.

### Drug use causes crime

A large proportion of the qualitative statements found in the literature refer to the causal effect of drug use on crime. The statements can be divided into: (a) economic necessity, (b) courage to offend, (c) pharmacological effects, (d) amplification and (e) crime by association.

#### Economic necessity

The economic necessity argument is based on the idea that drug users need money for drugs and resort to crime to obtain them. Most of the qualitative studies reviewed that provide quotations from individuals on the role of economic necessity in their offending were based on studies of prostitutes.

Erickson *et al.* (2000) explored the impact of crack addiction on women in Toronto who were, or who had become, involved in the sex trade. The study involved in-depth interviews with a sample of 30 women who were recruited on the basis of being known (by a local street worker) as being heavy crack users over several years. The study identified a clear link between drug use and prostitution. One respondent explained: 'I've been doing it [prostitution] since I was 16 years old, that's like what I know best. I started prostitution to support my habit for alcohol and marijuana' (Erickson *et al.* 2000: 775). Erickson *et al.* (2000) state that 'it is clear that they work in the sex trade to get money and/or crack to support their own usage when few other sources of income are available to them' (p. 784). Graham and Wish (1994) identified a relationship between drug use and prostitution in a study of female arrestees in the USA. They quote one arrestee who explained that:

> For the past year I have been hustling to support my habit. I started out hustling the men I met while hitchhiking into the city to cop

(purchase drugs) and I am now working the streets. All my proceeds go towards drugs.

(Graham and Wish 1994: 326)

Similarly, in a study of female crack users in the United States, Sterk *et al.* (2000) found some evidence of a causal relationship between crack use and prostitution. One subject is reported to have said: 'I wouldn't be out there doing what I'm doing if it wasn't because of getting high' (p. 359).

Maher and Curtis (1992) investigated the relationship between crack use and prostitution in an ethnographic study of 25 women in New York City. The sampling method is not described in the paper, but the reader is told that interviews were conducted with 'women in the field'. The subjects interviewed sometimes noted that one reason why they engaged in prostitution was to fund their drug use. One woman reported: 'That's mainly what the whole deal's about – drug using, you know what I'm saying. You not out there 'cause you need love' (Maher and Curtis 1992: 234).

Dalla (2002) investigated the relationship between drug use and prostitution in a qualitative investigation of 43 women involved in street walking prostitution. The results of this investigation showed that one of the reasons for prostitution was to fund the women's drug use:

> The girls out there now are not like we used to be. They're out there for drugs. That's why the business is so bad. It's not even worth it. They're crack-heads and will do anything for a little bit of money . . . they're not real ones [prostitutes].
>
> (Dalla 2002: 69)

The other studies provided quotations that referred to the economic links between drug use and other types of crime. One study provides an explanation about the economic links between drug use and shoplifting. Brain *et al.* (1998) interviewed crack cocaine users in the north of England. Sixty-three people were interviewed and were asked to comment on the relationship between their drug use and criminal behaviour. One male reported on the links between shoplifting and drug use: 'Now I wake up and I go out shoplifting and I don't come back in until I've got enough for at least a stone and a bag and then I'll be out again once or twice more' (Brain *et al.* 1998: 43).

The study by Rosenbaum (1981) includes a quotation on the links between drug use and the onset of burglary. The author conducted interviews with 100 female addicts in the United States. One addict explained: 'My bank accounts were exhausted. I had no more money. Everything was sold. And that's when I committed my first burglary' (Rosenbaum 1981: 68).

Other studies have found economic links between drug use and drug dealing. In an ethnographic study conducted in New York City, Sommers *et al.* (2000) investigated the lives of women drug dealers in two neighbourhoods. The research examined women's participation in the cocaine/

crack economy and involved interviews with women both in the community and in correctional facilities. During the course of their research, the authors noted that many of the women in their study (63 per cent) became dealers to support or subsidize their personal drug use. One woman explained: 'I started selling crack by me wanting to smoke . . . I was smoking a lot, needed money. So I took a couple of bundles and sold them. I made straight money. It was easy money' (Sommers *et al.* 2000: 57).

## Courage to offend

Some studies have argued that drug use can cause crime in the sense that drugs can be used to provide the necessary courage to offend. This argument is used more often to describe the links between alcohol use and crime. However, it is sometimes used to explain links between other types of drug and crime. The explanation is different from the 'pharmacological effects' argument in that the subject in a sense consciously chooses to use

**Amplification of cri**

Another argument is
offenders rather than ca
mit crimes they would not

Parent and Brochu (2002)
the drugs–crime relationship an
subjects were recruited from treatm
and through snowball sampling. Whe
tionship, one subject noted that his dru
behaviour: 'It's evident – if I wasn't using
been a criminal, but much less . . . Maybe I
as I did, but I would have always been a little b
Brochu 2002: 145).

view
include
few of the
that covered

Wright 1984b: 436). Another burglar noted: 'I used to have an idea that I'd go out [to commit a burglary], then I'd pop in the pub for a few drinks, which would give me the courage to take things further' (ibid.).

### Pharmacological effects

The pharmacological effect argument is based on the idea that the effect of certain kinds of drugs or certain combinations of drugs can lead to the commission of crime. The link may be direct (or almost direct), whereby the drug generates the immediate motivation for crime. For example, the consumption of alcohol might lead directly to a mood of aggression, which might lead to violent crime. The link may also be indirect, whereby drug use affects judgement, which in turn affects decision making. For example, drug use may result in the decision to commit a risky burglary that might not otherwise have been attempted.

Carpenter *et al.* (1988) conducted structured open-ended interviews with a sample of 100 youths in the United States. The sample was obtained following a period of fieldwork during which researchers became acquainted with a community of youths. Forty subjects were selected purposively, 40 more were selected randomly from lists of youths enrolled in the two study schools, and a further 20 were recruited from a local detention facility. The authors found that the youths in their study had a 'rich repertoire of common-sense theories about the association between drugs and crime' (p. 27). Eighty-four subjects answered a direct question about the relationship between drug use and crime. The authors report that the subjects emphasized the irrationality that results from drug use and the riminogenic aspects of drug addiction' (p. 37). Some of these youths ed drug and alcohol use as resulting in impulsive behaviour, which d a wide range of crime including theft and vandalism. However, subjects believed that there was a single or simple explanation everyone's behaviour.

e

that drug use serves to amplify crime among existing se people to begin committing crimes or to com- therwise commit.

conducted a study in Canada that explored ong 42 male regular cocaine users. The ent facilities in Quebec, from prisons asked about the drugs–crime rela- use exacerbated his offending I would have probably still wouldn't have gone as far it criminal' (Parent and

### Crime by association

The final explanation concerns the way in which drug use causes crime by association. Drug users often have to operate in a world of criminals to obtain illegal drugs. The study by Parent and Brochu (2002) includes an interview with one subject who explains the way in which drug users need to inhabit the criminal world and how this can result in criminality:

> Using drugs equals crime, that's sure and certain. Because you want to keep on being all right – well to keep on using – you have to hang round in places where it's being sold. People who sell dope are all criminals. Because they're all criminals, you get into that yourself and automatically become a criminal too.
>
> (Parent and Brochu 2002: 145)

### Crime causes drug use

The most common crime-causes-drug-use explanation is that the proceeds of crime are used to finance pleasure-seeking activities. In their study of street robbers in St Louis, Missouri, Wright and Decker (1997) used the concept of 'life as a party' to explain why offenders took drugs and the role of drugs in 'keeping the party going'. One of the robbers explained that money from crime might be used to buy drugs or alcohol:

> I'm walking around, sometimes if I have any money in my pocket I go get high, buy a bag of [marijuana], a forty-ounce (malt liquor) or something. Get high and then I ain't got no more money and then the highness makes you start thinking until you go out and do [a robbery].
>
> (Wright and Decker 1997: 36)

Another armed robber also mentioned that the money from crime could be used to purchase alcohol: '[I think about armed robbery when] I need some money. I like money in my pocket, I like going out and getting drunk' (Wright and Decker 1997: 36).

Brain et al. (1998) provide an example of a man who claimed that he would commit crime (burglaries) and only afterwards would think about using drugs: 'It's just that I've chosen to spend the proceeds on drugs' (p. 43).

### Crime and drug use are reciprocal

This explanation is based on the idea that drug use sometimes causes crime and crime sometimes causes drug use. The concept is usually applied within rather than between individuals. In other words, it usually refers to the idea that an individual might sometimes commit crime because of drug use and sometimes use drugs because of crime. This variation can be viewed over longer periods of time (at one point in time drug use caused crime and at another crime caused drug use) or over shorter periods of time (sometimes drug use leads to crime and other times crime leads to drug use).

One example of a reciprocal relationship over longer periods of time is provided by Simpson (2003) in an ethnographic study of 88 individuals in the north of England. One of the interviewees explained that the connection between drug use and crime in his case had changed over time. At first, he said that he committed burglary 'for the buzz'. Later on, he explained, 'it was just for the blow' (p. 315).

Hough (1996) provides an example of variations over shorter periods of time. In the case of prostitution and drug use, he argues, the two might be mutually reinforcing: 'There can be a complex dynamic between prostitution and drug dependence: prostitution can be a method of financing drug use, and drug use can be a palliative to prostitution' (Hough 1996: 14).

### No causal connection

The final group in this section concerns explanations based on the idea that there is no causal connection between drug use and crime.

A number of studies provide evidence from offenders' or drug users' accounts that drug use and crime are not connected. Bennett (2000), for example, found that the majority (58 per cent) of arrestees interviewed said that there was no connection between their drug use and offending behaviour. Liriano and Ramsay (2003) also found from a study of prisoners that almost half (45 per cent) believed that there was no connection between their offending and drug use. The study of crack users by Brain *et al.* (1998), mentioned earlier, provided an example of a drug user who thought that there was no connection between his drug use and crime. This subject stated: 'I know loads of blokes who don't dabble and are robbing night and day and so I can't blame my drug use for that [my crime]. I would be a dead-end kid even if I didn't take drugs' (Brain *et al.* 1998: 43).

### Summary

Qualitative studies provide evidence of a number of potential connections between drug use and crime. The greatest number of quotations fell under the heading of 'drug-use-causes-crime' explanations. However, within this category there were many different types of explanation ranging from economic necessity to crime by association. There are also examples of 'crime-causes-drug-use' explanations and 'reciprocal' connections. Some subjects argued that drugs and crime in their case were not connected.

The research was not designed to calculate the proportion of subjects across studies that gave causal explanations in each of the categories investigated. However, some studies have attempted to enumerate the proportion of subjects who give different kinds of explanation. Liriano and Ramsay (2003) found that the vast majority of individuals who thought there was a connection gave explanations that fell into the 'drug-use-causes-crime' category. A similar conclusion was drawn by Holloway and

Bennett (2004), who found that the majority of subjects who thought that there was a connection gave 'economic necessity' explanations. Among those arrestees who reported any drug use in the last 12 months, the majority (70 per cent) of those who saw a connection between drug use and acquisitive crime said it was because they needed money to buy drugs. The remainder said that they thought that drugs affected their judgement, which thereby caused them to commit crime (30 per cent of those who saw a connection) and/or that they used the money from crime to buy drugs (12 per cent). Users of both heroin and cocaine/crack were more likely than other arrestees to perceive a connection between their drug use and offending behaviour (78 per cent versus 40 per cent overall).

Overall, it appears that most (if not all) of the main academic hypotheses concerning the causal links between drug use and crime were recounted by offenders and drug users as explanations for the connection. This may be because these subjects were aware through everyday discourse of the range of potential explanations and were happy to recount these. However, it is also possible that there is no single connection between drug use and crime. Instead, it might be the case that under certain circumstances and in relation to certain individuals, almost all of the common explanations apply. The challenge for research is to understand more fully the nature of these variations.

## Conclusion

This chapter on the causal connection between drug use and crime is based on an analysis of the results of 'age-of-onset' studies, 'change-over-time' studies and qualitative studies. The main value of the 'age-of-onset' studies is that they can determine whether drug use preceded crime or crime preceded drug use. For a relationship to be causal, the cause needs to precede the effect. Hence, drug use cannot have caused crime if crime came before drug use. In the case of recreational drugs (typically cannabis), the majority of findings indicate that drug use preceded crime. Hence, drug use might have caused crime, but crime could not have caused drug use. In the case of more serious drugs (typically heroin, crack or cocaine), the majority of findings show that crime preceded drug use. Hence, crime might have caused serious drug use, but serious drug use could not have caused crime. This finding is consistent with the knowledge that the age of onset of recreational drugs is usually much younger than the age of onset of serious drugs. Hence, recreational drugs tend to be first used before the start of a criminal career, whereas heroin, crack and cocaine tend to be first used after the criminal career has already started. The review shows that few studies support the notion that serious drugs cause crime.

The 'changes-over-time' studies add support to the connection by investigating temporal order of changes in drugs and crime over time. They also have the advantage that they are often based on multiple measures and can plot a number of changes in drug use and crime. These studies tend to show that during periods of increased drug use criminal behaviour increased, and during periods of increased criminal behaviour drug use increased. However, few of these studies have disaggregated the data to show the effects of different drugs on different crimes.

The 'qualitative' studies add to the picture by providing information on the mechanisms and processes by which drug use and crime might be connected. The results showed that offenders and drug users provided a wide range of explanations about the way in which their drug use and crime were connected. A large proportion of these concerned the theory that drug use causes crime and many subjects provided statements in support of the economic necessity argument. However, it is likely that there is no single explanation of the link between drug use and crime and that on some occasions one explanation might apply and on other occasions another might apply.

In summary, studies of drug users, offenders and members of the general population have identified a number of ways in which drug use and criminal behaviour may be connected. It is common to end an evaluation of research on drug use and crime with the conclusion that the link between drug use and offending behaviour is 'complex'. In fact, it might be very simple. The main reason it seems complex is because the details of the relationship have not yet been worked out. Future research needs to focus on the details of the relationship so that it can be determined under what circumstances one type of explanation applies and under what circumstances another type of explanation applies.

## Further reading

Few studies provide overviews of research on the nature of the causal connection between drug use and crime. However, it would be worth looking at the general books on drugs and crime mentioned in the further reading section of the previous chapter. These address the causal connection, but are not dedicated to the task. However, there are some shorter publications that are more specific and are worth consulting. One of the most up-to-date UK studies of age-of-onset of drug use and crime is that of Pudney (2003), based on a survey of young people in the general population. The classic 'changes-over-time' study is that of Ball *et al.* (1981), which examines the criminality of heroin addicts when addicted and when not addicted. An interesting qualitative study that touches on some unusual connections between drug use and crime is that by Topalli *et al.* (2002) on violence in drug markets.

# chapter eight

# The effectiveness of interventions

## Introduction

This chapter looks at methods of tackling drug use and the problem of drug-related offending. In particular, it will examine the effectiveness of treatment approaches and criminal justice interventions in reducing criminal behaviour. The term 'treatment approaches' refers to traditional programmes aimed at drug users who voluntarily present themselves for treatment. These approaches are mainly aimed at controlling or reducing drug use. However, they may also serve to control or reduce offending. The term 'criminal justice interventions' refers to court orders or other criminal justice processes whereby drug-misusing offenders might receive treatment for drug misuse as part of the disposal. These programmes are sometimes described as 'coercive treatment' in that they are based on referral to treatment by the criminal justice system rather than self-referral. Criminal justice approaches are concerned with both reducing drug use and reducing crime. This chapter will look at the effectiveness of both types of programme in reducing criminal behaviour by reviewing the results of evaluative research.

### Previous reviews of treatment

There have been a number of reviews of the literature on the effectiveness of treatment programmes. Most of these have focused on the effects of the programme on drug use. However, there have been a few reviews that have looked at the effectiveness of medical treatment on offending. It is worth noting that there are different methods of reviewing the literature. Reviews sometimes include 'meta-analyses'. These are rigorous methods of comparing the results of studies by recalculating them to a standard unit of measurement. However, reviews can be quantitative without including meta-analyses. These are sometimes referred to as quantitative narrative reviews in that the results of studies are presented in a numerical form as presented in the original publication and described by the reviewer. Reviews can also be qualitative in that the results of previous research might simply be described without presentation of numerical results.

Some of these reviews have focused on a single type of treatment. Hall (1996), for example, reviewed the research evidence available on the effectiveness of methadone maintenance treatment and its impact on crime. The review was limited to the most rigorous research designs. The author located just three studies based on controlled trials of methadone maintenance (Dole *et al.* 1969; Newman and Whitehill 1979; Gunne and Grönbladh 1981). Each of these studies found that methadone maintenance treatment produced substantial reductions in drug use and crime. Hall (1996) concluded: 'A relationship between methadone treatment and reduced drug use and criminal behaviour has been consistently observed in controlled trials, quasi-experimental studies, comparative studies, and pre-post studies in the USA, Sweden, Hong Kong and Australia' (p. 6).

Marsch (1998) also conducted a review of the literature on the effectiveness of methadone maintenance using meta-analyses. The majority of the studies reviewed were undertaken in the United States and Canada. Forty-three studies were included in a meta-analysis. Twenty-four of these analysed the impact of methadone maintenance treatment on criminal activity. The results showed a statistically significant relationship between methadone maintenance treatment and the reduction of illicit opiate use, HIV risk behaviours, and drug- and property-related criminal behaviours.

Other reviews of the literature have looked at a broader range of treatment programmes. Pearson and Lipton (1999), for example, reviewed 1606 evaluations of various kinds of drug treatment programmes in prisons conducted during the period 1968–1996. Meta-analyses were used to examine evidence of their effectiveness in reducing recidivism among incarcerated drug-abusing offenders. The results of the meta-analysis showed that therapeutic communities were effective in reducing offending. They also showed that methadone maintenance treatment, substance abuse education and cognitive-behavioural therapy were 'promising' interventions (showing some evidence of success) in their abilities to reduce criminal behaviour. However, neither boot camps nor drug-focused counselling were found to be effective.

Chanhatasilpa *et al.* (2000) also looked at various kinds of drug treatment to determine their effectiveness among drug-dependent offenders in reducing recidivism. Their review was based on the results of 15 studies. They found that prison-based therapeutic communities with follow-up community treatment were effective in reducing recidivism. However, increased referral, monitoring and management in the community were not effective. The authors noted that it was not possible to determine which elements of the treatment regime (e.g. specific components of the treatment or the intensity of the treatment intensity) differentiated successful from unsuccessful programmes in terms of reducing criminal activity. Prendergast *et al.* (2002) conducted a meta-analysis of 78 studies of various kinds of drug treatment programmes published during the period 1965 and 1996 mainly in the United States and Canada. The kinds of treatment programme investigated included detoxification, methadone maintenance, therapeutic community and other miscellaneous techniques (e.g. acupuncture, anger management and relapse prevention). Outcomes for clients who received treatment were compared to clients who received minimal or no treatment. The authors concluded that there was no significant correlation between different kinds of treatment and measures of criminal behaviour.

Hence, the results of the reviews of treatment effectiveness are mixed. They range from almost everything works to almost nothing works. The reviews are also variable in terms of the combinations of programmes that are investigated. However, the majority of the reviews provide evidence that treatment can be effective in reducing criminal behaviour. They also suggest that not all programmes are effective and some are more effective than others.

### Previous reviews of criminal justice programmes

There have been very few reviews on the literature on the effectiveness of criminal justice programmes in reducing drug-related crime. Hough (1996) conducted one of the few selective reviews of the effectiveness of a range of criminal justice and treatment interventions. The programmes investigated were grouped into three categories: interventions before sentence, community penalties and interventions in prisons. In relation to interventions before sentence, it was concluded that low-level police enforcements can be successful in disrupting drug purchases. However, some of the demand for illegal drugs will be displaced to other suppliers. Arrest referral schemes tend to have low referral rates, but some might be cost-effective. With respect to community penalties, the author found that methadone maintenance reduced drug-related crime. However, schemes based on higher daily dosages tended to be more effective than those based on lower daily dosages. Detoxification and reduction prescribing are not as effective as maintenance prescribing. Therapeutic communities have high drop-out rates, but those who stay the full term do better than comparison groups. Other types of counselling and social skills training can sometimes be effective as long as the clients are retained in treatment. The review of interventions in prisons concluded that prisons reduce crime among drug users as a result of incapacitation. However, these offences might be deferred until release. Prison-based methadone maintenance may work if linked to other treatment. Research on the effectiveness of therapeutic communities is promising and 'drug-free wings' may prove of value. Cognitive-behavioural approaches and relapse prevention also seem promising.

In another UK review of research, Ramsay (2003b) looked at research on the effectiveness of interventions used in prisons to reduce drug use and offending. The review found that prisoners were often heavily involved in drug use in the year before they entered custody. Drug use tended to reduce during the period in custody compared with the period before or after custody. White women prisoners had particularly high rates of drug dependency compared with black or mixed-race women prisoners. The literature on drug treatment in prisons tends to show that good-quality treatment can be effective in reducing offending, particularly when it is of sufficient length, meets individual needs and is followed through by after-care. The Rehabilitation of Addicted Prisoners Trust (RAPt) abstinence programme has shown that graduates receiving the treatment show lower levels of drug use and offending following release. A process evaluation of the Prison Service drug strategy shows that treatment in prison can be successfully implemented.

Hence, the results of research on the effectiveness of criminal-justice-initiated programmes for drug-misusing offenders show that many of them can be effective in reducing criminal behaviour. They also show that the results vary depending on the quality of the programme and its suit-ability in relation to the current needs of the offender. However, the num-ber of reviews is small and few involve systematic methods of reviewing the literature, such as meta-analysis.

In the following sections, we shall conduct our own review of the litera-ture to determine the kinds of programmes that are available for drug users and to consider the effectiveness of these programmes in reducing offend-ing. The review will be influenced by our own systematic review of the literature conducted for the Home Office on the effectiveness of treatment and criminal justice programmes on reducing drug-related offending (Bennett and Holloway in prep.). However, the method of presentation and the selection of results will be structured to suit the needs of the current chapter. The results of the research will be divided into the outcomes of traditional treatment approaches for drug users and the outcomes of crim-inal justice programmes for offenders. The main aim of the review is to determine whether interventions of these kinds can help tackle the problem of drug-related crime.

## Treatment

As mentioned earlier, the term 'treatment' is used here to refer to traditional medical, social or psychological programmes for drug users. These are typically provided by doctors or other trained professionals working in appropriate settings for the treatment of drug misuse. Users are referred to these settings through self-referral or other medical or professional referral with the primary aim of treating their drug misuse.

### Description of programmes

Treatment programmes for drug users can be divided into six main categories: 'methadone treatment', 'heroin treatment', 'therapeutic communities', 'psychological, social and behavioural approaches', 'supervision and aftercare' and 'other' types of treatment.

*Methadone treatment* is based on replacing illegal opiates with prescribed methadone. Methadone is a synthetic opiate and produces similar effects to heroin and other opium-based products. However, it is manufactured rather than natural. It is regarded by the medical profession as a preferred alternative to heroin in that it is longer-lasting and can be taken orally. It can be used for purposes of withdrawal or maintenance. The most common form of methadone treatment is maintenance prescribing, whereby users are prescribed methadone as an alternative to heroin over extended periods of time. The aim of this method of treatment is to stabilize users and allow them to lead normal lives while drug dependent.

*Heroin treatment* is similar to methadone treatment in that an opiate is prescribed by a doctor usually over extended periods of time to stabilize drug dependence. However, in this case, the drug user's drug of choice is used rather than an alternative. It has been argued that heroin taken over long periods of time under controlled and sterile conditions is safe and is also preferred among drug users (Metrebian *et al.* 2001). However, heroin treatment is generally not preferred among doctors and relatively few heroin treatment programmes exist.

*Therapeutic communities* for substance abuse were first established in the late 1950s as a self-help alternative to existing treatments, particularly for heroin addicts (Nemes *et al.* 1999). They are now one of the most common residential treatment methods for substance misusers. Therapeutic communities are usually drug-free residential programmes based on peer influence and group processes. The aim of the programme is to encourage individuals to assimilate the norms of the group and to learn effective social skills to tackle their drug-use problems. The main agent of change is the community in which the individual lives and includes the treatment staff as well as other drug users at various stages in their recovery. Members of the community interact in various ways to influence attitudes, perceptions and behaviour associated with drug use. The programmes are also based on the principle of self-help in that the individual is seen as an important contributor to the change process.

*Psychosocial approaches* typically cover a range of programmes that use psychological, social or behavioural approaches in the treatment of drug misuse. The programmes can be quite wide-ranging and include psychotherapy, counselling, cognitive-behavioural approaches and family therapy. One of the most common psychosocial approaches is cognitive-behaviourism. These are approaches based on psychological theories of learning and behaviour. They tend to stress the role of the external environment in shaping an individual's actions. They also give importance to the individual's thought processes, such as reasoning, memory and problem solving. Programmes drawing on social learning theory stress the role of learning and social interaction. All of these approaches are based on the principle that drug users lack certain psychological or social skills that can be improved with suitable interventions.

*Supervision and aftercare programmes* are usually tagged onto other programmes such as supervision and aftercare following methadone treatment. However, these enhanced programmes have often been evaluated in their own right. *Other treatment* approaches are defined here as those that do not fit easily into any of the above groupings. They include multiple combination programmes, sheltered accommodation, alternative approaches and acupuncture.

## Effectiveness of programmes

What evidence is there that treatment approaches are effective in reducing criminal behaviour among drug users? To answer this question, we will look at the research evidence relating to each of the treatment categories described above and also comment on the results of our own systematic review of the literature on the effectiveness of interventions for drug misusers conducted for the Home Office. In the following sub-sections, we summarize two or three studies on each programme type and comment on the results of our own review as appropriate. The selection of the two or three studies is to some extent arbitrary and is designed mainly to give a flavour of the types of research being done. However, we have tried to include at least one study from the UK and one from another country, and have selected studies that have provided fairly standard versions of the programmes and clear results.

### Methadone treatment

Few evaluations of methadone treatment have been conducted in the UK. The study by Gossop *et al.* (2003) looked at the effects of methadone by drawing on data from the UK National Treatment Outcome Research Study (NTORS). The NTORS data are not ideal for the purpose of evaluation. However, they can be used to compare the effectiveness of methadone treatment and other programmes in their abilities to reduce criminal behaviour. The figures show that methadone treatment was more effective than residential care in reducing the mean number of drug crimes committed by patients over the 5-year period since treatment. However, residential care was more effective than methadone treatment in reducing the mean number of all crimes committed. Overall, the differences between the treatment types were small and both treatment options were associated with a reduction in crime. The authors conclude that reductions in crime were among the more striking findings from NTORS and that overall, 'both types of crime were reduced to about a quarter of the levels of intake' (p. 301).

The majority of evaluations of methadone maintenance have been conducted in the United States. French and Zarkin (1992), for example, used data from a longitudinal survey of 2420 drug abusers to explore the effects of drug abuse treatment on legal and illegal earnings. Individuals undertaking outpatient methadone treatment were compared with individuals who were drug-free outpatients. Illegal earnings among the methadone group decreased from $9324 in the year before treatment to $3383 in the year after treatment (a 64 per cent reduction). Among the drug-free group, illegal earnings decreased from $8179 before treatment to $3792 after treatment (a 54 per cent reduction). The authors conclude that, on average, clients in both groups experienced large changes in real illegal earnings from the year entering treatment to the year after leaving treatment.

Our own review of methadone treatment evaluations found that six of the seven studies that met the criteria for inclusion in the review reported that methadone treatment was more effective than at least one other comparison programme in reducing criminal behaviour (Bennett and Holloway in prep.). Overall, the review concluded that methadone treatment was effective in reducing criminal behaviour.

### Heroin treatment

Few studies have been undertaken that have assessed the effectiveness of heroin prescribing. In the UK, Hartnoll et al. (1980) investigated the effect of heroin treatment on 96 confirmed heroin addicts. The addicts were randomly allocated to treatment with injectable heroin or oral methadone. Progress was monitored by research workers operating independently of the clinic. Those offered heroin maintenance were less likely than those offered oral methadone to be arrested during the follow-up period (8 per cent of the former compared with 19 per cent of the latter). A similar result was found for the proportion spending time in prison during the follow-up period. During the first year, 19 per cent of the heroin maintenance group spent some time in prison compared with 32 per cent of the oral methadone group. The heroin treatment group who were imprisoned in the follow-up period spent less time in prison than the methadone treatment group who were imprisoned.

In Switzerland, Perneger et al. (1998) conducted an evaluation of an experimental heroin maintenance programme. Twenty-seven individuals who received intravenous heroin treatment were compared with 24 controls who received other forms of drug treatment. The results showed that heroin maintenance was more effective than conventional treatments in reducing crime. The proportion of subjects in the heroin group who reported committing drug-dealing offences decreased from 26 per cent in the 6-month period before treatment to 0 per cent during the 6-month follow-up period (a 100 per cent reduction). The proportion of subjects in the conventional drug treatment group who reported committing drug-dealing offences increased from 5 per cent to 10 per cent over the same period (a 100 per cent increase). A similar pattern of results was found for other offences with the heroin group reporting decreases and the conventional drug treatment group reporting increases. The authors conclude that heroin maintenance was better than conventional drug treatment in reducing criminal behaviour.

Our own systematic review found that all three of the studies that met our inclusion criteria showed that heroin was more effective than the comparison forms of treatment in reducing criminal behaviour among drug users (Bennett and Holloway in prep.). Hence, we concluded that, on the basis of the evidence, heroin was effective in reducing offending.

### Therapeutic communities

Wexler et al. (1999) evaluated the effectiveness of an in-prison therapeutic community in the United States. Seven-hundred-and-fifteen inmates were randomly assigned to either the prison therapeutic community group or to a no-treatment control group. The results show a greater reduction in criminal behaviour among prisoners offered therapeutic community treatment than those on the normal prison routine. At the 24-month follow-up, 14 per cent of subjects who had completed therapeutic community treatment and aftercare had been reincarcerated, compared with 67 per cent of subjects in the no-treatment group. The authors claim that their findings support the idea that therapeutic communities in prison can be effective in reducing reincarceration rates among inmates treated for substance abuse.

Hser et al. (2001) conducted an evaluation of drug treatments for adolescents in four US cities. Over 1000 adolescents aged 11–18 were interviewed in the year before commencing treatment and again in the year after treatment. The subjects were divided into three groups on the basis of the type of treatment they received: (a) residential treatment programmes (including therapeutic communities), (b) outpatient drug-free programmes and (c) short-term inpatient programmes. The proportion of residential subjects that reported committing any illegal act decreased from 79 per cent in the year before treatment to 50 per cent in the year after treatment (a decrease of 37 per cent). Comparable figures for the drug-free outpatients were 66 per cent in the year before treatment and 51 per cent in the year after treatment (a decrease of 23 per cent). The proportion of subjects reporting any arrests decreased by more than 50 per cent among the residential subjects, but increased by 7 per cent among the drug-free out-patients. These authors concluded that therapeutic communities can pro-duce greater reductions in criminal behaviour than outpatient drug-free programmes.

Our review conducted for the Home Office (Bennett and Holloway in prep.) found that nine out of ten studies that investigated therapeutic communities reported that they reduced criminal behaviour by a greater amount than the comparison group.

### Psychological, social and behavioural approaches

Most evaluations of psychosocial approaches have been conducted in the United States. Henggeler *et al.* (1991), for example, present findings from two independent evaluations of the efficacy of multi-systemic therapy in treating antisocial behaviour among serious juvenile offenders in Missouri. The results of the Missouri Delinquency Project (MDP) showed some evidence of success in reducing criminal behaviour among drug users. The participants in the MDP were 200 adolescents who had been referred to the project by juvenile court after a recent arrest. The offenders were randomly assigned to receive either multi-systemic therapy or individual counselling and were interviewed 4 years later. At the time of the follow-up interview, 4 per cent of subjects who received multi-systemic therapy had been arrested for a substance-related offence compared with 16 per cent of those who received individual counselling.

Woody *et al.* (1987) evaluated the effectiveness of psychotherapy among 93 male veterans who were addicted to opiates and were receiving metha-done maintenance treatment. The veterans were randomly assigned to one of three conditions: (1) drug counselling alone (Group 1), (2) counselling plus supportive-expressive psychotherapy (Group 2), or (3) counselling plus cognitive-behavioural psychotherapy (Group 3). Interviews were conducted with the subjects at intake and 12 months later. Among Group 2, the mean number of days spent committing crimes in the 30 days before interview decreased from five at baseline to three at 12-month follow-up. Among Group 1, the mean number of days spent committing crimes increased from two to four. The members of Group 2 also performed better than the members of Group 1 in terms of changes in overall criminality score. The mean score decreased from 219 to 117 among Group 2 members, but increased from 81 to 142 among Group 1 members. The authors conclude that the psychotherapy groups showed more improvements than the drug counselling group over a wider range of outcome measures, including criminal behaviour.

Our Home Office review (Bennett and Holloway in prep.) included four studies that evaluated psychosocial approaches. The review showed that all four studies reported that the psychosocial approaches investigated were more effective than the comparison interventions in reducing criminal behaviour.

### Supervision and aftercare

One evaluation of supervision and aftercare conducted in the UK (Ghodse *et al.* 2002) investigated the impact of aftercare among 49 patients who had undergone residential opiate detoxification. The comparison group received detoxification without aftercare. The results of this study suggest that detoxification plus aftercare is more effective than detoxification without aftercare in reducing criminal behaviour. Among subjects in the aftercare group, the mean number of drug-related crime days fell from 59 in the 3 months before treatment to 6 in the 3-month follow-up period (a 90 per cent reduction). Among subjects in the no-aftercare group, the mean number of drug-related crime days fell from 44 to 19 (a 57 per cent reduction). The authors conclude that significantly better treatment outcomes were observed among those who completed detoxification and went on to some kind of aftercare.

In the United States, Brown *et al.* (2001) evaluated the effectiveness of a stand-alone aftercare programme for 145 drug-involved offenders. The authors note that at the 6-month follow-up interviews, the aftercare group showed greater reductions in crime than the no-aftercare group. However, by the time of the 12-month follow-up interviews, the aftercare group had more arrests and a higher mean number of crime days than the no-aftercare group. The authors explained these findings by stating that the initial positive effect of the programme had been considerably attenuated by the time of the 12-month follow-up interviews.

Our own systematic review concluded that is was unknown, from the limited existing research, whether supervision and aftercare was effective in reducing criminal behaviour.

### Other types of treatment

Lam *et al.* (1995) conducted a study that evaluated the effectiveness of a short-term shelter and day treatment programme among subjects in the United States. Altogether, 294 males were randomly assigned to either the shelter programme or usual services. The study found that men in the shelter programme reported a larger decrease in mean illegal income than the other services group over the 21-month study period. At baseline, men in the shelter group reported obtaining $663 from illegal sources. This decreased to $256 at the 21-month follow-up (a 61 per cent reduction). Men in the usual services group reported obtaining $355 of illegal income at baseline and $182 at follow-up (a 49 per cent reduction). The authors conclude that the shelter programme had a positive impact, but point out that it would be wrong to consider the usual services to be of no value.

Latessa and Moon (1992) examined the effectiveness of acupuncture in an outpatient drug treatment programme. A sample of 274 chemically dependent offenders in a mid-western city in the United States were randomly allocated to one of three groups. The experimental group received acupuncture on a regular basis, the control group did not receive any form of acupuncture, and a placebo group received an acupuncture-like simulation. The 182 subjects in the experimental group were compared with the 45 subjects in the control group. Using official records, the authors compared the groups in terms of new arrests, convictions and technical violations incurred over the evaluation period (120–160 days). The figures show that a smaller proportion of subjects in the control group than in the acupuncture group had been convicted or arrested for a felony offence over the study period. There was little difference between the two groups in terms of the proportions with any conviction (15 per cent of the acupuncture group and 16 per cent of the control group). The authors conclude that there is no evidence that acupuncture had any appreciable effect on programme completion, arrests, convictions or probation outcome.

Our Home Office review of other treatment programmes (Bennett and Holloway in prep.) found that two of the four studies reviewed reported that the programme was successful in reducing offending. The review concluded that other treatment programmes were 'promising', but the results so far were inconclusive.

## Criminal justice programmes

The term 'criminal justice programmes' is used in the current review to include criminal justice orders or sentences that (among other things) aim to reduce drug-related crime. Criminal justice interventions of these kinds sometimes include treatment (e.g. drug treatment and testing orders) and sometimes do not (pre-conviction drug testing of arrestees).

### Description of programmes

Criminal justice programmes for drug-misusing offenders can be subdivided into four categories: 'drug testing', 'drug courts', 'probation and aftercare', and 'other' criminal justice interventions.

*Drug testing* or drug monitoring is a common component of community penalties used to control drug use among known offenders. There are a number of different types of programme that can be included under this heading. Drug treatment and testing orders were introduced as a new community sentence under the Crime and Disorder Act 1998. Other court orders involving drug testing introduced about the same time include drug abstinence orders and drug abstinence requirements. Drug testing provides a scientific measure of drug use and a means of identifying patterns of drug use. Drug testing is believed to be a deterrent to future drug use and criminal activity (Haapanen and Britton 2002).

*Drug courts* are special courts that provide judicially monitored treatment, drug testing and other services to drug-involved offenders. Diversionary drug courts usually enrol offenders into treatment shortly after arrest and determine outcomes on the basis of their graduation from the programme. In contrast, post-adjudication drug courts intervene after defendants have been convicted, and offer deferred or suspended sentences to those who complete treatment programmes. Some courts employ a combination of these approaches. The first drug court was established in the United States, in Florida in 1989 (Gottfredson and Exum 2002).

*Probation and parole supervision* interventions cover a wide range of court orders and judicial processes. In some US states, entering drug treatment can be a condition of parole. Similarly, a provision of probation supervision might be that the offender remains drug free. Drug-involved probationers might also be given some kind of intensive supervision that would involve surveillance and monitoring their drug use.

Other criminal justice interventions include multiple approaches based on combinations of conventional criminal justice programmes and various treatment programmes. These include juvenile drug treatment boot camps designed to deter offenders from both crime and drug use programmes based on both high levels and low levels of coercion.

## Effectiveness of programmes

### Drug testing

Drug treatment and testing orders were introduced in the UK specifically to tackle the perceived links between drug use and acquisitive crime. Hough *et al.* (2003) conducted one of the first evaluations of these orders. The study compared subjects on drug treatment and testing orders and subjects on similar schemes over a 2-year period. The results of the study showed that a slightly larger proportion of subjects on the comparison schemes than on drug treatment and testing orders were reconvicted over the comparison period (91 per cent compared with 80 per cent).

The effectiveness of drug testing has also been investigated at the pre-trial stage. Britt *et al.* (1992) conducted an experiment that explored the effects of drug testing on defendants on pre-trial release. Subjects were randomly allocated into either a drug testing group or a no-testing control group. The experiment was conducted in two counties in the United States. In Pima County, 2 per cent of subjects in the drug testing group were rearrested in the pre-trial period compared with 4 per cent of subjects in the no-testing group. In Maricopa County, a larger proportion of subjects in the testing group than in the no-testing group were rearrested. The authors concluded that there is no evidence from the research that monitoring the drug use of defendants on pre-trial release has a statistically significant effect in reducing pre-trial misconduct.

There have also been evaluations of drug testing at the post-release stage. Haapanen and Britton (2002) conducted an experimental study examining the parole outcomes and arrests for 1958 parolees in the United States. Subjects were randomly assigned to various levels of routine drug testing ranging from no testing to two tests per month. The results indicate that frequent drug testing was less effective than no testing in reducing criminal behaviour. At 42 months after treatment, the mean number of arrests for the drug testing group was 3.8 compared to 3.0 for the no-testing group. Similarly, the mean arrest rates for property crimes and drug crimes were also higher among the drug testing group than the no-testing group. Hence, the results do not suggest that drug testing was more effective than the comparison.

Our own review of the literature (Bennett and Holloway in prep.) found that four of the six studies with sufficiently rigorous research designs showed evidence that drug testing was more effective than the comparison method. However, only 4 of the 13 findings drawn from these showed that drug testing worked. The review concluded that the findings were mixed.

### Drug courts

All of the currently available evaluations of drug courts have been conducted in the United States. Turner et al. (1999), for example, compared the efficacy of drug courts with the efficacy of drug testing. They randomly allocated 506 subjects into either the drug testing group or the drug court group. At 36 months, a smaller proportion of subjects in the drug court group than in the drug testing group were found to have been arrested for any offence (33 per cent compared with 44 per cent) and for property offences (10 per cent versus 15 per cent). The drug court group was also associated with a smaller mean number of arrests (0.6 compared with 0.8). The authors conclude that drug courts were effective in reducing criminal behaviour.

Gottfredson et al. (2003) evaluated the outcome of the Baltimore Drug Treatment Court. Two-hundred-and-thirty-five subjects were randomly allocated into the drug court group or a treatment-as-usual group. The results showed that at the follow-up interviews, there were fewer mean arrests and convictions among the drug court group than among the treatment-as-usual group. The proportion of subjects who were reconvicted in the follow-up period was also lower among the drug court group than among the treatment-as-usual group (49 per cent compared with 53 per cent). The authors conclude that drug court subjects who participated in treatment were significantly less likely to relapse into crime than untreated drug court subjects and controls.

Our own study included just the two studies above in the quantitative review and concluded that drug courts were effective in reducing offending among drug users.

### Probation and parole supervision

There were few evaluations of probation and parole supervision and the small number that were conducted were based in the United States. Turner et al. (1992), for example, reported the results of a randomized experiment that tested the effects of intensive supervision under probation and parole (ISP) for drug-involved offenders in five sites across the United States.

Subjects were randomly allocated into either the ISP group or a routine supervision control group. The results were in the reverse direction to those hypothesized. At one-year follow-up, 28 per cent of subjects under routine supervision had been jailed compared with 39 per cent of subjects under intensive supervision. Similarly, 10 per cent of subjects under routine supervision had been imprisoned, compared with 13 per cent of subjects under intensive supervision. The authors explained that the result was likely to be due to the fact that ISP programmes are often surveillance-oriented and this tends to increase the number of violations of the sanction imposed by the courts. They conclude that their results lend 'serious doubt' to the belief that increased supervision will reduce recidivism.

Farabee et al. (2001b) examined criminal activity among 1167 adolescents who participated in a community-based substance abuse treatment study (DATOS-A). As part of the study, the authors explored the effect of criminal justice supervision on treatment outcome. Those subjects who were under criminal justice supervision at the time of treatment were compared with subjects who were not under such supervision. The proportion of subjects with arrests for any crime decreased by a larger amount among the supervised group than among the non-supervised group. However, with respect to drug dealing, the proportion of arrests increased among the non-supervised group.

Our review for the Home Office (Bennett and Holloway in prep.) found that three of the four studies that met the eligibility criteria (the above study being the exception) showed that probation and parole supervision can be effective in reducing criminal behaviour.

### Other criminal justice interventions

Other criminal justice interventions include various forms of legal coercion as a means of getting drug users into treatment. Brecht et al. (1993), for example, investigated the impact of legal coercion on treatment effectiveness among a sample of 618 methadone maintenance clients. Subjects were recruited from treatment programmes in six southern Californian counties and were divided into three groups on the basis of the level of legal coercion that they were under (high, moderate or low). Subjects in the high coercion group reported a decrease in the mean number of burglary-days a month from 3 days in the pre-treatment period to 1 day a month in the post-treatment period. Subjects in the low coercion group also showed evidence of a decrease in the mean number of property crime-days per month. The authors concluded that those coerced into treatment responded in similar ways to voluntary admissions.

Other interventions include drug treatment boot camps. Zhang (2000) conducted an evaluation of the Los Angeles County Juvenile Drug Treatment Boot Camp. As part of this evaluation, Zhang (2000) compared a sample of subjects who entered the drug treatment boot camp with a sample of subjects who entered regular boot camps. The two samples were interviewed at intake and again at 12 months following release. The drug camp participants experienced a 79 per cent decrease in the mean number of theft offences over the study period (from a mean of 4.8 offences to 1.0 offence). The regular camp subjects experienced an even larger reduction (85 per cent) in mean number of property offences (from a mean of 4.0 offences to 0.6 offences). The author concluded that there was no difference in the two regimes in terms of their effect on criminal behaviour.

The Home Office review found that only one out of three studies investigated showed that other criminal justice approaches for drug offenders worked. The review concluded that overall other approaches were not found to be effective in reducing criminal behaviour

## Variations by the type of programme

Overall, the review of the literature so far has shown that most of the broad groups of interventions appear to work in that they show at least some evidence of success. However, the proportion of studies showing success varies across the different types of intervention. Hence, some programmes appear to work better than others. This observation can lead to two broad conclusions.

The first broad conclusion is that there is more evidence of success among treatment interventions than criminal justice interventions. This is shown in the strong support for methadone and heroin programmes and the weak support for drug testing and other criminal justice interventions. Our own review of the literature concluded that 71 per cent of findings relating to treatment programmes showed evidence of success compared with 45 per cent of findings from the criminal justice programmes (Bennett and Holloway in prep.). Hence, there is a clear tendency for treatment programmes to fair better than criminal justice programmes in reducing crime among drug users. The conclusion is almost counter-intuitive in that criminal justice programmes should be better at reducing crime than drug programmes. However, it is not easy to explain this difference without knowing more about the processes involved. In theory, there should be no difference between subjects who enter treatment programmes voluntarily and those who enter as a result of referral from the criminal justice system. However, in practice, there are important differences between the two groups in that one is a group of known offenders and the other is a group of known drug users. Experienced offenders might be less willing or able to change their criminal behaviour than experienced drug users.

The second broad conclusion is that, within these broad categories, there is more consistent evidence of success for some programmes than others. In relation to treatment approaches, the vast majority of findings relating to methadone treatment, heroin treatment, therapeutic communities and psychosocial approaches showed that the programmes were effective in reducing offending. In relation to supervision and aftercare, and other treatment approaches, the results were inconclusive. In relation to the criminal justice programmes, the review has shown that drug courts and probation and parole supervision appear to be effective. However, there is less clear evidence that drug testing and other criminal justice approaches work.

## Variations by intensity of the programme

It is possible that some of the differences mentioned above might be the result of differences in intensity of the programme. Methadone maintenance programmes, for example, may last for many months or even years. Conversely, some drug-testing programmes (e.g. mandatory drug testing at the point of arrest) may last just a few minutes. Few studies have attempted to quantify the intensity of the programme or the extent to which subjects complete the treatment. However, some studies have included information on these topics and provide some indication of the influence of intensity on outcome. Intensity refers here to the length of the programme, the strength of the programme, or whether the respondent completed the programme.

Three of the studies reviewed investigated the effect of intensity on outcome in terms of different dosage levels (in this case, of methadone) and four studies investigated the effect of intensity on outcome in terms of the amount of the programme (one therapeutic community, one probation and parole programme, one supervision study and one psychosocial approach). All three studies that investigated different dosage levels concluded that higher dosages resulted in greater reductions in offending. Three of the four studies of different programme intensities found that higher-intensity programmes resulted in either a smaller increase or a larger decrease in criminal behaviour than lower-intensity programmes. It is also possible to investigate the effect of intensity by observing the authors' comments in the conclusions of the evaluation. We found 13 studies which provided general comments from the authors on the effect of the quality of the programme on criminal behaviour. Twelve of the 13 evaluations concluded that high-intensity programmes (using various measures) resulted in more favourable effects on criminal behaviour than low-intensity programmes.

Hence, overall, the research indicates that interventions for drug misuse are more effective when they are high dosage rather than low dosage, strong versions rather than weak versions, long term rather than short term, and completed rather than terminated.

## Variations by the characteristics of subjects

The discussion so far has focused only on whether or not the programme worked. In effect, this means whether or not the programme worked for the sample as a whole. In practice, a programme might work for some people and not for others. It would be useful to break down the findings of the research by the characteristics of the subjects. However, this is not quite as straightforward as it might seem, as most studies tend to report findings only for the sample as a whole. Nevertheless, there are a number of ways in which information on the effectiveness of a programme on sample sub-groups might be obtained.

Information on subject and programme characteristics can be found in the following types of studies:

1 studies that provide results for two or more sub-groups;
2 studies that provide results for a single sub-group;
3 studies that include regression analysis interaction terms for sub-groups; and
4 studies that include authors' comments on sub-groups.

Group 1 studies repeat the main analysis of the evaluation for particular sub-groups (e.g. males and females or young and old). This is one of the strongest methods of determining a differential programme effect. Group 2 studies comprise those based on a single sub-group of the population (e.g. all males or all females). While the individual study cannot tell us about sub-group differences, a number of studies, when viewed together, can indicate whether studies based on one sub-group tend to provide different results to those based on another sub-group. Group 3 studies include an interaction term relevant to sub-groups in a regression analysis. In these cases, it is possible to determine whether the programme has a differential effect by sub-group membership. Group 4 studies can be used when neither the raw data nor any other numerical data are included in the published results. In these cases, authors sometimes provide verbal comments on the outcome of the intervention for particular sub-groups in the conclusion or elsewhere in the text.

Only one study that we identified provided a breakdown of the results of the evaluation by gender (Magura *et al.* 1993). This evaluation of methadone treatment showed that the programme was more effective for males (who showed a 55 per cent reduction in offending following treatment) than females (who showed a 26 per cent reduction in offending). Differences between the sexes can also be investigated by studies that focus on just males or just females. We found six evaluations based on just males and one evaluation based on just females. These evaluations covered methadone maintenance and therapeutic communities. The average percentage reduction in offending following treatment was 50 per cent among the male-only studies and 0 per cent among the female-only study. Hence, this finding supports the previous finding that males tend to perform better than females in treatment evaluations. There was also one study that examined the effect of gender on outcome using regression analysis (Brecht *et al.* 1993). This study concluded that reductions in criminal behaviour following treatment were significantly greater among males than females. Finally, we found nine studies that included authors' conclusions that mentioned differences between the sexes. Four of these studies concluded that males performed better than females in terms of crime reduction and one concluded that females performed better than males. The remainder concluded that there was no difference. Hence, overall, the research tends to favour the conclusion that programmes for drug-misusing offenders are more effective for males than females.

We found no studies that provided a breakdown of treatment outcome by age. However, three studies (two of which were evaluations of therapeutic communities) provided results for young offenders only. These studies showed that, on average, the programmes were associated with a reduction in criminal behaviour of 53 per cent. This compares with a reduction of just 4 per cent among studies including adults only or a mix of ages. Hence, there is some evidence that programmes might be more effective for young people than older people. However, the results were not replicated when looking at non-random allocation studies. Three studies included a breakdown by age as an interaction term in a regression analysis. One of these studies concluded that the programme was more effective among young people than adults and two concluded that there was no difference between the two. Finally, we found six studies that included authors' comments on the differences in effectiveness of the programme by age. One of these studies showed that young people were more likely than adults to reduce offending following treatment. The remaining studies found no difference in terms of age. Hence, the results of the research tend either to show that young people are more likely to reduce their criminal behaviour following treatment or that there is no difference between young people and adults. No studies concluded that results were more favourable among adults.

Few studies have investigated differences in outcome by race. One evaluation of therapeutic communities (Gordon *et al.* 2000) provided a breakdown in the results by ethnic status and concluded that reductions in offending following treatment were greater for non-whites than whites. No studies focused only on one ethnic group. One study included an interaction term on race in a regression analysis. The study found that there was no significant difference between whites and non-whites in terms of programme effectiveness. Finally, six studies included comments on the effect of race in the authors' conclusions. One of these found that non-whites performed better than whites, while the remainder concluded that there was no difference between the two groups. Hence, overall, studies either show that programmes are more effective in reducing criminal behaviour among non-whites compared with whites or they show that there is no difference. No study concluded that whites performed better than non-whites in terms of reductions in criminal behaviour following treatment.

Hence, the results of the current review of study breakdowns suggests that interventions for drug misuse are at least sometimes more effective in reducing criminal behaviour among males than females, young drug users than adult drug users, and non-whites than whites.

## Conclusion

Overall, the research has shown that most interventions for drug users reduce offending at least some of the time. Our own systematic review of the literature conducted for the Home Office showed that programmes in eight of the ten treatment categories used in the research were found to be effective by at least half of the studies evaluating them. Hence, it is hard to avoid the conclusion that 'everything works' at least some of the time and perhaps even most of the time. However, these aggregate level results obscure important differences in the strength of the results obtained.

There are clear differences in the effectiveness of treatment compared with criminal justice interventions. Our review showed that the vast majority of findings relating to treatment programmes showed evidence of success compared with a minority of findings from the criminal justice programmes. However, these results are still based on aggregates of programmes and it is possible that some criminal justice programmes do work. The general finding is hard to explain without knowing more about the processes involved. There may be differences between the processes involved in voluntary and coercive treatment. The treatments received might be different in terms of quality and quantity. The subjects (who in the case of criminal justice referrals are all convicted offenders) may also be different in terms of their criminal propensities or their motivation to change.

The results also show that there are differences in effectiveness across specific programme types. Some interventions are more effective than others. In relation to the treatment programmes, methadone treatment, heroin treatment, therapeutic communities and psychosocial approaches all appear to be effective. In relation to supervision and aftercare, and other treatment approaches, the results were inconclusive. In relation to the criminal justice programmes, the review has shown that drug courts and probation and parole supervision are effective. However, there is less clear evidence that drug testing and other criminal justice approaches work. This is not to say that these programmes do not work some of the time in relation to some offenders.

There are also variations in findings in terms of the quality of the programme. The research findings suggest that greater reductions in offending occur among methadone programmes based on high dosages compared with those based on low dosages. It has also been shown that intensive versions of probation and parole supervision for drug users are more effective than routine supervision. Finally, there are also some differences in the effectiveness of programmes in terms of the characteristics of the subjects. The review has shown that males might be more favourably affected by treatment programmes than females. Young offenders might be more responsive than adult offenders and non-whites might be more responsive than whites.

## Further reading

It would be worth reading any of the existing published reviews of the evaluation literature on the effect of treatment or criminal justice approaches on criminal behaviour. The main UK reviews to date are those by Hough (1996) and Ramsay (2003b), although these are limited in certain ways in their terms of reference. The publications deriving from the NTORS study (e.g. Gossop *et al.* 2003) are also worth looking at. The authors might not claim that they are conducting an evaluation of different treatment methods. Nevertheless, the comparisons in outcomes of different treatment types are useful and relevant to understanding effectiveness.

# The nature of the solution

## Introduction

Here, we reflect on what has been learned about the relationship between drug misuse and crime from this review of the literature. First, we look at what we now know about the nature of the relationship and the extent to which the association is causal or non-causal. Second, we summarize the programmes and other interventions that have been used to tackle drug-related crime and draw some conclusions about their overall effectiveness. Third, we consider the lessons that can be learned for government policy and what more might be done to reduce crime among drug users. Fourth, we consider the lessons that can be learned for research on drug-related crime and evaluations of methods designed to reduce it. Finally, we reflect on the state of current knowledge about drugs and crime and comment on what more might be done to expand knowledge and effective practice.

## What do we know about the drugs–crime connection?

One of the aims of the book has been to answer fundamental questions about the nature of the relationship between drug misuse and crime. These include: 'What do we know about the extent of drug misuse?', 'What is the nature of the drugs–crime connection?', 'How can the connection be explained', 'What research evidence is there that drugs and crime are connected?' and 'What evidence is there that drug misuse causes crime?' It might be worth bringing together in this conclusion some of the answers to these questions that can be found in the research literature.

## What do we know about the extent of drug misuse?

The problem of the drugs–crime connection would be greater if drug misuse were widespread than if it were narrowly spread. If hardly anyone misused drugs, then the problems of a drugs–crime connection would be limited to this small group and the problems for society would be restricted. If almost everyone misused drugs, then the problems associated with the drugs–crime connection would be pervasive. The research findings reported in Chapter 3 show different results for different populations. When looking at the general population, it could be argued that drug misuse is widespread in that about one-third of adults were shown to have consumed at least one illegal drug type in their lives. However, only 2 per cent of the population had used the most serious drug types commonly associated with drug-related crime. When looking at the offender population, the picture is quite different. The research shows that the vast majority of offenders have consumed at least one drug and had done so recently. It also shows that a substantial minority of offenders had consumed one or more of the most serious drug types in the last year. Hence, the misuse of serious drugs is particularly widespread in the criminal population, which increases the chance that the effects of a drugs–crime connection among this group could be substantial, whereas the misuse of serious drugs is not particularly widespread in the general population, which reduces the chance that the effects would be pervasive.

### What is the nature of the drugs–crime connection?

The phrase the 'drugs–crime connection' is a shorthand term used to refer to the possible association between drug misuse and criminal behaviour. The definition of the term was discussed at some length in Chapter 1. The review showed that the term the 'drugs–crime connection' needs to be distinguished from 'drug-related crime'. The concept of 'drug-related crime' includes a number of crime types, including: 'drug offences', systemic crimes committed as part of the functioning of drugs markets, and crimes committed as a result of drug use or drugs consumed as a result of crime. The 'drugs–crime connection' refers mainly to this latter group. The second main finding relating to the 'drugs–crime connection' is that there are a number of different ways in which drugs and crime might be associated. It was noted that drugs and crime might be linked because drug use causes crime or crime causes drug use. The link could also be forged by a third variable, or cluster of variables, that explains both drug use and crime. However, the association between drug use and crime might not be causal at all. It is possible that drug use and criminal behaviour merely co-exist in perhaps rather chaotic lifestyles of some individuals: neither drug use can be seen as causing crime, nor can crime be seen as causing drug use. These distinctions are very important, as they have considerable implications for government strategy in tackling the drugs–crime relationship. If the relationship is non-causal, there is not much that the government can do about it.

## How can the connection be explained?

The main explanations for the drugs–crime connection tend to follow the causal and non-causal models described above. While there are a number of theories available to explain each of the connections, there are some that are more popular than others. The idea that drug use might cause crime can be explained by the pharmacological effects of the drugs. However, these are the least popular of the explanations. They are usually directed at the relationship between drug use and violent crime. Pharmacological explanations are rarely used to explain the connection between drug use and property crime. However, they have sometimes been used to explain drug use as a protective factor on crime, in that the effects of drug use might sometimes be so inhibiting that they reduce the risk of offending. The most popular explanations of the 'drugs-cause-crime' model are the economic explanations, the most common of which are the 'enslavement' or 'economic necessity' arguments. The idea that crime might cause drug use has also been explained using pharmacological approaches. These include the idea of 'chemical recreation' as a means of celebrating the successful commission of crime. However, economic explanations are currently the most popular. These include the idea that surplus funds from crime can be used to finance drug use. Perhaps the most popular of the 'crime-causes-drug-use' theories are the 'lifestyle' explanations. These suggest that drug use is part and parcel of the criminal lifestyle that revolves around criminal behaviour and having a good time. Overall, current thinking seems to be moving in the direction that each of these theories plays some part in explaining the drugs–crime connection some of the time.

## What research evidence is there that drugs and crime are connected?

A major aim of the book has been to look at the research evidence on the association between drug misuse and criminal behaviour. The issue of whether there was a statistical association between drug use and crime was tackled in Chapter 6. We found that the answers tended to vary by type of question asked. The answer to the question 'Is involvement in drug use associated with involvement in crime' was, broadly speaking, 'Yes'. The research was almost unanimous in finding that drug users were more likely than non-users to be criminals and that criminals were more likely than non-criminals to be drug users. The answer to the question 'Is frequency of drug use associated with frequency of crime?' was also 'Yes'. High-rate drug users (particularly daily users) were more likely than low-rate users to commit crimes and to commit them at a higher rate. Similarly, high-rate offenders were more likely than low-rate offenders to use drugs and to use them at a high rate. The answer to the question 'Are all drug types associated with all crime types' was 'No'. The association between recreational drug use and crime was weak. The strongest associations occurred in relation to use of heroin and crack. Similarly, there was little association between drug use and some offences, such as theft of a vehicle. However, there was a strong association between drug use and other offences, such as shoplifting. The answer to the question 'Does it matter whether drugs are used singly or in combination?' was 'Yes'. For example, heroin use in combination with no other drugs was only weakly associated with criminal behaviour, whereas heroin use in combination with crack was strongly associated with criminal behaviour. These variations are important, not only in terms of refining our knowledge about the nature of the connection between drug use and crime, but also in terms of doing something about it.

### What research evidence is there that drug misuse causes crime?

Perhaps the biggest issue of the whole debate on the drugs–crime connection is whether the two are causally connected. If they are not causally connected, then the reason for studying the connection and tackling the relationship through government interventions becomes less relevant. The issue of causality was discussed in Chapter 7. We argued that three main methods of determining causality are used in the literature.

The first are what are referred to as 'age-of-onset' studies. These compare the age of onset of drug use and the age of onset of crime to determine which came first. If crime comes before drug use, then drug use cannot cause crime. The review found that most studies reported that recreational drug use precedes criminal behaviour, but criminal behaviour precedes serious drug use (e.g. heroin, crack or cocaine use). So, what does this mean about causality? It is possible that it shows that there is no causal connection between the two variables. The differences in age of onset of drug use and crime might simply reflect the different ages of onset of the various forms of criminal behaviour and drug use (e.g. people tend to use recreational drugs before serious drugs). The results are also consistent with two causal connections: recreational drugs lead to (possibly minor) criminal behaviour and later criminal behaviour leads to serious drug misuse. However, the results are not consistent with the most popular drugs–crime explanation that serious drug use leads to crime, as most people who are likely to be involved in crime are already offending by the time they begin serious drug misuse.

Further information about the causal connection can be obtained from 'changes-over-time studies'. Most of these studies look at the effect of changes in drug use or changes in crime. In other words, if it can be shown that when drug use goes up crime goes up and when drug use goes down crime goes down, then this would provide strong evidence that the two were causally connected. In general, these studies show that the two variables are connected in the sense that changes in one appear to be associated with changes in the other. However, the research shows that this connection is not true for all drug types and all crime types. The changes are most noticeable in relation to heroin and crack use and theft and drug-dealing offences.

The cross-sectional and longitudinal research reviewed above provides only partial answers to the questions because these studies tend not to investigate the causal mechanisms involved. Studies based on interviews with drug users and offenders help bridge this gap by showing whether the individuals involved believe the relationship is causal. Most of the studies included showed that drug users and offenders tend to see their drug use and crime as causally connected. However, the manner of the connection is wide-ranging and examples were provided that covered most of the main theories of the nature of the connection.

## What do we know about methods for tackling drug-related crime?

Another aim of the book was to answer questions about the methods of tackling drug-related crime. These included 'What laws and policies address the drugs–crime connection?' and 'How effective are these laws and policies in reducing drug-related crime?'

### What laws and policies address the drugs–crime connection?

The development of laws relating to drug use and crime was discussed in Chapter 2. It was noted that it is only in recent years that any form of drug use has been defined as illegal. It was also noted that the first attempts to control drug misuse by law were instigated by the medical profession rather than the Home Office. This began a period of what has been referred to as the 'medicalization' of drug use. However, by the beginning of the twentieth century, the connection between drug misuse and other aspects of social disorder became apparent and the Home Office stepped in and helped guide legislation in what has been referred to as the period of 'criminalization' of drug misuse. However, early 'criminalization' of drug use did not address the drugs–crime connection as such. Instead, it focused on the manufacture, distribution and supply of illegal drugs. It was not until the 1990s that drug legislation began to tackle explicitly the association between drug misuse and crime. The most notable piece of legislation was the Crime and Disorder Act 1998, which introduced drug treatment and testing orders designed specifically for offenders who were also drug users. More recent legislation has continued this trend and has introduced a range of measures, including drug testing and other requirements designed specifically for drug-misusing offenders.

The development of government policy in relation to drug use and crime has a slightly longer history. The policy link between drug use and crime grew out of the concept of harm reduction that was introduced in the Advisory Council on Misuse of Drugs (ACMD) 1984 report. One of the harms caused by drug misuse was crime. However, the biggest policy push in terms of addressing both drug misuse and crime came with the government policy document *Tackling Drug Misuse: A Summary of the Government's Strategy* (Home Office 1985). The strategy focused mainly on controlling the supply of drugs, but did so in recognition of the social harms that drug misuse caused. This document preceded a line of policy documents leading up to the present-day *Updated Drug Strategy 2002* (Home Office 2002), which gives particular prominence to the idea of 'breaking the link' between drug misuse and crime.

### How effective are these laws and policies in reducing drug-related crime?

Out of the laws and policies that have been generated over the last 20–30 years have emerged a series of programmes and other interventions designed to reduce drug misuse and drug-related crime. The current review investigated the findings of research that has evaluated this broad range of programmes. The review concluded that the results of evaluative research were broadly positive. However, they varied somewhat depending on the type of programme and type of subject.

The main methods that might impact on drug-related crime can be broadly grouped into traditional treatment services and more recent criminal justice interventions. Traditional treatment services include a range of medical, social and psychological programmes. They include methadone maintenance, heroin maintenance, therapeutic communities and other approaches. They are designed primarily to reduce or eliminate drug misuse, but might also serve to reduce criminal behaviour. Criminal justice programmes include a number of court orders and sentences directed at drug-misusing offenders. They include drug treatment and testing orders, drug courts, interventions linked to probation or parole, and other methods. These interventions are designed primarily to reduce criminal behaviour among drug-misusing offenders.

The review of the literature on the effectiveness of these programmes showed generally positive findings, However, traditional treatment programmes appeared to be more effective than criminal justice programmes. This is somewhat surprising, since it is one of the central aims of drug-related criminal justice programmes to reduce crime, whereas it is one of the central aims of traditional treatment programmes to reduce drug use.

There was also some variation in effectiveness of programmes within each of these two broad categories. Some programmes such as methadone treatment, heroin treatment and therapeutic communities were found to be effective by the majority of evaluations. Other programmes such as supervision, drug testing and some of the more individual programmes were less well supported in the evaluation research. Even within individual programmes, there were signs of variation in results by programme intensity. Generally speaking, high-intensity programmes were more effective than low-intensity programmes. Finally, there was some evidence that there was variation in outcome by type of subject. Overall, males were more likely than females to show reductions in criminal behaviour, young offenders more so than older offenders, and non-white subjects were slightly more responsive than white subjects.

## What lessons can be learned for current government policy?

It was noted in Chapter 2 that the current government anti-drugs strategy is based firmly on the view that there are strong links between drug use and crime and its central aim is to break these links. The strategy is summarized in the *Updated Drug Strategy 2002* document (Home Office 2002), which amends the previous strategy outlined in *Tackling Drugs to Build a Better Britain* (Home Office 1998a). In fact, the two documents are closely linked and to some extent the most recent document continues the same broad principles outlined in the earlier report. It proposes four main courses of action for tackling drug-related crime: (1) preventing young people from using drugs, (2) reducing the availability of drugs on the streets, (3) reducing drug-related crime, and (4) reducing the number of problematic drug misusers.

### Has the anti-drugs strategy worked?

It is probably too early to tell whether the updated strategy has been effective. However, there was some doubt expressed about the effectiveness of the earlier strategy that began in 1998. Within the first 2 years of its inception, there was considerable concern raised by the government and the Home Office about whether it was realistic to achieve the objectives that had been set for it. These concerns were so great that some of the major elements of the original strategy were disbanded, which resulted in the need for an updated strategy. The main concerns related to the performance targets set. The whole issue of performance assessment was investigated by a Select Committee on Home Affairs, which was set up to consider the viability of the government's drugs strategy. The Committee reported back in a report titled *The Government's Drugs Policy: Is it Working?* (Home Office 2001). The report concluded, 'We believe it is unwise, not to say self-defeating, to set targets which have no earthly chance of success. We recommend . . . that the Government distinguishes explicitly between aspirational targets and measurable targets'. Reports from witnesses summoned by the Committee indicated that they were not impressed by the early outcomes. Representatives from the association of Chief Police Officers reported that there was no evidence that any of the desired results were being achieved. One retired chief constable reported to the Committee that, in his view, all four major indicators of drug misuse and drug-related crime had moved in the opposite direction to that proposed in the strategy documents. There is some support for this view in the trend results of the New English and Welsh Arrestee Drug Abuse Monitoring (NEW-ADAM) programme, which investigated drug misuse among arrestees during the period 1999–2002 (the period immediately following the implementation of the strategy) (Holloway *et al.* 2004). The report found that, during this early period, the proportion of arrestees testing positive for opiates and/or cocaine increased across the eight sites investigated. This is not to say that the early or later versions of the strategy have failed. The most that can be said is that the performance targets have not yet been met. There has been substantial ground work carried out in setting the conditions for future outcomes and it is possible that some of the more favourable results might take more time to be realized. Nevertheless, the early signs are not good.

## The importance of type of intervention

The current review has addressed some issues that might be relevant to government drugs policy. One thing that has been learned is that not all programmes are equally effective. However, the current policy documents described above do not give any clear direction on the types of treatment that should be used to reduce drug-related crime. The documents provide support for the new criminal justice interventions. However, the document does not discriminate between different kinds of criminal justice programme or different kinds of treatment. It could be argued that there is nothing wrong with this, as the review has shown that most programmes work at least some of the time. However, this ignores the fact that some programmes might work better than others. For example, there is strong evidence that therapeutic communities and drug courts reduce criminal behaviour. There is less strong evidence that supervision and aftercare following drug treatment, and drug testing reduce offending. Hence, there might be something to be gained in prioritizing certain kinds of interventions over others.

## The importance of the quality of the intervention

The summary of evaluative research presented in Chapter 8 shows that there is some variation in the effectiveness of programmes depending on the quality or intensity of the programmes. More intensive interventions tend to produce stronger evidence of success than less intensive programmes. This applies to most of the common measures of intensity, including dosage levels, whether the programme is continuous or interrupted, time in treatment, whether the subject completes or terminates the programme, and whether treatments are combined in some way. The quality of the treatment might be an important factor to take into consideration in determining which kinds of programme to use. It would appear from these findings that government drugs policy is likely to be more effective if it focuses on promoting the best quality and most intensive treatment programmes. This could be done by giving some kind of priority to the development and use of the strongest versions of these programmes.

### The importance of matching subjects and treatments

There is some evidence that more favourable results are sometimes obtained for males compared with females, young compared with old, and (in one study at least) non-whites compared with whites. There is insufficient research available to determine which programmes perform better for one group of subjects over another. Further research should be done in this area. However, in the meantime, some attempt might be made to match more closely the needs of particular offenders and the type of programme made available to them. This would be very resource intensive. Nevertheless, the case remains that in order to obtain the best results from criminal justice and treatment interventions, it might be necessary to match provisions and clients.

## What lessons can be learned for research methods?

### Lessons from research on the drugs–crime connection

The review of research on the drugs–crime connection has identified a number of gaps in the research literature. First, there are a large number of relevant studies on the statistical association. However, there are very few rigorous reviews of these studies. In particular, there are no systematic reviews that have used meta-analysis techniques. This is unfortunate because it is important that the body of knowledge can be viewed as a whole. This would help lessons to be learned and it would also help to direct future research. One reason for the absence of meta-analyses might be that traditionally these have been used only in studies of treatment effectiveness. However, the principles of the approach can be applied to other bodies of research and studies on the drugs–crime connection are particularly suitable for this. It would be useful to know, for example, whether the association between drug use and crime were significantly stronger when looking at certain kinds of drugs and certain kinds of users.

Second, there are relatively few relevant studies on the causal connection. We mentioned in Chapter 7 that the main quantitative methods found in the literature were 'age-of-onset' studies and 'changes-over-time' studies. However, there are relatively few of these studies and most of these have been conducted in the United States. In particular, there have been very few longitudinal studies of any kind that have investigated the connection between drug use and crime and none to our knowledge that have been designed specifically for this purpose. This kind of research is invaluable for both 'age-of-onset' and 'changes-over-time' research. It can help identify the temporal order of onset of different kinds of drugs and different kinds of crime. It can also be helpful in monitoring continuation of drug use and crime and the factors that influence variations in drug use and variations in crime. The research could ultimately be used to assist in understanding the desistance process. Very little longitudinal research has addressed the issue of desistance from drug use or the temporal order of terminating drug use and terminating crime.

Third, there is a need for more qualitative research in the area. There are few studies that have addressed the causal mechanisms from the subject's perspective. Some studies have tapped the views of offenders and drug users. However, these attempts have been unsystematic. More qualitative research needs to be done which can help distinguish details of the causal connection. This could provide breakdowns of differences between different types of drugs and crime and different kinds of drug users and offenders. Qualitative research could also be used to investigate onset, continuation and termination in drug use and crime. It is possible that different explanations might be required at different points in the drug-using and criminal career.

## Lessons from evaluations of interventions

One problem that emerges from reviewing the research evaluations on the effectiveness of treatment and criminal justice programmes is that insufficient attention is paid to the causal mechanisms involved. This is a similar point to that made in relation to the drugs–crime connection studies mentioned above. Few of the studies have tackled the problem of causality beyond identifying the three statistical markers of a causal connection (association, temporal order and non-spuriousness). However, it is important to know more precisely how the programme worked. This would require knowing more about the mechanisms and processes involved by which cause is linked to effect. It is usually considered good practice when conducting quasi-experimental or experimental evaluation designs to build into the research a method for determining the causal mechanisms. This requires constructing hypotheses about the ways in which the cause and effect might be connected. It might also involve collecting additional information about potential intermediary factors. There is also an opportunity for more qualitative research in this area. Qualitative research can help identify the relationship between cause and effect from the subject's perspective. This might be done through qualitative research that follows drug users through the treatment process and monitors their progress over time. It would be useful to know whether the users' thought that their drug use and offending had reduced and what they thought were the causes of the reduction.

Another problem is the familiar issue of research quality. In our own systematic review of the literature on both the drugs–crime connection and the evaluation of effectiveness, many studies initially selected were rejected on grounds of weak methodology. The most common weakness lay in the research design and the omission of any kind of comparison group. Without a comparison, it is not possible to determine whether the experimental group performed better or worse than might have been expected in the absence of the intervention. In terms of causality, the design fails to rule out the possibility than any correlation might be the result of extraneous factors. Another problem is that of potential non-equivalence of experimental and comparison groups in quasi-experimental designs, especially when they have been selected by medical staff rather than the evaluators to receive particular treatment types. It is possible that the most promising clients are selected to receive the most promising treatment option. Such differences are likely to affect the study outcome. One solution is to conduct more controlled trials and to allocate clients randomly to experimental and control conditions.

The third problem is the problem of research coordination. It is clear from this review that research in this area is varied and largely uncoordinated. It is characterized by different research teams exploring different outcomes, among different populations, over different time periods, using different methods. Drawing conclusions from such a variable body of studies is particularly difficult. A great deal would be gained from adopting greater consistency across research studies to facilitate systematic reviews. It is accepted that it is hard to coordinate the output of research conducted by different individuals in different locations. However, it is feasible to encourage a research culture that works to agreed standards of evaluation design. The use of guidelines developed by bodies such as the Campbell Collaboration should be encouraged. The major funding bodies might also consider building minimum requirements into bona fide evaluations of treatment programmes.

## Where now?

We are entering a period of time in which the connection between drug use and crime is probably stronger than it has ever been. The vast majority of prisoners are drug users and the vast majority of drug users in treatment are criminals. There is no doubt that drug use and crime are connected. However, the absence of effective research on the causal nature of the connection means that we still do not know why.

It is implausible to think that the vast majority of drug-misusing prisoners and arrestees are all new recruits to crime as a result of a recent engagement in drug misuse. If this were so, then where have all the traditional criminals gone who would have otherwise filled the prisons? It is somewhat more plausible to believe that some of the traditional criminals who would have been there anyway have started using drugs. Hence, for some reason, some criminals have begun using drugs. We also know that a large proportion of drug users in treatment are criminals. As before, it is implausible to think that the vast majority of drug users in treatment are there solely because of their criminal behaviour. At least some of them would have been drug users anyway, regardless of their involvement in crime. Hence, for some reason, some drug users have begun committing crimes. It is enormously important that researchers begin to come up with some convincing answers as to why this has happened.

It is also important that somebody comes up with an effective solution to the drugs–crime problem. Effective solutions are likely to derive from effective research that can provide fundamental knowledge about the processes that link drug use and crime and practical knowledge about what works and why. There are signs that research is developing in these areas and that effective programmes are being implemented. However, neither task can be considered satisfactorily completed. Much more work needs to be done in terms of both research and practice before more noticeable progress can be made.

## Further reading

The main current policy document in the UK is the *Updated Drug Strategy 2002* (Home Office 2002). General news about government drugs policy can be found on the Home Office website (http://www.homeoffice.gov.uk). The DrugScope guide to UK drug policy is also worth looking at http://www.drugscope.org.uk. The DrugScope site is also useful for keeping up-to-date with news about the current UK drugs strategy and policy developments.

# References

Advisory Council on the Misuse of Drugs (1984) *Prevention*. London: HMSO.
Advisory Council on the Misuse of Drugs (1988) *AIDS and Drug Misuse, Part 1*. London: HMSO.
Alcohol Concern (2004) *Hangover Cure for Londoners at Alcohol Summit: Almost 250,000 Engaging in Risky Drinking – Costing the Capital £294m per annum* (www.alcoholconcern.org.uk/servlets/doc/800: accessed 31 August 2004).
Anglin, M.D. and Speckart, G. (1986) Narcotics use, property crime, and dealing: structural dynamics across the addiction career, *Journal of Quantitative Criminology*, 2(4): 355–75.
Apospori, E., Vega, W.A., Zimmerman, R., Warheit, G.J. and Gil, A.J. (1995) A longitudinal study on conditional effects of deviant behavior on drug use among three racial/ethnic groups of adolescents, in H.B. Kaplan (ed.) *Drugs, Crime, and Other Deviant Adaptations*. New York: Plenum Press.
Ashton, R. (2002) *This is Heroin*. London: Sanctuary.
Aust, R., Sharp, C. and Goulden, C. (2002) *Prevalence of Drug Use: Key Findings from the 2001/2002 British Crime Survey*. Findings #182. London: Home Office.
Balding, J. (2002) *Young People in 2002*. Exeter: Schools Health Education Unit.
Ball, J.C., Rosen, L., Fluceck, J.A. and Nurco, D.N. (1981) The criminality of heroin addicts when addicted and when off opiates, in J.A. Inciardi (ed.) *The Drugs–Crime Connection*. Beverly Hills, CA: Sage.
Ball, J.C., Shaffer, J.W. and Nurco, D.N. (1983) The day-to-day criminality of heroin addicts in Baltimore: a study in the continuity of offense rates, *Drug and Alcohol Dependence*, 12: 119–42.
Baumer, E., Lauritsen, J.L., Rosenfeld, R. and Wright, R. (1998) The influence of crack cocaine on robbery, burglary, and homicide rates: a cross-city longitudinal analysis, *Journal of Research in Crime and Delinquency*, 35(3): 316–40.
Bean, P. (2001) *Drugs and Crime*. Collumpton: Willan.
Bennett, T. (1988) The British experience with heroin regulation, *Law and Contemporary Problems*, 51(1): 299–314.

Bennett, T. (1990) Links between drug misuse and crime, *British Journal of Addiction*, 85(7): 833–40.

Bennett, T. (2000) *Drugs and Crime: The Results of the Second Developmental Stage of the NEW-ADAM Programme*, Home Office Research Study #205. London: Home Office.

Bennett, T. and Holloway, K. (2004) Possession and use of illegal guns among offenders in England and Wales, *The Howard Journal of Criminal Justice*, 43(3): 237–52.

Bennett, T. and Holloway, K. (in press) Disaggregating the relationship between drug misuse and crime. *Australian and New Zealand Journal of Criminology*.

Bennett, T. and Holloway, K. (in prep.) *The Effectiveness of Criminal Justice and Treatment Programmes in Reducing Drug-Related Crime: A Systematic Review*, Home Office Research Study. London: Home Office.

Bennett, T. and Wright, R. (1984a) *Burglars on Burglary: Prevention and the Offender*. Aldershot: Gower.

Bennett, T. and Wright, R. (1984b) The relationship between alcohol use and burglary, *British Journal of Addiction*, 79(4): 431–7.

Bennett, T. and Wright, R. (1986) The drug-taking careers of opioid users. *The Howard Journal of Criminal Justice*, 25(1): 1–12.

Berridge, V. (1984) Drugs and social policy: the establishment of drug control in Britain 1900–1930, *British Journal of Addiction*, 79(1): 17–29.

Berridge, V. and Edwards, G. (1981) *Opium and the People: Opiate Use in Nineteenth-Century England*. London: Allen Lane.

Best, D., Sidwell, C., Gossop, M., Harris, J. and Strang, J. (2001) Crime and expenditure among polydrug misusers seeking treatment, *British Journal of Criminology*, 41: 119–26.

Biron, L.L., Brochu, S. and Desjardins, L. (1995) The issue of drugs and crime among a sample of incarcerated women, *Deviant Behaviour*, 16(1): 25–43.

Borrill, J., Maden, A., Martin, A. *et al.* (2003) Substance misuse among white and black/mixed race female prisoners, in M. Ramsay (ed.) *Prisoners' Drug Use and Treatment: Seven Studies*, Home Office Research Study #267. London: Home Office.

Brain Committee (1961) *Report of the Interdepartmental Committee on Drug Addiction*. London: HMSO.

Brain, K., Howard, P. and Bottomley, T. (1998) *Evolving Crack Cocaine Careers: New Users, Quitters and Long Term Combination Drug Users in N.W. England*. Manchester: University of Manchester.

Bramley-Harker, E. (2001) *Sizing the UK Market for Illicit Drugs*, Research, Development and Statistics Directorate Occasional Paper #74. London: Home Office.

Braucht, G.N., Kirby, M.W. and Berry, G.J. (1978) An empirical typology of multiple drug abusers, in D.R. Wesson, A.S. Carlin, K.M. Adams and G. Beschner (eds.) *Polydrug Abuse: The Results of a National Collaborative Study*. New York: Academic Press.

Brecht, M.L., Anglin, M.D. and Wang, J.C. (1993) Treatment effectiveness for legally coerced versus voluntary methadone maintenance clients, *American Journal of Drug and Alcohol Abuse*, 19(1): 89–106.

Britt, C.L., Gottfredson, M.R. and Goldkamp, J.S. (1992) Drug testing and pretrial misconduct: an experiment on the specific deterrent effects of drug monitoring dependents on pretrial release, *Journal of Research in Crime and Delinquency*, 29(1): 62–78.

Brochu, S. (1994) Intoxication and violence: aggression or excuse, *Deviance and Society*, 18: 431–45.

Brochu, S. (2001) *The Relationship Between Drugs and Crime*. Montreal: University of Montreal (www.parl.gc.ca/37/1/1/parlbus/commbus/senate/Com-e/ille-e/presentat . . . /brochu-e.ht: accessed 10 July 2003).

Brown, B.S., O'Grady, K.E., Battjes, R.J. *et al.* (2001) Effectiveness of a stand-alone aftercare program for drug-involved offenders, *Journal of Substance Abuse Treatment*, 21: 185–92.

Brownstein, H. and Crossland, C. (2002) *Drugs and Crime Research Forum: Introduction*. Washington, DC: National Institute of Justice, US Department of Justice (www.ojp.usdoj.gov/nij/drugscrime/Introduction.pdf: accessed 1 September 2004).

Bushman, B. (1997) Effects of alcohol on human aggression: validity of proposed explanations, in M. Galanter (ed.) *Recent Developments in Alcoholism, Vol. 13: Alcoholism and Violence*. New York: Plenum Press.

Byqvist, S. (1999) Criminality among female drug abusers, *Journal of Psychoactive Drugs*, 31(4): 353–62.

Cabinet Office (2001) *Tackling the Diseases of Poverty*. London: Performance and Innovation Unit, Cabinet Office.

Cabinet Office (2004) *Alcohol Harm Reduction Strategy for England*. London: Strategy Unit, Cabinet Office.

Carpenter, C., Glassner, B., Johnson, B.D. and Loughlin, J. (1988) *Kids, Drugs, and Crime*. Toronto: Lexington.

Chaiken, J.M. and Chaiken, M.R. (1990) Drugs and predatory crime, in M. Tonry and J.Q. Wilson (eds.) *Drugs and Crime*. London: University of Chicago Press.

Chanhatasilpa, C., MacKenzie, D. and Hickman, L. (2000) The effectiveness of community-based programmes for chemically dependent offenders: a review and assessment of the research, *Journal of Substance Abuse Treatment*, 19: 383–93.

Clayton, R.R. (1986) Multiple drug use epidemiology, correlates and consequences, *Recent Developments in Alcoholism*, 4: 7–38.

Collins, J.J. and Messerschmidt, P.M. (1993) Epidemiology of alcohol-related violence, *Alcohol Health and Research World*, 17(2): 93–100.

Collins, J., Hubbard, R. and Rachal, J. (1985) Expensive drug use and illegal income: a test of explanatory hypotheses, *Criminology*, 23(4): 743–64.

Condon, J. and Smith, N. (2003) *Prevalence of Drug Use: Key Findings from the 2002/2003 British Crime Survey*, Home Office Findings #229. London: Home Office.

Corkery, J.M. (2002) *Drug Seizure and Offender Statistics, United Kingdom 2000*. London: Home Office.

Corkery, J.M. and Airs, J. (2003) *Seizures of Drugs in the UK 2001*, Home Office Findings #202. London: Home Office.

Cromwell, P.F., Olson, J.N., Avary, D.W. and Marks, A. (1991) How drugs affect decisions by burglars, *International Journal of Offender Therapy and Comparative Criminology*, 35(4): 310–21.

Cross, J.C., Johnson, B.D., Rees, D.W. and Liberty, H.J. (2001) Supporting the habit: income generation activities of frequent crack users compared with frequent users of other hard drugs, *Drug and Alcohol Dependence*, 64: 191–201.

Curruthers, S. and Loxley, W. (2002) Attitudes of novice heroin injectors towards non-injecting routes of administration to prevent the transmission of blood borne viruses, *International Journal of Drug Policy*, 13(1): 69–74.

Dalla, R.L. (2002) Night moves: a qualitative investigation of street-level sex work, *Psychology of Women Quarterly*, 26: 63–73.

Datesman, S. (1987) Women, crime, and drugs, in J.A. Inciardi (ed.) *The Drugs–Crime Connection*. Beverly Hills, CA: Sage.

De Micheli, D. and Formigoni, M.L.O.S. (2002) Are reasons for the first use of drugs and family circumstances predictors of future use patterns?, *Addictive Behaviors*, 27(1): 87–100.

Department of Health (2002) *Prevalence of HIV and Hepatitis Infections in the United Kingdom: Annual Report of the Unlinked Anonymous Prevalence Monitoring Programme*. London: Department of Health.

Department of Health (2003) *Statistics on Alcohol: England 2003*. Statistical Bulletin 2003/20. London: Department of Health.

Department of Health and Human Services (2003) *National Survey of Substance Abuse Treatment Services (N-SSATS): 2002. Data on Substance Abuse Treatment Facilities*. Rockville, MD: National Clearinghouse for Alcohol and Drug Information.

Dobinson, I. and Ward, P. (1984) *Drugs and Crime: A Survey of NSW Prison Property Offenders*. Sydney, NSW: Bureau of Crime Statistics and Research.

Dole, V.P., Robinson, J.W., Orraca, J. *et al.* (1969) Methadone treatment of randomly selected criminal addicts, *New England Journal of Medicine*, 280: 1372–5.

Dolin, B. (2001) *National Drug Policy: The Netherlands*. Report prepared for the Senate Special Committee on Illegal Drugs, Library of Parliament.

Domier, C.P., Simon, S.L., Rawson, R.A., Huber, A. and Ling, W. (2000) A comparison of injecting and noninjecting methamphetamine users, *Journal of Psychoactive Drugs*, 32(2): 229–32.

Drug Enforcement Agency (2002) *Chapter 13 – Drug Abuse Prevention and Control*. Washington, DC: DEA (www.dea.gov/pubs/csa/841.htm: accessed 31 August 2004).

Drug Policy Alliance (2003a) *Drug Policy Around the World: The Netherlands* (www.lindesmith.org/global/drugpolicyby/westerneurop/thenetherlan/: accessed 31 August 2004).

Drug Policy Alliance (2003b) *Drug Policy Around the World: Switzerland* (www.lindesmith.org/global/drugpolicyby/westerneurop/switzerland/: accessed 31 August 2004).

Drug Policy Alliance (2003c) *Drug Policy Around the World: Sweden* (www. lindesmith.org/global/drugpolicyby/westerneurop/sweden/: accessed 31 August 2004).

Drug Policy Alliance (2003d) *Drug Policy Around the World: United States* (www.lindesmith.org/global/drugpolicyby/northamerica/unitedstates/: accessed 31 August 2004).

DrugScope (2004) *Drug Abuse/Misuse/Use* (www.drugscope.org.uk/druginfo/drugsearch/ds_results.asp?file=%5Cwip%5C11%5C1%5C1%5Cdrug_abuse_misuse_ use. html: accessed 31 August 2004).

Edwards, G. (1969) The British approach to the treatment of heroin addiction, *Lancet*, i: 768–72.

Edwards, G. (1981) Drug problems in Britain – the background, in G. Griffiths and

C. Busch (eds.) *Drug Problems in Britain: A Review of Ten Years*. London: Academic Press.

Ekblom, P. (1999) Towards a discipline of crime prevention: a systematic approach to its nature, range and concepts, in T.H. Bennett (ed.) *Preventing Crime and Disorder, Targeting Strategies and Responsibilities*. Cambridge: Institute of Criminology.

Elliott, D.S. and Huizinga, D. (1984) *The Relationship between Delinquency Behavior and ADM Problems*. Report prepared for the Alcohol, Drug Abuse, and Mental Health Administration/Office of Juvenile Justice and Delinquency Prevention State-of-the-Art Conference on Juvenile Offenders with Serious Drug, Alcohol, and Mental Health Problems, April.

Elliott, D.S., Huizinga, D. and Menard, S. (1989) *Multiple Problem Youth: Delinquency, Substance Use and Mental Health Problems*. New York: Springer-Verlag.

Erens, B. and Laiho, J. (2001) Alcohol consumption, in B. Erens, P. Primatesta and G. Prior (eds.) *Health Survey for England – The Health of Minority Ethnic Groups 1999*. London: The Stationery Office.

Erickson, P.G., Butters, J., McGillicuddy, P. and Hallgren, A. (2000) Crack and prostitution: gender, myths and experiences, *Journal of Drug Issues*, 30(4): 767–88.

European Monitoring Centre for Drugs and Drug Addiction (2003) *The State of the Drugs Problem in the European Union and Norway*. Luxembourg: EMCDDA.

Fagan, J. (1990) Intoxication and aggression, in M. Tonry and J.Q. Wilson (eds.) *Drugs and Crime*. London: University of Chicago Press.

Fagan, J. (1993) Set and setting revisited: influence of alcohol and illicit drugs on the social context of violent events, in S.E. Martin (ed.) *Alcohol and Interpersonal Violence: Fostering Multidisciplinary Perspectives*. Rockville, MD: US Department of Health and Human Services, National Institutes of Health.

Farabee, D., Joshi, V. and Anglin, D.M. (2001a) Addiction careers and criminal specialization, *Crime and Delinquency*, 47(2): 196–220.

Farabee, D., Shen, H., Hser, Y., Grella, C. and Anglin, M. (2001b) The effect of drug treatment on criminal behavior among adolescents in DATOS-A, *Journal of Adolescent Research*, 16(6): 679–96.

Faupel, C.E. and Klockars, C.B. (1987) Drug–crime connections: elaborations from the life histories of hard core heroin addicts, *Social Problems*, 34: 54–68.

Fergusson, D.M., Horwood, L.J. and Swain-Campbell, N. (2002) Cannabis use and psychosocial adjustment in adolescence and young adulthood, *Addiction*, 97(9): 1123–35.

Fitzgerald, J. and Chilvers, M. (2002) *Multiple Drug Use Among Police Detainees*, Crime and Justice Bulletin #65. Sydney, NSW: NSW Bureau of Crime Statistics and Research.

Fortson, R. (2002) *Misuse of Drugs and Drug Trafficking Offences*. London: Sweet & Maxwell.

Fountain, J., Griffiths, P., Farrell, M., Gossop, M. and Strang, J. (1997) Diversion tactics: how a sample of drug misusers in treatment obtained surplus drugs to sell on the illicit drug market, *International Journal of Drug Policy*, 9(3): 159–67.

French, M. and Zarkin, G. (1992) Effects of drug abuse treatment on legal and illegal earnings, *Contemporary Policy Issues*, 10(2): 98–110.

French, M.T., McGeary, K.A., Chitwood, D.D. *et al.* (2000) Chronic drug use and crime, *Substance Abuse*, 21(2): 95–109.

Gandossy, R.P., Williams, J.R., Cohen, J. and Harwood, H.J. (1980) *Drugs and Crime: A Survey and Analysis of the Literature*. Washington, DC: US Department of Justice.

Ghodse, H., Reynolds, M., Baldacchino, A. *et al.* (2002) Treating an opiate-dependent inpatient population: a one-year follow-up study of treatment completers and noncompleters, *Addictive Behaviors*, 27: 765–78.

Giannini, J., Miller, N.S., Loiselle, R.H. and Turner, C.E. (1993) Cocaine-associated violence and relationship to route of administration, *Journal of Substance Abuse Treatment*, 10(1): 67–9.

Goldstein, P.J. (1985) The drugs/violence nexus: a tripartite conceptual framework, *Journal of Drug Issues*, 39: 143–74.

Goode, E. (1997) *Between Politics and Reason*. New York: St Martin's Press.

Gordon, J., Moriarty, L. and Grant, P. (2000) The impact of a juvenile residential treatment center on minority offenders, *Journal of Criminal Justice*, 16(2): 194–208.

Gossop, M. and Roy, A. (1977) Hostility, crime and drug dependence, *British Journal of Psychiatry*, 130: 272–8.

Gossop, M., Marsden, J., Stewart, D. and Treacy, S. (2000) Routes of drug administration and multiple drug use: regional variations among clients seeking treatment at programmes throughout England, *Addiction*, 95(8): 1197–1206.

Gossop, M., Marsden, J., Stewart, D. and Kidd, T. (2003) The national treatment outcome research study (NTORS): 4–5 year follow-up results, *Addiction*, 98: 291–303.

Gottfredson, D. and Exum, M. (2002) The Baltimore City Drug Treatment Court: one-year results from a randomized study, *Journal of Research in Crime and Delinquency*, 39(3): 337–56.

Gottfredson, D.C., Najaka, S.S. and Kearley, B. (2003) Effectiveness of drug treatment courts: evidence from a randomized trial, *Criminology and Public Policy*, 2(2): 171–96.

Gottfredson, M.R. and Hirschi, T. (1990) *A General Theory of Crime*. Stanford, CA: Stanford University Press.

Goulden, C. and Sondhi, A. (2001) *At the Margins: Drug Use by Vulnerable Young People in the 1998/99 Youth Lifestyles Survey*, Home Office Research Study #228. London: Home Office.

Graham, N. and Wish, E.D. (1994) Drug use among female arrestees: onset, patterns, and relationships to prostitution, *Journal of Drug Issues*, 24(2): 315–29.

Groom, C., Davies, T. and Balchin, S. (1998) Developing a methodology for measuring illegal activity for the UK national accounts, *Economic Trends*, 356: 33–71.

Gunne, L.-M. and Grönbladh, L. (1981) The Swedish methadone maintenance program: a controlled study, *Drug and Alcohol Dependence*, 7: 249–56.

Haapanen, R. and Britton, L. (2002) Drug testing for youthful offenders on parole: an experimental evaluation, *Criminology and Public Policy*, 1(2): 217–44.

Hall, W. (1996) *Methadone Maintenance Treatment as a Crime Control Measure*, Crime and Justice Bulletin #29. Sydney, NSW: NSW Bureau of Crime Statistics and Research.

HAPPY EASTER 😊

Hall, W., Bell, J. and Carless, J. (1993) Crime and drug use among applicants for methadone maintenance, *Drug and Alcohol Dependence*, 31: 123–9.

Hammersley, R. and Morrison, V. (1987) Effects of polydrug use on the criminal activities of heroin-users, *British Journal of Addiction*, 82: 899–906.

Hammersley, R., Forsyth, A., Morrison, V. and Davies, J.B. (1989) The relationship between crime and opioid use, *British Journal of Addiction*, 84: 1029–43.

Hammersley, R., Ditton, J., Smith, I. and Short, E. (1999) Patterns of ecstasy use by drug users, *British Journal of Criminology*, 39(4): 625–47.

Hammersley, R., Marsland, L. and Reid, M. (2003) *Substance Use by Young Offenders: The Impact of the Normalisation of Drug Use in the Early Years of the 21st Century*, Home Office Research Study #261. London: Home Office.

Hanlon, T.E., Nuren, D.N., Kinlock, T.M. and Duszynski, K.R. (1990) Trends in criminal activity and drug use over an addiction career, *American Journal of Drug and Alcohol Abuse*, 16: 223–38.

Harrison, L.D. and Gfroerer, J. (1992) The intersection of drug use and criminal behavior: results from the national household survey on drug abuse, *Crime and Delinquency*, 38(4): 422–43.

Hartnoll, R.L., Mitcheson, M.C., Battersby, A. *et al.* (1980) Evaluation of heroin maintenance in a controlled trial, *Archives of General Psychiatry*, 37(8): 877–84.

Hawke, J.M., Jainchill, N. and De Leon, G.J. (2000) Adolescent amphetamine users in treatment, client profiles and treatment outcomes, *Journal of Psychoactive Drugs*, 32(1): 95–105.

Henggeler, S.W., Borduin, C.M., Melton, G.B. *et al.* (1991) Effects of multisystemic therapy on drug use and abuse in serious juvenile offenders: a progress report from two outcome studies, *Family Dynamics of Addiction Quarterly*, 1(3): 40–51.

Holloway, K. and Bennett, T. (2004) *The Results of the First Two Years of the NEW-ADAM Programme*, Home Office Online Report #19/04. London: Home Office (www.homeoffice.gov.uk/rds/pdfs04/rdsolr1904.pdf).

Holloway, K. and Bennett, T. (in prep.) *The Statistical Association and Causal Connection between Drug Use and Crime: A Systematic Review*. Mid-Glamorgan: University of Glamorgan.

Holloway, K., Bennett, T. and Lower, C. (2004) *Trends in Drug Use and Offending: The Results of the NEW-ADAM Programme 1999–2002*, Home Office Findings #219. London: Home Office.

Home Affairs Committee (2002) House of Commons Home Affairs Committee Press Notice #18, 22 May 2002.

Home Office (1985) *Tackling Drug Misuse: A Summary of the Government's Strategy*. London: Home Office.

Home Office (1990) *UK Action on Drug Misuse: The Government's Strategy*. London: Home Office.

Home Office (1995) *Tackling Drugs Together: A Strategy for England 1995–1998*. London: HMSO.

Home Office (1998a) *Tackling Drugs to Build a Better Britain: The Government's 10-Year Strategy for Tackling Drug Misuse*. London: The Stationery Office.

Home Office (1998b) *Tackling Drugs to Build a Better Britain: The Government's 10-Year Strategy for Tackling Drug Misuse – Guidance Notes*. London: The Stationery Office.

Home Office (2001) *The Government's Drug Policy: Is it Working?* Home Affairs Select Committee Inquiry (www.publications.parliament.uk/pa/cm200102/cmselect/cmhaff/318/31802.htm: accessed 6 September 2004).

Home Office (2002) *Updated Drug Strategy 2002.* London: Home Office.

Hough, M. (1996) *Drug Misuse and the Criminal Justice System: A Review of the Literature.* London: Home Office.

Hough, M., Clancy, A., McSweeney, T. and Turnbull, P.J. (2003) *The Impact of Drug Treatment and Testing Orders on Offending: Two Year Reconviction Results*, Home Office Research Findings #184. London: Home Office.

Hser, Y., Longshore, D. and Anglin, M.D. (1994) Prevalence of drug use among criminal offender populations: implications for control, treatment, and policy, in D.L. MacKenzie and C.D. Uchida (eds.) *Drugs and the Criminal Justice System: Evaluating Public Policy Initiatives.* Thousand Oaks, CA: Sage.

Hser, Y., Boyle, K. and Anglin, M.D. (1998) Drug use and correlates among sexually transmitted disease patients, emergency room patients and arrestees, *Journal of Drug Issues*, 28(2): 437–53.

Hser, Y.I., Grella, C.E., Hubbard, R.L. *et al.* (2001) An evaluation of drug treatments for adolescents in 4 US cities, *Archives of General Psychiatry*, 58: 689–95.

Hunt, D.E. (1991) Stealing and dealing: cocaine and property crimes, *NIDA Research Monograph Series*, 110: 139–50.

Hunt, D.E., Lipton, D.S. and Spunt, B. (1984) Patterns of criminal activity among methadone clients and current narcotics users not in treatment, *Journal of Drug Issues*, 14(4): 687–702.

Inciardi, J.A. (1981) *The Drugs–Crime Connection.* London: Sage.

Inciardi, J.A. (1995) Crack, crack house sex, and HIV risk, *Archives of Sexual Behavior*, 24(3): 249–69.

Inciardi, J.A. and Pottieger, A.E. (1986) Drug use and crime among two cohorts of women narcotics users: an empirical assessment, *Journal of Drug Issues*, 16(1): 91–106.

Inciardi, J.A. and Pottieger, A.E. (1991) Kids, crack and crime, *Journal of Drug Issues*, 21(2): 257–70.

Inciardi, J.A. and Surratt, M.A. (2001) Drug use, street crime and sex-trading among cocaine-dependent women: implications for public health and criminal justice policy, *Journal of Psychoactive Drugs*, 33(4): 379–89.

Inciardi, J.A., McBride, D.C., McCoy, H.V. and Chitwood, D.D. (1994) Recent research on the crack/cocaine/crime connection, *Studies on Crime and Crime Prevention*, 3: 63–82.

International Center for Alcohol Policy (2002) *Drinking Age Limits*, ICAP Report #4. Washington, DC: ICAP.

Jacobs, B.A. (1999) Drug markets and transition, *British Journal of Criminology*, 39(4): 555–74.

Jarvis, J. and Parker, H. (1989) Young heroin users and crime: how do the new users finance their habits, *British Journal of Criminology*, 29(2): 175–85.

Jay, M. (2000) *Emperor of Dreams: Drugs in the Nineteenth Century.* Sawtry: Dedalus.

Johnston, L.D. (1998) *Reasons for Use, Abstention, and Quitting Illicit Drug Use by American Adolescents*, Monitoring the Future Occasional Paper #44. Ann Arbor, MI: Institute for Social Research, The University of Michigan.

Johnston, L.D., O'Malley, P.M. and Eveland, L.K. (1978) Drugs and delinquency: a search for causal connections, in D.B. Kandel (ed.) *Longitudinal Research on Drug Use*. Washington, DC. Hemisphere.

Jones, A. and Millar, T. (2000) *Mortality and Drug Misuse: Making Sense of Mortality Data*. Manchester: University of Manchester Drug Misuse Research Unit.

Kaminski, D. and Decorte, T. (2004) *Problematic Drug Use*. Wetenschapsstraat, Brussels: Belgian Federal Science Policy Office (www.belspo.be/belspo/fedra/ proj.asp?l=en&COD=DR/11: accessed 31 August 2004).

Kaplan, H.B., Tolle, J.R. and Yoshida, T. (2001) Substance-use induced diminution of violence: a countervailing effect in longitudinal perspective, *Criminology*, 39(1): 205–24.

Kenny, D.A. (1979) *Correlation and Causality*. Chichester: Wiley.

Klee, H. (1997) *Amphetamine Use: International Perspectives on Current Trends*. Amsterdam: Harwood Academic.

Kokkevi, A., Liappas, J., Boukouvala, V. *et al.* (1993) Criminality in a sample of drug abusers in Greece, *Drug and Alcohol Dependence*, 31: 111–21.

Kraemer, H.C., Kazdin, A.E., Offord, D.R. *et al.* (1997) Coming to terms with risk, *Archives of General Psychiatry*, 54: 337–43.

Kuhns, J.B., Heide, K.M. and Silverman, I. (1992) Substance use/misuse among female prostitutes and female arrestees, *International Journal of the Addictions*, 27(11): 1283–92.

Lafrenière, G. (2002) *National Drug Policy: Sweden*. Report prepared for the Senate Special Committee on Illegal Drugs, Library of Parliament.

Lam, J.A., Jekel, J.F., Thompson, K.S. *et al.* (1995) Assessing the value of a short-term residential drug treatment program for homeless men, *Journal of Addictive Diseases*, 14(4): 21–39.

Latessa, E.J. and Moon, M.M. (1992) The effectiveness of acupuncture in an outpatient drug treatment program, *Journal of Contemporary Criminal Justice*, 8(4): 317–31.

Leri, F., Bruneau, J. and Stewart, J. (2003) Understanding polydrug use: review of heroin and cocaine co-use, *Addiction*, 98(1): 7–22.

Levine, H.J., Reif, S., Lee, M.T., Ritter, G.A. and Horgan, C.M. (2004) *Alcohol and Drug Services Study (ADSS). The National Treatment System: Outpatient Facilities*. Rockville, MD: Substance Abuse and Mental Health Services Administration.

Lindesmith, A.R. (1968) *Addiction and Opiates*. Chicago, IL: Aldine.

Lipsey, M.W., Wilson, D.B., Cohen, M.A. and Derzon, J.H. (1997) Is there a causal relationship between alcohol use and violence? A synthesis of evidence, in M. Galanter (ed.) *Recent Developments in Alcoholism, Vol. 13: Alcoholism and Violence*. New York: Plenum Press.

Liriano, S. and Ramsay, M. (2003) Prisoners' drug use before prison and the links with crime, in M. Ramsay (ed.) *Prisoners' Drug Use and Treatment: Seven Research Studies*, Home Office Research Study #267. London: Home Office.

Lupton, R., Wilson, A., May, T., Warburton, H. and Turnbull, P.J. (2002) *A Rock and a Hard Place: Drug Markets in Deprived Neighbourhoods*, Home Office Research Study #240. London: Home Office.

MacCoun, R., Kilmer, B. and Reuter, P. (2002) *Research on Drugs–Crime Linkages: The Next Generation*. Washington, DC: National Institute of Justice (www.ncjrs.org/pdffiles1/nij/194616c.pdf: accessed 1 September 2004).

Maddux, J.F. and Desmond, D.P. (2000) Addiction or dependence?, *Addiction*, 95(5): 661–6.

Maden, A., Swinton, M. and Gunn, J. (1992) A survey of pre-arrest drug use in sentenced prisoners, *British Journal of Addiction*, 87: 27–33.

Magura, S., Rosenblum, A., Lewis, C. and Joseph, H. (1993) The effectiveness of in-jail methadone maintenance, *Journal of Drug Issues*, 23(1): 75–99.

Maher, L. and Curtis, R. (1992) Women on the edge of crime: crack cocaine and the changing contexts of street-level sex work in New York City, *Crime, Law and Social Change*, 18(3): 221–59.

Makkai, T. (2001) Patterns of recent drug use among a sample of Australian detainees, *Addiction*, 96: 1799–1808.

Makkai, T., Fitzgerald, J. and Doak, P. (2000) Drug use among police detainees, *Crime and Justice*, 49(March). Sydney, NSW: NSW Bureau of Crime Statistics and Research.

Marsch, L. (1998) The efficacy of methadone maintenance interventions in reducing illicit opiate use, HIV risk behaviour and criminality: a meta-analysis, *Addiction*, 93(4): 515–32.

Maruna, S. (2001) *Making Good: How Ex-convicts Reform and Rebuild their Lives*. Washington, DC: American Psychological Society.

Mason, W.A. and Windle, M. (2002) Reciprocal relations between adolescent substance use and delinquency: a longitudinal latent variable analysis, *Journal of Abnormal Psychology*, 111(1): 63–76.

Matsumoto, T., Kamijo, A., Miyakawa, T. *et al.* (2002) Methamphetamine in Japan: the consequences of methamphetamine abuse as a function of route of administration, *Addiction*, 97(7): 809–17.

McCoy, V., Inciardi, J.A., Metsch, L.R., Pottieger, A.E. and Saum, C.A. (1995) Women, crack, and crime: gender comparisons of criminal activity among crack cocaine users, *Contemporary Drug Problems*, 22: 435–51.

Menard, S., Mihalic, S. and Huizinga, D. (2001) Drugs and crime revisited, *Justice Quarterly*, 18(2): 269–99.

Metrebian, N., Shanahan, W., Stimson, G. *et al.* (2001) Prescribing drug of choice to opiate dependent drug users: a comparison of clients receiving heroin with those receiving injectable methadone at a West London drug clinic, *Drug and Alcohol Review*, 20: 267–76.

Mitcheson, M. (1994) Drug clinics in the 1970's, in J. Strang and M. Gossop (eds.) *Heroin Addiction and Drug Policy: The British System*. Oxford: Oxford University Press.

Moser, C.A. and Kalton, G. (1993) *Survey Methods in Social Investigation*. Aldershot: Dartmouth.

Mott, J. (1991) Crime and heroin use, in D.K. Whynes and P.T. Bean (eds.) *Policing and Prescribing the British System of Drug Control*. London: Macmillan.

National Centre for Social Research and National Foundation for Educational Research (2004) *Drug Use, Smoking and Drinking Among Young People in England in 2003*. London: Department of Health.

National Commission on Marihuana and Drug Abuse (1972) *Marihuana: A Signal of Misunderstanding* (www.druglibrary.org/schaffer/Library/studies/nc/ncmenu.htm: accessed 27 June 2003).

National Criminal Intelligence Service (2003) *U.K. Threat Assessment: The Threat from Serious and Organised Crime 2003* (www.ncis.co.uk/ukta/2003/ukta2003.pdf: accessed 31 August 2004).

National Institute of Justice (2003) *Annual Report 2000: Arrestee Drug Abuse Monitoring*. Washington, DC: US Department of Justice.

Nemes, S., Wish, E. and Messina, N. (1999) Comparing the impact of standard and abbreviated treatment in a therapeutic community, *Journal of Substance Abuse Treatment*, 17(4): 339–47.

Netherlands Institute of Mental Health and Addiction (1999) *Drugtext Information Services: The Netherlands* (www.drugtext.org/count/nl1.html: accessed 31 August 2004).

Netherlands Ministry of Foreign Affairs (2002) *Q and A. Drugs: A Guide to Dutch Policy* (http://www.ukcia.org/research/DutchDrugPolicy.pdf).

Newman, R.G. and Whitehill, W.B. (1979) Double-blind comparison of methadone and placebo maintenance treatments of narcotic addicts in Hong Kong, *Lancet*, 2: 485–8.

Norström, T. (1998) Effects on criminal violence of different beverage types and private and public drinking, *Addiction*, 93(5): 689–99.

Nurco, D.N., Shaffer, J.W., Ball, J.C. and Kinlock, T.W. (1984) Trends in the commission of crime among narcotic addicts over successive periods of addiction and non-addiction, *American Journal of Drug and Alcohol Abuse*, 10: 481–9.

Nurco, D.N., Kinloch, T. and Balter, M.B. (1993) The severity of pre-addiction criminal behaviour among urban, male narcotic addicts and two non-addicted control groups, *Journal of Research in Crime and Delinquency*, 30(3): 293–316.

Office for National Statistics (2002) *Statistics from the Regional Drug Misuse Databases for Six Months Ending March 2001*. London: Department of Health.

Office for National Statistics (2004) Deaths related to drug poisoning: England and Wales, 1998–2002, *Health Statistics Quarterly*, 21: 59–65.

Ong, T. (1989) Peers as perceived by drug abusers in their drug-seeking behaviour, *British Journal of Addiction*, 84: 631–7.

Osler, W. (1892) *The Principles and Practice of Medicine*. New York: Appleton & Co.

Parent, I. and Brochu, S. (2002) Drug/crime pathways among cocaine users, in S. Brochu, C. Da Agra and M. Cousineau (eds.) *Drugs and Crime Deviant Pathways*. Aldershot: Ashgate.

Parker, H. (1996) Young adult offenders, alcohol and criminological cul-de-sacs, *British Journal of Criminology*, 36(2): 282–98.

Parker, H. and Bottomley, T. (1996) *Crack Cocaine and Drugs–Crime Careers*. London: Home Office.

Parker, H., Aldridge, J. and Measham, F. (1998) *Illegal Leisure: The Normalization of Adolescent Recreational Drug Use*. London: Routledge.

Parker, H., Aldridge, J. and Egginton, R. (2001) *UK Drugs Unlimited: New Research and Policy Lessons on Illicit Drug Use*. Basingstoke: Palgrave.

Parker, H., Williams, L. and Aldridge, J. (2002) The normalization of 'sensible' recreational drug use: further evidence from the North West England Longitudinal Study, *Sociology*, 36(4): 941–64.

Parker, R.N. and Auerhahn, K. (1998) Alcohol, drugs and violence, *Annual Review of Sociology*, 24: 291–311.

Parry, C.D.H., Louw, A. and Pluddemann, A. (2000) *The MRC/ISS 3-Metros Arrestee Study (Phase 3)*. Pretoria, South Africa: Medical Research Council and Institute for Security Studies.

Pearson, F. and Lipton, D. (1999) A meta-analytic review of the effectiveness of corrections-based treatments for drug abuse, *Prison Journal*, 79(4): 384–410.

Pearson, G. (1999) Drugs at the end of the century, *British Journal of Criminology*, 39(4): 477–87.

Pearson, G. and Hobbs, D. (2001) *Middle Market Drug Distribution*, Home Office Research Study #227. London: Home Office.

Pedersen, W. and Skrondal, A. (1999) Ecstasy and new patterns of drug use: a normal population study, *Addiction*, 94(11): 1695–1706.

Pennings, J.M., Leccese, A.P. and de Wolff, F.A. (2002) Effects of concurrent use of alcohol and cocaine, *Addiction*, 97(7): 773–83.

Perkonigg, A., Lieb, R., Hofler, M. *et al.* (1999) Patterns of cannabis use, abuse and dependence over time: incidence, progression and stability in a sample of 1228 adolescents, *Addiction*, 94(11): 1663–78.

Pernanen, K. (1982) Theoretical aspects of the relationship between alcohol use and crime, in J. Collins (ed.) *Drinking and Crime: Perspectives on the Relationship between Alcohol Consumption and Criminal Behavior*. New York: Guilford Press.

Perneger, T.V., Giner, F., del Rio, M. and Mino, A. (1998) Randomised trial of heroin maintenance programme for addicts who fail in conventional drug treatments, *British Medical Journal*, 317: 13–18.

Potterat, J.J., Rothenberg, R.B., Muth, S.Q., Darrow, W.W. and Phillips-Plummer, L. (1998) Pathways to prostitution: the chronology of sexual and drug abuse milestones, *Journal of Sex Research*, 35(4): 333–40.

Preble, E. and Casey, J. (1969) Taking care of business: the heroin user's life on the streets, *Journal of the Addictions*, 4: 1–24.

Prendergast, M., Podus, D., Chang, E. and Urada, D. (2002) The effectiveness of drug abuse treatment: a meta-analysis of comparison group studies, *Drug and Alcohol Dependence*, 67(1): 53–72.

Proctor, P. (1995) *Cambridge International Dictionary of English*. Cambridge: Cambridge University Press.

Pudney, S. (2002) *The Road to Ruin? Sequences of Initiation into Drug Use and Offending by Young People in Britain*, Home Office Research Study #253. London: Home Office.

Pudney, S. (2003) The road to ruin? Sequences of initiation to drugs and crime, *Economic Journal*, 113(486): 182–98.

Ramsay, M. (2003a) *Prisoners' Drug Use and Treatment: Seven Studies*, Home Office Findings #186. London: Home Office.

Ramsay, M. (ed.) (2003b) *Prisoners' Drug Use and Treatment: Seven Research Studies*, Home Office Research Study #267. London: Home Office.

Ramsay, M., Baker, P., Goulden, C., Sharp, C. and Sondhi, A. (2001) *Drug Misuse Declared in 2000: Results from the British Crime Survey*, Home Office Research Study #224. London: Home Office.

Riley, S.C.E., James, C., Gregory, D., Dingle, H. and Cadger, M. (2001) Patterns of recreational drug use at dance events in Edinburgh, Scotland, *Addiction*, 96: 1035–47.

Robson, P. (1999) *Forbidden Drugs*. Oxford: Oxford University Press.

Rolleston Committee (1926) *Report of the Interdepartmental Committee on Morphine and Heroin Addiction*. London: HMSO.

Roncek, D.W. and Maier, P.A. (1991) Bars, blocks, and crimes revisited: linking the theory of routine activities to the empiricism of 'hot spots', *Criminology*, 29(4): 725–53.

Rosenbaum, M. (1981) *Women on Heroin*. New Brunswick, NJ: Rutgers University Press.

Ross, J., Darke, S. and Hall, W. (1997) Transitions between routes of benzo-diazepine administration among heroin users in Sydney, *Addiction*, 92(6): 697–705.

Sanchez, J.E., Johnson, B.D. and Israel, M. (1985) *Drugs and Crime Among Riker's Island Women*. San Diego, CA: American Society of Criminology.

Shaw, C. and McKay, H. (1942) *Juvenile Delinquency and Urban Areas*. Chicago, IL: University of Chicago Press.

Shaw, V.N., Hser, Y., Anglin, D.M. and Boyle, K. (1999) Sequences of powder cocaine and crack use among arrestees in Los Angeles County, *American Journal of Drug and Alcohol Abuse*, 25(1): 47–66.

Shewan, D., Dalgarno, P., Marshall, A. *et al.* (1998) Patterns of heroin use among a non-treatment sample in Glasgow (Scotland), *Addiction Research*, 6(3): 215–34.

Simpson, M. (2003) The relationship between drug use and crime: a puzzle inside an enigma, *International Journal of Drug Policy*, 14: 307–19.

Singleton, N., Bumpstead, R., O'Brien, M., Lee, A. and Meltzer, H. (2001) *Psychiatric Morbidity Among Adults Living in Private Households, 2000*. London: The Stationery Office.

Skog, O.J. (1992) Correlation and causality: notes on epistemological problems in substance abuse research, in M. Lader, G. Edwards and D.C. Drummond (eds.) *The Nature of Alcohol and Drug Related Problems*. Oxford: Oxford University Press.

Smart, R.G. and Ogborne, A.C. (2000) Drug use and drinking among students in 36 countries, *Addictive Behaviours*, 25(3): 445–60.

Smith, D.A. and Polsenberg, C. (1992) Specifying the relationship between arrestee drug test results and recidivism, *Journal of Criminal Law and Criminology*, 83(2): 364–77.

Sommers, I., Baskin, D. and Fagan, J. (2000) *Workin' Hard for the Money: The Social and Economic Lives of Women Drug Sellers*. New York: Nova Science.

South, N. (1994) Drugs: control, crime, and criminological studies, in M. Maguire, R. Reiner and R. Morgan (eds.) *The Oxford Handbook of Criminology*. Oxford: Oxford University Press.

Spear, H.B. (1969) The growth of heroin addiction in the United Kingdom, *British Journal of Addiction*, 64: 245.

Spear, H.B. and Mott, J. (2002) *Heroin Addiction, Care and Control: The British System*. London: DrugScope.

Speckart, G. and Anglin, M.D. (1985) Narcotics and crime: an analysis of existing evidence for a causal relationship, *Behavioral Sciences and the Law*, 3(3): 259–82.

Sterk, C.E., Elifson, K.W. and German, D. (2000) Female crack users and their sexual relationships: the role of sex-for-crack exchanges, *Journal of Sex Research*, 37(4): 354–60.

Stewart, D., Gossop, M., Marsden, J. and Rolfe, A. (2000) Drug misuse and acquisitive crime among clients recruited to the National Treatment Outcome Research Study (NTORS), *Criminal Behaviour and Mental Health*, 10(1): 10–20.

Stimson, G.V. (1987) The war on heroin: British policy and the international trade in illicit drugs, in N. Dorn and N. South (eds.) *A Land Fit for Heroin*. London: Macmillan.

Stimson, G.V. and Lart, R. (1991) HIV, drugs, and public health in England: new words, old tunes, *International Journal of the Addictions*, 26: 1263–77.

Stimson, G.V. and Metrebian, N. (2003) *Prescribing Heroin. What is the Evidence?* York: Joseph Rowntree Foundation.

Stimson, G.V. and Oppenheimer, E. (1982) *Heroin Addiction: Treatment and Control in Britain*. London: Tavistock.

Strang, J., Griffiths, P. and Gossop, M. (1997) Heroin smoking by 'chasing the dragon': origins and history, *Addiction*, 92(6): 673–83.

Swedish Ministry of Health and Social Affairs (2002) *National Action Plan on Narcotic Drugs*. Stockholm: Printing Works of the Government Offices.

Swift, W., Hall, W. and Teesson, M. (2001) Cannabis use and dependence among Australian adults: results from the National Survey of Mental Health and Wellbeing, *Addiction*, 96(5): 737–48.

Swiss Federal Office of Public Health (2002) *Swiss Drugs Policy*. Berne: Swiss Federal Office of Public Health.

Taylor, B. and Bennett, T. (1999) *Comparing Drug Use Rates of Detained Arrestees in the United States and England*. Washington, DC: US Department of Justice.

Taylor, L. (1972) The significance and interpretation of replies to motivational questions: the case of sex offenders, *Sociology*, 6(1): 23–39.

The White House (2003) *National Drug Control Strategy*. Washington, DC: The White House.

Thornberry, T.P. (1987) Toward an interactional theory of delinquency, *Criminology*, 25(4): 863–91.

Tonry, M. and Wilson, J.Q. (eds.) (1990) *Drugs and Crime: A Review of Research*. London: University of Chicago Press.

Topalli, V., Wright, R. and Fornango, R. (2002) Drug dealers, robbery and retaliation: vulnerability, deterrence and the contagion of violence, *British Journal of Criminology*, 42(2): 337–51.

Towberman, D.B. and McDonald, R.M. (1993) Dimensions of adolescent drug-avoidant attitude, *Journal of Substance Abuse Treatment*, 10(1): 45–52.

Trachtenberg, A.I. and Fleming, M.F. (2004) *Diagnosis and Treatment of Drug Abuse in Family Practice*. Bethesda, MD: NIDA, National Institute of Health.

Turner, S., Petersilia, J. and Deschenes, E.P. (1992) Evaluating intensive supervision probation/parole (ISP) for drug offenders, *Crime and Delinquency*, 38(4): 539–56.

Turner, S., Greenwood, P., Fain, T. and Deschenes, E. (1999) National Drug Court Institute review: perceptions of drug court: how offenders view ease of program completion, strengths and weaknesses, and the impact on their lives, *National Drug Court Review*, 2(1): 61–86.

Turpeinen, P. (2001) Outcome of drug abuse in a 20-year follow-up study of drug-experimenting school children in Finland, *Nordic Journal of Psychiatry*, 55(4): 263–70.

US Department of Justice (1994) *Fact Sheet: Drug-Related Crime*. Rockville, MD: ONDCP Drugs and Crime Clearinghouse.

Waldorf, D., Reinarman, C. and Murphy, S. (1991) *Cocaine Changes: The Experience of Using and Quitting*. Philadelphia, PA: Temple University Press.

Walker, A., O'Brien, M., Traynor, J. *et al.* (2002) *Living in Britain: Results from the 2001 General Household Survey.* London: The Stationery Office.

Walters, G.D. (1994) *Drugs and Crime in Lifestyle Perspective.* London: Sage.

Wexler, H., De Leon, G., Thomas, G., Kressel, D. and Peters, J. (1999) The Amity Prison TC evaluation, *Criminal Justice and Behavior*, 26(2): 147–67.

White, H.R. (1990) The drug-use–delinquency connection in adolescence, in R. Weisheit (ed.) *Drugs, Crime, and Criminal Justice.* Cincinnati, OH: Anderson Publishing Co.

White, H.R. and Gorman, D.M. (2000) Dynamics of the drug–crime relationship, *Criminal Justice*, 1: 151–218.

Wilkinson, D.A., Leigh, G.M., Cordingley, J., Martin, G.W. and Lei, H. (1987) Dimensions of multiple drug use and a typology of drug users, *British Journal of Addiction*, 82: 259–73.

Wilson, W.J. (1987) *The Truly Disadvantaged: The Inner City, the Underclass, and Public Policy.* Chicago, IL: University of Chicago Press.

Winick, C. (1962) Maturing out of addiction, *Bulletin on Narcotics*, 14(1): 1–7.

Woody, G.E., McLellan, T., Luborsky, L. and O'Brien, C.P. (1987) Twelve-month follow-up of psychotherapy for opiate dependence, *American Journal of Psychiatry*, 144(5): 590–6.

Wright, R. and Decker, S. (1997) *Armed Robbers in Action: Stickups and Street Culture.* Boston, MA: Northeastern University Press.

Yacoubian, G.S. and Kane, R.J. (1998) Identifying a drug use typology of Philadelphia arrestees: a cluster analysis, *Journal of Drug Issues*, 28(2): 559–74.

Yacoubian, G.S., Urbach, B.J., Larsen, K.L., Johnson, R.J. and Peters, R.J. (2001) A comparison of drug use between prostitutes and other female arrestees, *Journal of Alcohol and Drug Education*, 46(2): 12–25.

Zhang, S.X. (2000) *An Evaluation of the Los Angeles County Probation Juvenile Drug Treatment Boot Camp.* San Marcos, CA: California State University at San Marcos.

# Index

*Passim* indicates numerous scattered mentions within page range.

## UNDERSTANDING VICTIMS AND RESTORATIVE JUSTICE

### James Dignan

Two of the principal and most influential developments within criminal justice policy in the last thirty years have been the rise of the 'victim movement' and the emergence of a distinctive set of practices that have become associated with the term 'restorative justice'. *Understanding Victims and Restorative Justice* examines the origins of and the relationship between these two sets of developments, and assesses their strengths and weaknesses in meeting the needs of victims as part of the response to crime.

Written in a lively and accessible style, this book benefits students from a range of disciplines, including criminology, sociology and the law. Also helpful to professionals, practitioners and policymakers working in voluntary agencies within the criminal justice system.

### Contents
*Preface – Introducing victims, victimisation, victimology and victim-focused policy-making – Victims and the criminal justice system – Reforming the criminal justice system: 'traditionalist' and welfare reformist' approaches – Reforming the criminal justice system: 'restorative justice approaches' – Restorative Justice reforms in practice – The limits of Restorative Justice and the way ahead? – Glossary of key terms – Index.*

c.160 pp     0 335 20979 3 (Paperback)     0 335 20980 7 (Hardback)

# UNDERSTANDING PSYCHOLOGY AND CRIME
## PERSPECTIVES ON THEORY AND ACTION

### James McGuire

- What contributions can psychology make to the understanding of crime?
- How can theories of crime that focus on the individual be integrated in a wider social perspective?
- How can psychological models and research be applied in crime prevention and the reduction of repeat offending?

This book bridges the gap between criminology and psychological perspectives and ideas concerning crime. It sets this in historical context and provides an outline of the contributions that psychological approaches can make understanding crime and how to respond to it. It is argued that some objections to the use of psychology within criminology are based on outdated or erroneous conceptions about psychology itself.

Throughout the book there is an emphasis on the close relationships between theory, research and practice, and a central part of this is to demonstrate how a methodical approach to the study of criminal behaviour can generate both systematic findings and practical solutions to problems. This authoritative and stimulating text provides essential reading for courses in criminology and psychology alike, moving from theory and research to how such ideas can be applied in crime prevention and reduction, and concluding with discussion of the ethical and political implications.

**Contents**
*Series editor's foreword – Why psychology? – Explaining crime – Psychological processes in crime – Individual factors in crime – Crime and punishment: a psychological view – Preventing and reducing crime – Values in criminology and psychology – Glossary – Index.*

192pp     0 335 21119 4 (Paperback)     0 335 21120 8 (Hardback)